GOD, JESUS, AND SPIRIT

GOD, JESUS, AND SPIRIT

Edited by
Daniel Callahan

HERDER AND HERDER

1969
HERDER AND HERDER NEW YORK
232 Madison Avenue, New York, N.Y. 10016

Library of Congress Catalog Card Number: 70-75256
© 1969 by Commonweal Publishing Co., Inc.
Manufactured in the United States

Contents

Introduction

DANIEL CALLAHAN

THE ORIGIN of the articles collected here is the first three *Commonweal* Papers, published in that magazine during 1967 and 1968. During my own years with the magazine, I doubt that anything was as satisfying as the work, with my colleagues, of conceiving, commissioning and editing these Papers. There was a quick receptiveness to the idea among potential authors and an unusual interest on the part of the American theological audience.

The idea behind the *Commonweal* Papers was a simple one. We felt an important though unexpected consequence of the Second Vatican Council had been to push the Church back to fundamentals, to issues much deeper and more critical than reform of the Church. What, we asked, were the most basic questions of all for the Christian? The question of God was an obvious first choice and thus the topic of the first of the Papers. The choice of the second was not quite so easy, but it seemed both logical and desirable to deal with the problem of Jesus. There had been much talk during the Council of the need for a Scripture-centered and Christ-oriented theology to replace the arid rationalism of nineteenth-century manual theology. But who was Jesus and what can he mean to us today? The answer to that question is critical to the meaning of Christianity. But after the problem of Jesus, then what? Here our own thinking coincided with the suggestions of a number of readers: the Holy Spirit. Not only was the increasing interest in Pentecostalism (Protestant and Catholic) a goad, but the constant invocation of "the Spirit" in much recent theology and polity made it clear that the Holy Spirit was coming once again, though all too belatedly, into the center of theological speculation.

As these brief words on the background of the *Commonweal* Papers might suggest, they were not conceived as a unit, but were planned one at a time. We wanted to leave ourselves free to respond to public interests as well as to the changing emphases of the theological landscape. Thus the problems of God, Jesus and the Holy Spirit as discussed here do not constitute, in sum, a study of the doctrine of the Trinity. Curiously enough, no one suggested that we have a Paper devoted to "God the Father," and it never occurred to us to do so. This was not, I think, the result of an oversight on anyone's part but, more plausibly, a reflection of what can only be called a considerable disinterest in the topic, both on the part of the public and of the professional theological community. The issue on "God" was published at the height of the debate on the "death of God," a debate which did not, in the end, manage to show a widespread conviction that God was, indeed, dead. But it might well be worth asking just how much life is left in the concept of, and belief in, God the Father. The evidence might suggest there is very little, at least at present. Just why would be a worthy subject for someone's exploration.

It is probably no accident as well that the three Papers were not conceived as an extended treatment of the Trinity. That subject also seems, at the moment, to be of little interest. Despite the wide range of authors in the three Papers, and the obvious pertinence of much of what they say to the Trinity, the doctrine is barely mentioned at all. Part of the explanation for this is undoubtedly the relatively narrow focus of each author, who wrote his particular article on request, and who could not in a relatively short compass take up everything. But part is likely a manifestation of an important characteristic of present-day Catholic theology: a relative disinterest in the kind of system-building theology which feels obliged to relate a discussion of one Christian belief to every other Christian belief. There seems to be a pronounced tendency to take up issues seriatim, sometimes in an almost ad hoc way, leaving the various conclusions (though often there are none) floating in independence of each other.

I am not saying this by way of criticism, but only to note a salient characteristic of the contemporary scene. It may, in any case, be the only way possible for the time being. The rapid changes in exegesis and hermeneutics, the influx of a large host of non-scholastic philosophical perspectives, the impact of the social and historical sciences, have made available more material and methods than can immediately be integrated. It is not at all clear, for instance, how the various new ways of thinking about God as a philosophical problem can be brought to bear on the Christian belief that Christ is God; too little has been written on that point. Nor is it clear whether, and how, the language of prayer can be made compatible with the language of linguistic or phenomenological analyses which have had much to do with shaping recent thought on the problem of God. In an important sense, of course, there are differences between the language of piety and prayer and that of theology; but the former will be significantly influenced by the latter. If, for instance, it was seriously believed—with the Harvey Cox of *The Secular City*—that we should declare a moratorium on the word "God," waiting for a better word to make an appearance, this would mean the formulation of prayers which did without the word. But what would such prayers be like, and how would they be received by those in the community for whom the word "God" is still central and meaningful? The implications of Leslie Dewart's contention that we should cease thinking of God as "being" are no less unsettling for the life of prayer and worship.

Any full attempt, however, to catalogue the still-pending issues brought to the surface by the contemporary theological upheaval would run into many pages. There is scarcely a single aspect of the present theological enterprise which is not overburdened with puzzles and difficulties. One problem, though, seems to me central: that of theological method. A reading of the articles collected in this book makes unmistakably clear how varied are the styles, the perspectives and the methodologies not only of different theological disciplines but also of theologians themselves. In part this is attributed to the exigencies of the different disciplines themselves; the method of the exegete is bound to be different from that of the philosopher of religion. But in part it is attributable to the very rich range of secular insights being mined today, not all of them by any means homogeneous with each other.

As a value, theological pluralism is commended nowadays; and it might as well be since it is a fact of life, made inevitable by a pluralism of methods and interests. At the same time, though, it would undoubtedly be helpful if some greater coherence could be brought into the theological arena. One of the drawbacks of this pluralism is that different theological camps often go their own way, failing to profit from the discoveries in each other's work, either because they don't understand it ("that's not my field") or because they are unaware of it. The very commendation of theological pluralism, which allows a valuable freedom, can also serve, unwittingly, to justify a mutual isolation of different theological schools.

In theology as in other disciplines, a cross-disciplinary approach is more praised then practiced. And it is easy to understand why. The very multiplicity of the disciplines bearing on theology, the technical competence required to master even one of them, and the endemic nervousness of academics about wading out beyond their depth, all serve to intimidate anyone who tries to mix theological genres and methods. Nonetheless, it is imperative that more theologians run the risk, whether to their sanity or their professional reputation, of trying to integrate and work with a variety of approaches simultaneously. As David Tracy has pertinently remarked, "All practitioners of theology must attempt to find some methodological means to allow, once again, some kind of scientific collaboration. Hopefully, then, theologians may be able at once to share the scientific results of their several disciplines and of others, and, of perhaps equal importance, to avoid the totalitarian temptations that beset us all" (*Continuum,* Summer 1968). To this I would add the opposite kind of temptation, that of an excessive modesty, deterring efforts synthetic and sweeping in scope.

Beyond the internal needs of theology for cooperative efforts and "scientific collaboration" there is an even greater need, and opportunity, beginning to make its appearance. It is a long time since anyone has been able to say, with an entirely straight face, that "theology is the queen of the sciences." Secularity and pluralism have succeeded in making it simply one more of the "sciences" (on those relatively rare occasions when people are willing to accord it any status at all), and theologians have been willing in their own right to accept a humble and diminished role for their work. One unfortunate consequence of this diminishment is that there now exists no one discipline which tries to make sense of life as a whole, which is able and positioned to draw together the many, many strands of human thought, feeling and aspiration. The result of this malaise is felt most critically in the universities. Students feel, with considerable justice, that the large questions of meaning and value, the most important questions of all, are slighted or ignored. They seem, for one thing, to fall within the range of no one's discipline or department. For another, students discover that their professors, bound by apparently fixed canons of method and competence, are often personally at a loss to deal with the human, non-academic problems of their students. The narrowness of the professional disciplines seems to spill over into the personalities of their practitioners.

With nerve and imagination, theology could begin to fill some of the gaps here. In principle, theology is open to the whole range of human experience and human questions. In principle, theology is concerned with problems of meaning and value. In principle, theology is supposed to make some sense of the totality of life. In principle, theology is receptive to all the findings of the discrete disciplines: the humanities, the social and natural sciences. But in actuality theology too often presents a very different face. Once out of the pulpit, it usually retreats into a constricted world, with a jargon, a methodology and a set of concerns which make it just one more specialized branch of human learning. The very defensiveness of theology, induced by the seemingly higher prestige of just about any discipline one can think of, appears only to exacerbate its present weaknesses.

During the past decade or so, theology has made something of a comeback in American intellectual and academic life. Religion and religious studies departments are proliferating. It is no longer considered inherently ridiculous for an intelligent person to be concerned with religion. But theology has purchased this fresh respectability at a high price. For the sake of regaining a foothold in the secular universities, it has felt compelled to demonstrate its academic purity, seriousness and distinctiveness. It has tried to demonstrate its purity by disavowing any intention of dominating or stepping upon the toes of other disciplines; it sticks to its own trade. It has tried to demonstrate its seriousness by upgrading the quality of its graduate training, a training heavy in a narrow technical competence in specialized aspects of theology: exegesis, dogmatics, Church history and so on. It has tried to demonstrate its distinctiveness by arguing that theology is a separate discipline which can only be handled by those with degrees in religion or theology. By and large, it has succeeded with these demonstrations. The kinds of snickers once heard in the secular university when the words "theology" or "religion" were mentioned are increasingly uncommon.

But has theology enriched itself or really enriched others in the process? In some instances it undoubtedly has. Theologians are invited to conferences now of a kind which wouldn't have welcomed them a decade ago. Many more students are being exposed to theological problems, theological authors and theological practitioners. But is any of this to say that theology has once again become "queen." Hardly. It is anything but, if only because the price of achieving academic respectability was to take an oath that it had abandoned its earlier monarchical pretensions.

While not suggesting that the oath should be repudiated, there is no reason why theology today cannot take up once again its traditional work of trying to provide a synthesis of and a focal point for the most basic of human concerns. That no other discipline is trying to do this means that the field is open. More importantly, there is a desperate need not only in the universities but also in the culture generally for the field to be tilled in some orderly fashion. The questions of meaning, purpose and value have once again come to the fore in the culture, particularly among students but increasingly among their elders as well. If theology cannot make the most of this fresh opportunity, then surely it must be abandoned forever; it is not likely to have as good a chance again.

In order, however, for it to become a central and valuable discipline, certain requirements seem to me imperative. It must become (1) less specialized and more general; (2) cross-disciplinary; (3) less denominational.

(1) *Less specialized and more general.* Strictly taken, the word "theology" suggests the study of God, and is usually construed as including such problems as that of revelation, the Church, eschatology and the like. To be judged competent in theology one is supposed to have studied Scripture, Church history, religious ethics, dogmatics, among other things. The presumption here is that the discipline of theology has a coherent history, its own traditions and a characteristic methodological canon. And this is undoubtedly true; there has been, historically, a field known as "theology." But at this juncture, theologians need to risk the integrity of their discipline, bringing to clearer focus the larger and not the smaller problems of human life. Where the theologian now is trained to explore some facet or other of

theology well, perhaps the emphasis of future training should be on the making of broad, non-specialized judgments, the linking together of the human and the scholarly/academic, and on the probing of those fundamental questions given short shrift by other disciplines. I don't want to make another plea here for "relevance," a tricky and sometimes tawdry notion anyway. But I would make a plea that theology resist going any further than it has in sub-dividing the field. Theology is rarely most significant and interesting when it pushes some small point to the nth degree. Instead, the source of whatever human interest it has or is worthy of is that it deals with perennial questions. When these questions are lost sight of, even for the sake of "scholarship," there may be no remaining point in theology. Of course if theologians want only to keep proving that their academic credentials and methods are as good as anyone else's, then narrowness is the approved route. But something more than that ought now to be sought.

(2) *Cross-disciplinary.* Theologians ought to get over any worries they may have about treading in other people's territory. On the contrary, they should make it a special point to move into other fields, adopt other methods and pass judgment on the fruits of other disciplines. This is only to say that the concern of the theologian should be everything human (and that includes everything academic and professional). But this concern will be nothing more than an empty slogan unless theologians display some nerve: the nerve to trespass, the nerve to be cross-disciplinary, the nerve to mix their metaphors and their language. Take the problem of man, surely a major concern of theology. Man in community can only be understood with the help of sociology; theology must thus incorporate the language of sociology, weaving its concepts into those of theology more narrowly taken. Man as a bundle of instincts, drives, passions and dispositions can only be understood with the help of psychology, and not just theological psychology of the elevated kind but behavioral psychology as well. Again, theology must

learn how to do some language- and concept-splicing, running the risk of foolishness in order that a higher synthesis might be devised. The good theologian of the future, assuming he takes the necessary risks, will not be easily categorized, for he will move in and out of a variety of fields, stretching the word "theology" to cover whatever he believes requires thought and unity.

In an important sense, the theologian should do with his own culture what the biblical scholar has done with biblical times: analyze every aspect of its life and thought to gain an insight into patterns and meanings. Recently, for instance, there has been a resurgence of interest in astrology, especially in the women's magazines. This is a perfect field for the theologian, who ought to be bringing to bear on this phenomenon the insights of history, philosophy, sociology, psychology and whatever other disciplines seem relevant. Other aspects of contemporary life call for a like analysis: the arms race (treated not only as a problem in moral theology but also as a problem bearing on the search for community), cybernetics, automation, sexual fashions, clothes, sports and on and on. In each instance, the theologian would attempt to discern what these things say about human life and what they portend for the future. In part, of course, this is already being done, but only fitfully and rarely in any systematic fashion. Generally speaking, the "serious" theologians ignore such issues or speak of them only in their lighter moments.

Finally, as part of a cross-disciplinary approach, there needs to be what I would like to call a "total methodology" which could be applied to particular problems. That would be a methodology which brought a variety of disciplines to bear simultaneously, involving both objective and subjective analysis. If one chose, say, to deal with astrology, such a method would require historical analysis, a study of the sociological setting of present interest in the subject, psychological analyses of those drawn to it, cultural analysis of its present significance, self-analysis by the author(s) of the study, probing their own emotions about the topic (including autobiographical data), a self-critique of the method(s) of analysis chosen and the like. Put another way, the ideal theological study of astrology would be at once a brilliant study which passed the norms of a variety of different disciplines and, at the same time, provided brilliant insight into the personality of the person doing the study. In an age which is beginning to discover the riches of personal experience, it is discouraging to see so much theology still written in the detached, analytic mode (the most horrible expression of which is the persistence of authors who say "we" when they mean "I").

(3) *Less denominational.* It almost goes without saying that theology must be less denominational today, cutting across Church lines as well as across the line between believer and unbeliever. Yet, once that is said, it is also necessary to add that the necessity of a personal standpoint means that people will write and think out of some community setting. This community setting ought not to be disguised; indeed, it should be brought out and exposed to full view—the full view of the public and the full view of the one doing the writing and thinking. The price of a genuinely "post-ecumenical" stance is likely to be either self-delusion (as if roots could be entirely transcended) or a bloodless theology, uninformed by the fruits of working through the implications of one tradition or another in a personal way. Good theology (at least as I am defining it here) is not "scientific theology," if by that expression is meant a cool, crisp toeing of some tight methodological norm system. Good theology must be a living activity, with all the rough edges of human life, thought and feeling, while at the same time an activity carried on in community with others (not all of them by any means theologians). To be genuinely open is at once to have gone beyond the parochial in aspiration while shrewdly recognizing that to be a concrete human being is to be unfailingly parochial.

As the essays published in this book indicate, however, there still remains a huge variety of problems connected with particular theological topics. They must surely be explored further, and I would not want to suggest that such explorations be fore-shortened. But I believe it ought to be possible even for those working on particular problems to give some of their energy and attention to the larger problem of revitalizing theology in general. As a specialized discipline, theology has a decent enough future. But it is bound to remain a very modest future if it is nothing more than a congeries of different sub-specialties. Of all people, the theologian should be the most wide-ranging, the least bound by tradition, the most imaginative, the most alive. Theology has had, or is in the midst of, its academic, intellectual renewal. What remains is the need for a moral renewal, a renewal which will require, first of all, that it eschew much of its newly gained respectability. A moral and human renewal is the pressing need.

GOD, JESUS, AND SPIRIT

PART ONE

God

I.

The God of Revelation

GABRIEL MORAN

AT THE BEGINNING of his talk at the St. Xavier symposium in the spring of 1966, Edward Schillebeeckx remarked that a Catholic answer has not yet been given to modernism. The modernist movement was an attempt to rethink the foundations of Catholic doctrine in a way that would take more account of historical development and the conscious subject. Unfortunately, the movement did not have the tools to carry out its project. The Church's magisterium, realizing that this could not lead to a right answer, simply closed the door to further development in that direction. The step which may have been necessary at that time did not solve the problem; it only covered it up momentarily.

One might go beyond the modernist movement and say that orthodox Catholic tradition has never adequately answered a constantly recurring heresy. The frequency of this heresy is indicative of the legitimate demand implicit in the error. Eventually, orthodoxy must face this issue and deal with it in an adequate way. What I refer to is the existence throughout the centuries of countless sects of people who wished to "experience" God, or at least to search for a God who would speak in their lives. In its classical form, this is the heresy of the third age, the age of the Spirit, in which institutional forms will fall away and each individual will be immersed in the Spirit.

This demand is not solely an ancient or a medieval problem. One need not go beyond the limits of any large city in the United States to find religious sects whose appeal is a revelation of the

3

Spirit. More important than these small groups, however, is the search by millions of people for some kind of experience in their lives that would be ultimately satisfying or meaningful. In the book of Jeremiah, the king Zedekiah asked the prophet: "Is there any word from the Lord?" This question has never entirely disappeared. Moreover, what had been implicit in that question has come more to the forefront in our day: "Is there any word from the Lord *for us?*"

It is possible to dismiss this demand of a present revelatory experience as due to a lack of sophistication on the part of the masses. Theologians and bishops have often done just that. Of course, religious experience is not altogether outlawed in Catholicism. As a matter of fact, the liturgy is currently being revamped to encourage it. The only trouble with this concession to fleshly, temporal, social man is that his experience is not taken with any ultimate seriousness. It is measured against "revealed data" that God has bestowed upon the Church. Because religious experience must therefore be an essentially brainless affair, it is exposed to manipulative techniques that destroy its significance.

It is quite acceptable for one to say that in the liturgy we meet God or that God acts in human history. But it would be considered rather dangerous to say that God reveals himself in personal experience today. One must qualify that statement by adding that strictly speaking the divine public revelation ended with the death of the last apostle. Whatever strange happenings go on in the world and whatever playing with liturgy occurs in the Church, the real revelation of God is contained in the carefully preserved truths. Thus, no one gets upset by a writer saying that God speaks to us in the liturgy, because almost no one believes this. For to take the phrase seriously would require a revolution in thinking about revelation that has not occurred in the Catholic Church.

The religious question today is not whether there is revealed data but whether there is a God who reveals. A God who once spoke but now speaks no more is not only uninteresting but un-

4

intelligible. Possibly this is a fault of our contemporary era. It may be an error traceable to the narrowness of men who identify the "meaningful with the instantaneously incandescent" (Sittler). The Christian may perhaps judge as egocentric and blasphemous the remark of Rousseau, that if God wanted to talk to Jean-Jacques then why did he go speak to Moses. Yet the question is not wholly irrelevant.

These questions have answers, of course, that have been formulated in well-worn phrases. But even if the answers are the right ones, each person who repeats them must think out his own conclusions or risk clouding the issue with meaningless words. It is somewhat painful to read the exchanges that took place between the modernist George Tyrrell and his more orthodox opponents. On the part of some of these people it did not take great courage or intelligence to repeat traditional formulas. That kind of stance is not very dangerous, but neither is it very helpful for the Church's task of coming to understand her mission in the world.

Catholic theology in recent centuries presupposed that there were two rather distinct ways to know about God. God can be known by reason and by revelation. From the universe a right thinking man can read off God's existence. From the revealed data in the scriptures and in tradition, one can know things about God's character. The basic assumption was that Christianity possessed a revelation and from this it could know about God.

During the past century, under the pressure of critical examination, this picture was gradually altered. The number of revealed truths was carefully honed down, the interplay of reason and revelation was more subtly worked out, and the revealed truths of scripture and tradition were squeezed into some kind of unity. The fundamental attitude, however, has not greatly changed: somewhere, somehow, in some number, the Church has revealed truths about God. But it must be admitted that the tactic of shrinkage has not really helped; nor would the lopping off of a few more doctrines improve conditions. What many men

5

find inconceivable is the assumption that there are any truths that are unquestionable and are a norm to which men are to submit their freedom of inquiry. Whether there are two or twenty-two hundred of these revealed truths is not the paramount issue.

An English writer, F. Gerald Downing, recently published a book entitled *Has Christianity a Revelation?* Partly on the basis of his empiricist's learnings and partly on the basis of the bible, Downing seems to think that the answer should be in the negative. Although it would be for different reasons, I think that I would agree with his conclusion. Christianity does not *have* a revelation because this would presuppose that revelation is something men might have or possess. Instead, Christianity might *be* a revelation, or at least a community of people becoming aware of a God who is revealing, a God who is always in front of man and inviting him forward. Our language predisposes us to think of revelation as an object. It is easy to move from speaking of the truths through which God reveals to the truths which God has revealed. The difference in phraseology is slight, but the difference in resulting attitudes is enormous.

It is highly ambiguous to speak of faith as a response to revelation. It would be better to speak of faith as an attitude within the revelational process or an act directed to the God who is revealing. Traditional Catholic teaching has asserted that faith terminates not in the proposition but in the reality, not in the truths but in the person. What has not been obvious in this teaching is that a present act of believing must be correlated with a present act of revealing. It is not sufficient to keep saying that biblical faith is more a verb than a noun. Faith still ends up as a body of truths and this happens inevitably because revelation is still assumed to be something that the Church possesses rather than what God is now doing.

Some people may protest that this view of revelation has been recovered in recent years. It is true that it is now often said that revelation is an "event" as well as a truth, a happening in history as well as the prophetic interpretation. This insight provided by contemporary exegesis represents a great advance in our understanding of revelation. It is seldom recognized, however, what this biblical teaching implies. If one really wishes to say that revelation is an event, then one must say that revelation exists today as a present event. A happening is happening only when it is happening. This is the crucial issue that has not been faced in all radicalness even in much writing that appears to take a radical approach.

The Constitution on Divine Revelation represents an excellent statement on scriptural research into the question of revelation. The approved Constitution is an immeasurably better document than the one that was first presented to the Council in 1962. Yet it does not pose, let alone answer, the question of God's revelation happening in the contemporary world. Given the present shape of Catholic theology, this limitation was probably both wise and necessary. The Constitution on Divine Revelation can be of great help so long as we remember that it is as much a starting point as it is a conclusion.

The Second Vatican Council did work with wider and deeper notions of revelation. Intimations of this are found in the Constitution on the Church, the Constitution on the Church in the Modern World, the Declaration on Religious Freedom, the Decree on Ecumenism, and the Declaration on Non-Christian Religions. These documents are filled with marvelous insights for the Catholic trying to live his faith in the world of today. These insights, however, rest upon a more developed notion of revelation than that which has yet surfaced. There is nothing surprising or deceitful in the movement from pastoral concern to theological depth. What would be unfortunate would be to stop with the practical, pastoral statements. The result would be that in no time at all the assertions would be trivialized into pious sayings that would not have to be taken too strictly.

I would cite as an example here the question of Christian-

Jewish relations. This example is so decisive that it is more than an example; it is the index of whether we understand the whole present issue in relation to our past and future.

At the present time, many Catholics and Jews are working diligently to break down some of the barriers that have been constructed over the centuries. A first stage of ordinary social relationships inevitably leads to the raising of theological questions. As Catholics have recovered a greater appreciation of the Old Testament they have felt a growing bond with the people of Israel. The increased knowledge of the Old Testament has undoubtedly been a great help to the Catholic in encountering Judaism.

The ironic and sometimes tragic thing, however, is that the more the Catholic concentrates on the Old Testament, the more this can strain relations with the contemporary Jew. For the stress upon old as opposed to new is a source of continuing irritation. The Jew has no *Old* Testament. He does have a Hebrew scripture. He also has a post-biblical history with which most Catholics are not very familiar. The questions which rabbis repeatedly pose to Catholic audiences today is not what do you think of the Old Testament, but what do you think of contemporary Jewish people.

The Catholic has difficulties in understanding contemporary Judaism because of many historical and social factors. But beneath the other problems there is a continuing theological inadequacy on the part of Catholicism. Because revelation is conceived to be something that came in the past and stopped, then the Old Testament cannot be anything but old. Despite all our contrary pleas, the Old Testament becomes that part of revelation that was supplanted or at least completed by the New Testament. It was once the revealing God at work but now it has been fulfilled. In this conception the Jewish people were once the bearers of revelation, but now they are an incongruous remnant. This line of thinking is very strong among Catholics despite the insistence of St. Paul (Rom. 11) and Vatican II that God has not revoked

8

the promises to his people. Unless one were to interpret this in a collectivistic sense, this can only mean that Jews retain a special mission in the revealing of God today.

The problem in saying this is that the Catholic cannot believe that God is still revealing himself to the Jewish people because the Catholic does not believe that God is revealing himself to anybody. Insofar as Catholics believe that revelation was sealed and delivered in the New Testament, there is no theological reason for a special study of post-biblical Judaism. If, on the other hand, God is still working in the world and revealing himself to men, it becomes imperative for the Christian to be attentive to the mission of Judaism. When Christian and Jew take each other's position with theological seriousness they can search together for the God in whom they both believe, the one who is glimpsed under different aspects in the lives of Jews and Christians. In such an undertaking the Christian will have to ask himself with candor where the most striking witness to the suffering servant of Yahweh has been found in the twentieth century.

The point of this discussion is that Catholics can hardly begin to look for God in the lives of all men if they do not even have a meaningful theology of Judaism. Obviously, no Catholic theology is going to be wholly acceptable to the Jew. This is not what is demanded. What is required is a developed theological position that will aid Catholic self-understanding and at the same time reveal the urgent need for dialogue. It is useless to encourage dialogue unless there is the prior conviction that one can learn from the other. So long as the Catholic believes that a perfected revelation has been delivered into his possession, then he will not look to the contemporary Jew for meaningful theological exchange.

One of the underlying difficulties here is the paradoxical notion of a chosen people. Running throughout the scriptures is the assumption that God chooses particular people and particular moments of time. This idea of choice can be easily misinterpreted. The peculiar character of God's choice is that in choosing one he

9

includes rather than excludes all the others. This is so because of the nature of the choice which is a call to serve and not to dominate the others. The chosen one has not merited some special gift; rather, something inexplicable happens in his life, something not so much for himself as for the other. The chosen ones are continually reminded by the prophet that they are not the good people who possess God as opposed to all other people who are cut off from God.

If God was to meet the real existing man, he had to deal with the particular man who lives moment by moment with his brothers. The religious faiths that men can live by are necessarily particular and concrete. It must be especially insisted upon today that particular religious faiths are not less than the general ideals that can be abstracted from them. The revelation of God is not a set of lofty ideals for men to conform their lives to.

The problem of Christian and Jewish faiths is not that they are particular and limited, but that they interpret particularity in an exclusive or negative way. Rightly understood, Judaism and Christianity need not negate any human value because their claim is not to possess all truth but to be receptive to all truth. Claiming to be the chosen of God does not necessitate the belief that God is not revealing himself among all men. The exact contrary is true. The Jew and Christian must recognize that God reveals himself to all men and that no man and no institution possesses the whole truth. Precisely by not trying to dominate with the truth, by not claiming to possess all truth already, the Jew and Christian can be points around which the unification of truth can occur. This position is not one of bland indifference or utter relativism. The Catholic can be tolerant of another's beliefs because he is passionately committed to his own truth.

Belief in a chosen people includes, therefore, a belief that God is with all people. Likewise, belief in chosen moments of time means that God is revealing himself in every moment of time. It cannot be denied that there have been crucial moments of the past that influence the present. If one wishes to understand the

10

present, he cannot do so except through the past and future. Nevertheless, if one wishes to begin looking for a God of revelation, one simply cannot overemphasize the present. It is only there that God can be God for us.

Given the receptiveness and search by the believer, it may be asked whether any special knowledge of God can be pointed to as achieved by revelation. The Christian claims that he has been found by another so that a new demand is made upon his life and a distinctive quality is to be found in his activity. As to the question of knowing more things about God, the Christian would have to qualify his answer. There are not a certain number of things that one can know of God by reason and an additional number that are known by revelation. If the word "knowledge" connotes the gathering in of objective data and the quantitative increase of facts about the world, then God's revelation cannot be identified with knowledge. God does not compete with infinite objects for man's attention; he does not fit into our schema of known things.

On the other hand, if "knowing" can designate man's primordial receptiveness to being and man's thrust forward to the fullness of life, then the Christian would claim that he knows and is known by God. Man's quest for some ultimate meaning has been met by God's loving gift of himself. This communion at the most intimate level of man's life has found objective historical expression in all human life. It has been expressed in a privileged way in the history of the Jewish people, in the history of Jesus of Nazareth, and in the lives of those who try to follow him in the way of God. In all human experiences this God is to be sought although some of the expressions within a continuing tradition have a special role in the listening to God. The professions of faith of the community are not truths revealed by God but they are of special importance in helping to unveil the God who reveals himself in all human life. Stories, poetry, or rituals may achieve this result more effectively than a logically constructed system of abstract truths.

The danger to which faith is continually exposed is that God will no longer be sought but that his revelation will be identified with something finite. The distinctive character of Judaic-Christian revelation is that God has left us no revelation. He is himself still here. The most subtle enemy of faith and revelation, Bonhoeffer and Barth have recently taught us, is religion. In this context, religion would be the supposition that revealed truths are a substitute for a revealing God. When such a notion of revelation gains ascendancy, the role of the community leader becomes that of dispenser of revealed truths. The rest of the community is then under pressure to accept these truths and conform to them. Not only is this notion of revealed truth inhibitive of personal faith and mature freedom, it is creative of an idolatrous situation. For a revealed truth in Christianity can be nothing but an idol. God reveals and conceals himself in the naming of every truth. Every human formulation testifies to its own inadequacy and forbids the equation of any doctrine with revelation.

Nothing of itself is divine. Even the greatest works of man cannot be guaranteed to reveal God. Man is not God; that is not the whole truth but it is an important truth that man must struggle to retain. To preserve the transcendence of God it is necessary to insist just as strongly on a complementary truth. God does not depend upon man but he is freely in our history, concerned with each event in human life. He is not an abstract God above the heavens but a God who is for us. Some men try to protect the true God by keeping him removed from the contamination of history. In pushing God out beyond man's power of description, they succeed only in introducing a substitute god to whom men can be related. Whoever tries to save God from involvement in present history usually ends by idolizing elements of past human history.

God's utter sovereignty is therefore inseparable from his intense concern with man's history. There must be on our part a readiness *always* to look for God in historical happenings but *never* to equate our human judgment of the event with the

12

divine will. This constant tension and striving forward requires the strictest self-criticism. The clearer became God's intention in the demands laid upon man, the more difficult it became to ascertain the next historical step in realizing his will for man. The closer God drew, the less conceptualizable he became.

Christianity is not or should not be the reversal of this fundamental belief of Judaism. It would be a wrong impression to think that in Jesus the veils were taken away and God became known. It is incorrect to assume that Christians should not be in doubt because God himself has told us in plain language what to believe and what to do. Not only is this notion of divine revelation not the consequence of the incarnation; it is a direct denial of it. The Word became flesh, the Word did not do away with flesh. God did not become obvious and comprehensible in Christ. He became more confusing or at least more paradoxical; that is, we are driven to re-examine our most basic presuppositions of what God should be like. In Christ the contrast of good with evil is put into sharpest focus. At the same time we are cautioned that the line of demarcation does not run between creator and creature, nor between creature and creature, but between the good and the bad in each man's heart.

Christ does not supply any ready-made answers for the questions of contemporary men. His life is proposed as an answer to the question which man's being presupposes. He gives no revealed doctrines about God nor any revealed precepts for leading a proper life. He does suggest the examples and he himself becomes the example for other human beings to live before God. Whatever Christ was, he was not just a very, very good man who left some idealistic teachings to be followed. He was at the least a strange and incomprehensible character in whom a unique call to other men occurs.

The last glimmering hopes of man for sacred messages and divine institutions were extinguished with Christ. What had been implicit has now become an unavoidable fact, namely, that man is the high point of creation and that there are no messages

13

or truths above him. If God is to be sought, it can only be in human life. God can be for man only as man takes up his own responsibility and frees himself from every form of slavery.

The God of revelation is the one who can be reached only by belief. In belief one stakes his life on a person rather than on submission to the bounded truths of nature. To believe is to be in restless search for the one who guarantees that it is not absurd to seek. The belief is restless but it is also serene to the extent that one knows a presence and an absence that cannot be lost. In knowing God as present, the believer is confident of this truth for a presence of love is simply a positive reality that asserts itself. No argument brings about a presence and no argument can take it away. As to the experience of God's absence, the believer is painfully aware of this fact but knows too that absence is significant only in contrast to presence.

The undeniable reality of evil and suffering is the most inexplicable fact that the believer must live with. He knows that the affirmation of God is no solution to the problem of evil, but neither is the denial of God. The struggles and sufferings that men are involved in surely must have some seriousness and meaning. To try to maintain the opposite and merely take a stand against the absurdity of life is still to affirm some value of heroism and to approve the taking of a stand on something ultimate.

For those who think that Christianity gives answers of naïve optimism, it might be emphasized that it is Christianity which maintains that there is no final solution except in death. What is more, death in Christianity is not of body alone as distinct from soul nor is it simply escape from life. Death is the shattering apart of man's personal existence in which he becomes receptive to the sufferings of all men. Only he who is willing to die daily, only he who is willing to lay down his life for his brother is a follower of Jesus to the revelation of God. This cannot be assumed of everyone who calls himself Christian; it can be attributed to every man who believes that love is stronger than hatred

14

and death and who is willing to back that belief with his life. Here is the supreme paradox for the Christian believer: he must believe that the man who is denying God with his lips may have more truly found God than the believer who is confessing God and working in his name.

There is no way out for the believer in a revealing God. He must continue to strive forward after God although he knows that his strivings will of themselves never attain to God. Other men demanded: Where is your God? Can you not at least give us a working definition of him? The believer will be tempted to change the One Who Cometh into the truths that are or the things that have been handed down. To fall into this trap would be to close off history and introduce a god above man. Every impatient attempt to make God appear results in a false god that competes with human freedom. The God who reveals himself is the one who lets himself appear, choosing the ways and the times. He is the one who keeps open the future so that man may become more himself.

Thus man is allowed to live his life with its joys and sorrows, its ups and downs; he is not to cling convulsively to life nor frivolously toss it aside. The revealing God who draws near is the judge, the hunter, the lover. Either to accept this God or to try to build still another god is the choice man is always faced with. God is not the answer to any human problems but he is the demand for an answer and the promise that it is not useless to seek a better world.

II.

The God of the Bible

BRUCE VAWTER

WHAT IS VALID about the death-of-God theology, if this is to use
the right word, is of course that the God of theology is what we
make him. This has always been true, as true in the theology of
Chalcedon or Augsburg or Vatican II as in the mythologies of
Canaan or Mesopotamia or Phrygia, which fashioned very satisfactory gods for themselves out of an experience of life that some
men found adequate and real. To paraphrase St. Thomas, when
we name God we speak our experience, our understanding of
man and of ourselves (*S.T.*, I, xiii, 1). This is only to say what
has been said many times before and since—though by some it
is now being said as for the first time—that a good theology must
begin as a good anthropology. Therefore, while one may question the judgment on which an analysis of the human condition
leads to the conclusion that contemporary man stands in no need
of redemption but only of reconciliation with his fellows, he
should not fault the logic by which in this view of man God is
proclaimed dead. With Schubert Ogden he may agree that it is
wildly implausible to claim that this can ever become a genuine
theology of Christian faith, but that is another question entirely.

To take up that other question, I begin, as I suppose I can,
with the assumption that a genuine theology of Christian faith
will be a biblical theology (though not, obviously, merely a
theology of the bible). Such a theology I cannot conceive if it
does not have at its heart the true God whom the Israel of the
bible claimed to worship—that is, the God who had *proved* him-

16

self true, trustworthy, reliable, in Israel's historical experience, who conformed to the realities of life as Israel knew them. When Israel branded the gods of the Gentiles "lies," it was not necessarily to deny their existence; a theoretical monotheism was of late development in its thought and really has little to do with the bible. Rather, it was meant that such gods were unreliable, unsuitable for faith and trust, since they did not correspond to the realities.

The superior cultures on which Israel thus sat in judgment, and which admittedly it never made much effort to understand, would have regarded the Israelite attitude as one of incredible arrogance. As Mircea Eliade, the Frankforts, and many other scholars have shown most convincingly in their studies of mythopoeic thought, the mythological religions of Mesopotamia and Egypt, the twin foci of all that was civilized in the ancient world, were highly serious and pragmatically successful attempts to come to grips with life's deepest problems and man's most earnest questionings. They were, before their time, the scholastic syntheses of the middle ages or of nineteenth-century scientism, in which everything in a closed universe was identified and put in its place where it harmonized with everything else. The mythological worldview was an organized, hierarchical structure of great complexity which on its premises made admirable sense and reflected faithfully the mentality of its age just as surely as Peter Lombard did that of the semi-mythical Christian world of the age of faith. It is in keeping that the art of such otherwise alien cultures should so often show striking parallels, and that the Sumerian organization of temple and city should resemble nothing so much as a medieval abbey town.

It was doubtless the very consistency of the mythological religions that first roused Israel's mistrust. The way that Israel had gone had given it an experience that did not coincide with these neat, tidy, pat answers to life's problems. The record of that experience is the Old Testament, which because of it is rather different from any other literature of man. Despite careless or deliberately sensationalist titles like "the Babylonian Job" or "the Egyptian Koheleth," in point of fact there is nothing in the literatures of the great nature religions of antiquity that really resembles Job or Ecclesiastes. There was hardly room there for these images of a God who does the unexpected, who is totally unpredictable, who is Raymond Nogar's "Lord of the Absurd."

It was not the way of mythology only that Israel renounced because of its experience. As Joseph Ratzinger has brought out in a recent study, in his journey beyond myth man generally took (with some deviations at times) one of three paths: that of mysticism, of monotheism, or of philosophical enlightenment. The last re-integrated him in nature in just the way the old myths had done, but now without the gods, who were dispensable. This is the great liberation of human thought that is sometimes ascribed to the pre-Socratic Thales of Miletus. The way of mysticism was that of the great religious personalities, whose names remain as exemplars to other men of the ultimate meanings that can be discovered within their own selves. As the early church fathers already recognized, and as we recognize better from a study of comparative religions they had not made, biblical religion produced no great religious personalities of this kind, no Buddha, no Confucius, no Lao-tse. Biblical monotheism took the path neither of nature nor of that inward turning that seeks absorption in the All, but of faith in a received word.

We don't disparage other men in the other ways in which they seek meanings in life when we insist that Israel's path was true. Acceptance, even very dogmatic acceptance, of the way of Israel ought never to have precluded the recognition that the designs of God can be broader than its own vision of God could tell. Nor did it always. Arnold Toynbee has ascribed the doctrinal intolerance of Christians to their Judaistic origins. Yet the great Pentateuchal traditions (the Priestly *ex professo,* the older Yahwistic more than equivalently) prefaced to their belief in a unique and unrepeatable Sinaitic covenant with Israel, the divine covenant with all mankind in Noah. And as Jean Daniélou has shown, in

18

its dealings with "holy pagans" the Old Testament made good on the possible conclusions from this premise. From later on in the same tradition, we might remember the often perversely misunderstood *angelus ex machina* whom Aquinas imagined the Christian God might send in order to guarantee the universality of his salvific will.

Nevertheless, the force of Pascal's discovery remains, that the God of the philosophers is no God of Christians. Here I would firmly dissociate from Schubert Ogden by specifying the philosophers as both modern *and* classical; Pascal, it is not always remembered, added "scholars" to his "philosophers." He is not such a God, I believe, simply because he is a God who has appeared in the experience of a people, and there has never been a people of philosophers. Judged by this standard the God of philosophers must always be a suspect deity: it is hard to credit the idea that a God who has revealed himself to such a few really cares enough about man that man should care much about him. He is an ideal deity to the same extent that Plato's Republic of philosophers was an ideal polity, extending to no real condition of man. There is no question here, obviously, of arguing about or against philosophical objectivation: no one should presume to challenge another man's philosophy unless he is prepared, if he can, to retrace the path that led the other to it. It is only that there is such little likelihood that it will ever be the path of any other men. The God of Bultmann, Heidegger, of, I strongly suspect, Paul Tillich, of, I would venture to say, Bishop Robinson (the theologian rather than the exegete), certainly of Professor Whitehead, will always remain a very personal deity, necessary, no doubt, a true God for his true believer, but just as irrelevant to the larger world of man as the *Protos Aion* was to the man in the streets of Periclean Athens.

The God of the bible is the God of a people's historical experience. Acceptance of his word begins, as does any other truly human attitude towards life, with an act of faith. Faith in the biblical God is, first and foremost, faith in a God of salvation: it

19

was as a saving God that Israel first experienced Yahweh and that Paul experienced Christ and the God revealed in Christ. And it was in terms of salvation that all the other works of God were understood, not excluding creation when, somewhat tardily, a theology of creation was evolved which, in both the Old and the New Testaments, appears as the divine saving act *par excellence.*

If we ask, from what is God supposed to have saved man, the answer would have to be, at its most basic, from the meaninglessness of existence—existence which, only when it has taken on meaning and purpose, does the bible know as "life."

Existence without this faith the bible does consider meaningless, and in this respect the bible has a far clearer title to the assent of universal human experience than any God of the philosophers can have. Bishop Robinson quotes Professor Huxley, a voice from the past with which he seems to have been strangely impressed, on the inevitability of science's producing in the end the grand synthesis in which the need of God will be no more. But as we know very well, science has not made the world more comprehensible and rational, but quite the reverse. The thinking man's response to the world science has given him has been no grand synthesis, but that existentialist decision and renunciation which is the humanistic *credo quia absurdum.* Biblical faith is itself such a decision and renunciation, but in favor of a saving God.

One element in the biblical anthropology that necessitated a saving God is what we in Christian terminology have long known as original sin. However it may have been or is now articulated, this notion corresponds to something that seems to be a universal human experience on which man is agreed, as long as he is left to his experience and not, as St. Paul would say, deceived by philosophy. The Yahwistic author of the tenth pre-Christian century articulated it in the beautiful paradise myth which has contributed the adjective "original" to our traditional vocabulary. Elsewhere in the bible it has been articulated otherwise and without recourse to the myth, which in any case is peripheral; St. Paul alone in the New Testament returns to the Yahwist's story, without making a point of it as a story.

Here as elsewhere the bible has used myth on occasion because it is the bible, "because it is only Christian men who guard even heathen things." Its use of myth, however, does not make the bible a mythology. Already in its own way and for its own reasons it had begun to do what Father Hulsbosch has seemingly demonstrated we must do again and for other reasons in this Teilhardian age. But when we do what we must, when the myth has been sorted away, we can still recognize ourselves ineluctably in the biblical word: "the inner longing for eternity and the impotence to fulfill this longing . . . a wanderer who, in the depths of his heart, longs for the Tree of Life, but sees that the gate is closed."

The historical experience in which Israel encountered its saving God is the revelation that constituted it a light to the nations and is the most meaningful sense in which Israel was and is an elect people. It was its unrefracted view of man who knows good and evil, in whose members there is this war of interests, that made Israel reject the attempt to project a macrocosm more logical of itself than the microcosm. It remains a touchstone of this biblical faith that man and the world he inhabits cannot save themselves, that they must be saved from without. Neither has this situation been altered as an experiential fact for everyman because of the incarnation and atonement which Christian faith understands to be the epitome of the revealing and saving word: they have but delineated the culmination of a way of salvation that Israel already knew. If, as Father Hulsbosch says, Christ has opened the gate, if the New Testament preaches a realized eschatology, it is only in virtue of our hope in an eschatology that remains final and future. With Oscar Cullmann I believe that an abandonment of true eschatology is the sure and infallible sign of apostasy from Christianity and a reversion to the myth of timelessness from which the bible once saved us.

It is, therefore, to an authentic human condition that the biblical word continues to speak. There is a place in it for the healthy skepticism of Ecclesiastes and the healthy eroticism of the Song of Songs as well as for Amos' cry for justice and Hosea's vision of a God of love, for these too are part of that human condition to which and in which God reveals himself; these too are the word of God. An unerring instinct brought them into the canon of scripture, to the scandal of those who will not take man as he is and therefore will not hear God as he has spoken. There is a place in it for Paul's friendly note to Philemon as well as for his letter to the Romans, for the inspired grotesquerie of the Apocalypse along with the Sermon on the Mount. It is in this sense that *sola scriptura* does somehow sum up all that we expect to know abut God, because it is so true to all that we know about man.

By knowing the human condition to which it speaks, the biblical word is really capable of offering salvation, of conferring that meaningful existence which it presents as true life. It reaches man in his twin loci of time and place and frees him from both of these by transforming them both. As Brevard Childs has argued, what is really unique about the biblical concept of time is the qualitative discontinuity it ascribes to it. "The new is not a mere renewal, but the entrance of the unexpected." In this concept is the seed of progress, of hope, for man and for his world. As with time, so with place. Places are important to the bible because there something happened; it was not that something happened because of the place. The biblical word liberates man from the pretended sureties of time and place by destroying their natural autonomy over him, by historicizing them. Or, put in other words, biblical faith sets man free of what Erich Fromm calls his narcissism, his natural attachment to the womb that gave him birth, and sends him forth on pilgrimage to find what it assures him is the real meaning of life.

Abraham passing from Ur to Canaan, Jacob from Canaan to Egypt, Moses and Israel from Egypt back to Canaan again, Jesus on pilgrimage from Galilee to Jerusalem, Paul from Jerusalem to Rome: the bible is not only a history of salvation but its itinerary as well, yet only as time and place are conditions to be used and themselves the causes of nothing. In the New Testament the liberating word achieves its perfection in the person of one who regarded not even a divine primal condition as a thing to be clung to, but emptied himself of it to obtain through pilgrimage a name above every other name and in whom was therefore revealed the supreme paradox of Christian faith, that life is to be found not in cherishing it but in throwing it away.

The *synkatabasis* that is biblical revelation sometimes hangs the exegete and theologian on the horns of a hermeneutical dilemma. Has the biblical word been predetermined by a view of God and man that was a Semitic cultural phenomenon of a number of pre-Christian and the first Christian centuries, or has it been the word itself that formed the biblical categories? Often it may be quite impossible to establish the priorities. In many details I am sure that it does not matter much whether we can establish them or not, though in certain vital areas it is very important indeed that we should. Certainly the bible itself was in no doubt about the priorities at least as regards the key affirmations of biblical faith. As the Second Isaiah reminded Israel, "My thoughts are not your thoughts, nor are your ways my ways, says Yahweh. As high as the heavens are above the earth, so high are my ways above your ways and my thoughts above your thoughts." The continual newness of the bible's historical experience in which time and place were transformed, the bible saw as the continued inbreaking upon its consciousness of a word from without. Jesus is the Word to the Fourth Evangelist precisely because he has revealed the God whom no man has ever seen.

It may seem that there is a somewhat unresolved epistemology in these biblical concepts. The perennial newness of the prophetic word, the guarantee of a theology of progress and human freedom the very opposite of a myth of eternal return or of any determinism ethical or historical, at the same time asks to be judged and accepted on the basis of the already known, the *tradita*. John's

23

and Paul's exhortations to test the spirits merely echo the protestations of the great prophets and of Deuteronomy, and the grounds of the testing are the same: "If a prophet or a dreamer of dreams arises among you and offers to do a sign or wonder for you, and the sign or wonder comes about; and if he then says to you, 'Come, then, let us follow other gods (whom you have not known) and serve them,' you are not to listen to the words of that prophet or to the dreams of that dreamer . . . That prophet or that dreamer of dreams must be put to death, for he has preached apostasy from Yahweh your God who brought you out of the land of Egypt and redeemed you from the house of slavery." On a more positive note, the author of Hebrews and the New Testament in general appeal for the credibility of the Christian word to the many different times and ways in which the same word had come to the fathers of the Israelite and Jewish past.

The resolution of the epistemological difficulty apparently lies in the biblical conviction of a consistent historical process to which human experience was warrant. It is this historical process, I feel, that remains the *locus standi vel cadendi* of biblical faith today, and it is shocking to find that at times it is made of such little account in the very name of the faith it underlies. This is said not as an appeal for historicism or in the thought that historical criticism can of itself validate any of the interpretations the bible has given to any event in history. I insist only that for the biblical authors the interpretations they offered *were* of events and not "cleverly devised tales" (2 Peter 1:16); and an idea of "salvation history" that treats as irrelevant our ability, or the degree of it, to get at these underlying events I fail to see as much concerned about the difference between history and cleverly devised tales. The studies of Alt and Albright, de Vaux and Gordon, Speiser and Glueck on the God of the fathers and the fathers themselves; of Noth and L'Hour on the Israelite amphictyony; of Mendenhall, Beyerlin, Baltzer, and McCarthy on the Mosaic age and Israel's covenant—all of these I consider to be matters of pressing contemporary concern for biblical faith,

24

as are the studies of Dodd and Jeremias and the post-Bultmann-ians in the kerygma of New Testament Christianity.

The late T. W. Manson once wrote: "It is easy to laugh at those who, a couple of generations ago, saw in Jesus a good nineteenth-century humanist with a simple faith in a paternal deity. It is less easy to see the joke when the Jesus of history is a twentieth-century existentialist, a kind of pre-existent Heidegger . . . But if God does reveal himself in history, it is there if any-where that we must find him. If God did in fact speak through the prophets we cannot absolve ourselves from the task of finding out as exactly as we can what was said and what is meant. If God did in fact speak to us through the life, death, and resurrec-tion of Jesus, it is vitally important to know as fully and as accurately as possible what sort of life and death and resurrection became the medium of the divine revelation. There is no escape from the historical inquiry."

The historical inquiry will continue as long as we do. To the extent that it can continue, biblical religion can remain relevant, translatable into the historically changing condition of man. And to this extent, too, it can remain a constant challenge to historical man. Some*thing* happened in the exodus, some*thing* in the resur-rection. If we believe what the bible says this something meant, it is our task to find out better what indeed it was, the better to understand it in relation to our own needs and responses. If neces-sary—as sometimes it is inevitable—this must be done at the sacrifice of outworn biblical categories. Karl Rahner is quite in the right when he warns against confusing biblical theology with a pious biblicism. A word—any word—demands continual trans-lation if it is to continue to be a word. What is to be translated is the bible and not, as some seem to imagine, the contemporary hearer of the word, whose head they want to cram with "Semitic thought patterns." Translation of this kind is a rather more com-plicated process than simple "demythologizing."

If, on the other hand, we are no longer concerned at all with the biblical something as an experienced reality that can speak to

25

us, we had better stop thinking in terms of a biblical faith altogether. Some*one* acted in the exodus, in the resurrection. We cannot read the psalms or the prophet Jeremiah or the apostle Paul without recognizing how this conviction is all of the bible. Unless we can share that conviction, we had better move on to some better source of religious inspiration than the bible. This, I think, is not for the bible to ask too much, that we take it for what it is or leave it alone.

III.

The Human God: Jesus

JOHN S. DUNNE

"THE PASSION of man," Sartre has said, "is the reverse of that of Christ, for man loses himself as man in order that God may be born." What Sartre means, I think, is that man attempts to do away with the concerns and anxieties which make him human, either by fulfilling his desires or else by hardening himself to pain and deprivation or else by renouncing his hopes and fears, in order that the fulfilled or hardened or detached being which he conceives to be divine may be born.

Something hinders us, if this is true, from entering fully into the A.D. period and finding our way to the present. We lose ourselves as human beings in order that God may be born. We are like the two bums, Vladimir and Estragon, who are waiting for Godot in the tragicomedy by Samuel Beckett. We are oriented towards the future, waiting for the future to dawn. We live in B.C., waiting for A.D. to come, waiting for God to be born. Vladimir and Estragon wait and wait again, but Godot never comes. The future is always ahead, always still to come. Complete fulfillment, complete hardening, complete detachment are always out of reach. "We lose ourselves in vain," Sartre has concluded, "man is a useless passion."

What is missing here, I believe, is the humanity of Christ, the idea that the passion of God, God losing himself as God in order that man may be born, the reverse of what Sartre called the "passion of man," would also be a human passion. It would be, in fact, the passion to be human, just as the passion of man is the

27

passion to be divine. Although man is not God and therefore in a sense cannot lose himself as God, he can very well have the desire to be God, to be God through fulfillment or through hardening or through renunciation, and so he can lose himself as God by aiming at being man rather than at being God. The lost pathway into the present, according to this, would have to be the path of the "kenosis," the "emptying" of self described in the great hymn about Christ in Philippians 2:7. We can understand what it is to desire to be God through fulfillment of desire or through hardening against pain and deprivation or through re-nunciation of hope and fear, and so we can understand conversely what it is to aim at being man rather than God.

When we make humanity our aim, however, and enter thereby into a sympathetic understanding of the passion of Christ, we come to believe that the fulfilled or hardened or detached being which we had imagined to be divine on the basis of our own de-sire to be God is not the genuine God, but the genuine God is the one who loses himself as God in order that man may be born. This is my way of stating that central theme of contemporary theology which Karl Barth has called "the humanity of God."

If we may expect to discover the genuine God when we dis-cover the humanity of Jesus, how do we go about discovering the humanity of Jesus? This has been one of the chief theological problems of recent times. One approach to it has been the famous "quest of the historical Jesus" which was criticized by Albert Schweitzer and which has been renewed in a somewhat changed form more recently by some of the followers of Rudolf Bult-mann. Another has been Søren Kierkegaard's project of "becom-ing contemporary with Christ." The quest of the historical Jesus was essentially a quest of the true standpoint on Jesus. The trouble was that there were many possible standpoints, that of Matthew, that of Mark, that of Luke, that of John. Which was the true one? On the whole it seemed that the true standpoint was that of Mark. In the last analysis, though, the quest of the true standpoint appeared to be hopeless, and the historical Jesus seemed to be forever hidden in the past. This result was obtained on Jesus, but it could also have been obtained on other personages if the same zeal and rigor and exactitude were applied to finding the true standpoint on them. For instance, which was the true standpoint on Socrates? That of Plato, that of Xenophon, or that of Aristophanes? Or is Socrates too, as has also been suggested, hidden forever in the past?

The real upshot, if the relativity of standpoints is taken into account, is not that Jesus and Socrates and, for that matter, every other personage of the past and even of the present is simply hidden. It is rather that the kind of knowledge we can have of ourselves and others is a "knowledge of ignorance" instead of a "knowledge of knowledge." We can know what was true about Jesus from the standpoints of Matthew, Mark, Luke, and John, and we can know what was true about Socrates from the standpoints of Plato, Xenophon, and Aristophanes, even though we know that each of these standpoints is relative. We can pass over, furthermore, from these standpoints, relative as they are, to the standpoints of Jesus and Socrates themselves, while realizing that these two are relative. This is how I would propose to carry out Kierkegaard's project of "becoming contemporary with Christ."

But can we say that the standpoint of Jesus is relative? Is this not tantamount to denying his divinity? Actually, to say this neither affirms nor denies his divinity. It does affirm his humanity. Let us consider, at any rate, what the life of Jesus would look like if we should assume that his standpoint on his own life was relative. The relativity of a person's standpoint on his own life is the fact that there are as many different standpoints on his life as there are different moments in his life. These standpoints always differ quantitatively, the past and future being longer or shorter according to the point where the person stands in his life, but they differ qualitatively, the past and future being taken differently, before and after the turning points of the person's life. The turning points in the life of Jesus, I would suggest, concern his

29

relations to John the Baptist. At any rate, here again, let us consider what the life of Jesus would look like if we should assume that this is so.

The first great turning point in the life of Jesus would have been his meeting with John the Baptist. What this meeting did, it appears, was to raise in his life the issue of being God's son, God's beloved. He came to John apparently in a considerably less exalted state of mind, ready to undergo John's baptism of repentance and to be one among many sinners. When he was baptized, however, he had a vision of the Spirit descending upon him, and a voice was heard declaring him God's beloved son in whom God was well pleased. Then he went into the desert and was tempted, some of the temptations taking the form "if you are God's son . . ." The meaning of "God's son" here is probably the one suggested by the words "beloved" and "in whom I am well pleased," namely one who is God's beloved and in whom God is well pleased. What happens here, this would imply, is that Jesus, who is ready at this point to take his place among sinners, receives and experiences unconditional acceptance from God.

Now from the standpoints of Matthew, Mark, Luke, and John, there can be no question of Jesus taking his place among sinners, and then too he is God's son in a somewhat different sense for each of them but always in a stronger sense than this. It is possible, nonetheless, to pass over from their respective standpoints to that of Jesus at this point in his life by attending closely to the fact that he does, however paradoxical it seems, present himself to John for a baptism of repentance, and that the words declaring him God's son can be understood, however weak this seems in the light of later events, simply as God's favor.

Jesus evidently did not presume to be his own judge, either to condemn himself or to approve of himself. He came ready to accept condemnation of his past and received instead unconditional acceptance. Acceptance, however, was not without its problems as the temptations immediately following demonstrated.

The story of these temptations as it was told from the standpoints of Matthew and Luke was probably meant to show how Jesus overcame the temptations to which Israel had succumbed in the desert. This does not prevent them from having been very real and personal from the standpoint of Jesus himself. Ready to undergo the baptism of repentance, he had been ready to accept condemnation of the past and to set the future against the past. Unconditionally accepted and looking towards the future anew, he was tempted to take advantage of his acceptance, but he refused to do so. Although he had been declared God's beloved like King David, he renounced the thought of an earthly kingdom, he resolved to live by God's word rather than by bread alone, and he determined not to presume upon God's acceptance or to put it to the test.

The second great turning point in the life of Jesus would have been the imprisonment of John the Baptist. When John was imprisoned, as Mark tells us, or when Jesus heard that John was imprisoned, as Matthew tells us, Jesus went into Galilee and began to preach. The imprisonment of John, the stopping of John's preaching, was the signal for the beginning of Jesus' preaching. Significantly too, as Matthew reports it, the message with which Jesus began was the same as the message of John, "Repent, for the kingdom of heaven is at hand." It is as though Jesus felt called upon to take John's place, to proclaim the message which John was now prevented from proclaiming.

The purport of John's message, however, would have been quite transformed when it came from the mouth of Jesus, transformed by the familiar relationship with God which grew out of unconditional acceptance. Jesus called God not merely "Father," in formal terms as we translate it, but "*Abba*," the familiar form in Aramaic, an unprecedented usage. What is more, he taught other men to speak of God and to God in this way, as though they too were unconditionally acceptable to God.

What Jesus saw himself as doing at this period of his life comes out, it seems, in his reply to the disciples of John the Bap-

31

tist who were sent by John from prison to ask Jesus "Are you the one coming or are we waiting for another?" Jesus replied "Go and tell John what you hear and see: the blind see, the lame walk, the lepers are cleansed, and the deaf hear, and the dead are raised, and the poor receive the good news, and happy is he who is not scandalized at me."

This reply by Jesus suggests a passage from the prophecy of Isaiah, the same passage with which Luke has Jesus begin his preaching. It probably describes what Jesus at this time conceived to be the coming of the kingdom of God. From the standpoints of the evangelists the coming of the kingdom was probably much more than the coming of Jesus in his public life, it was his coming in glory, risen from the dead. From the standpoint of Jesus himself at this period, though, the coming of God's kingdom would be the new situation which comes about as he communicates to other men what he himself received at his baptism, God's unconditional acceptance.

The third great turning point in the life of Jesus would have been the death of John the Baptist. "When Jesus heard of it," Matthew tells us, "he withdrew from there in a boat to desert country by himself." In John's death Jesus probably saw his own impending death. As John the Baptist was put to death by Herod, so also, Jesus and his contemporaries could see, was Jesus himself likely to be put to death. To begin his ministry, after the imprisonment, to continue it now, after the execution of John, was to risk death. As a matter of fact, Herod, thinking that Jesus was John the Baptist risen from the dead, wished to kill him. When Jesus was told of this, he said "Go and tell that fox, Behold, I cast out devils and do works of healing today and tomorrow, and on the third day I am finished. Yet today and tomorrow and the day after I must go on because it is not appropriate for a prophet to die outside of Jerusalem." Perhaps he meant by this that he would presently finish his work in Galilee, Herod's jurisdiction, but that he was going on to Jerusalem where he expected to die as had most of the prophets who were put to death. He dreaded the prospect. "*Abba,*" he prayed in the garden of Gethsemani, "all things are possible to you, take away this cup from me, but not what I will but what you will."

This prayer reveals the genuine attitude of Jesus towards his own death during this last period of his life. The death of Jesus probably made a great deal more sense from the standpoints of the evangelists than it did from his own standpoint at this time. It was not without meaning, however, from his own point of view, with his attitude towards God's will and his filial confidence in God. From the standpoints of the evangelists, Jesus had to die so that by raising him from the dead God could reveal that Jesus was the Lord. From his own standpoint Jesus could probably have said something like what John the Evangelist said: "Beloved, we are now children of God and it has not yet been manifested what we shall be."

Jesus had already received and experienced unconditional acceptance from God and lived on familiar terms with God, calling him "*Abba,*" but from his present standpoint it had not yet been manifested what he was ultimately to be. He was led into temptation and his relationship with God put to the test upon the cross where he cried out "*Eli Eli, lamma sabachthani?*"—"My God, my God, why have you forsaken me?" Still he did not despair, but was praying at the end, "*Abba,* into your hands I commend my spirit."

Thus if we assume that the standpoint of Jesus was relative, manifold, changing from period to period in his life, he appears to be fully and unequivocally human. His divinity, nevertheless, is not denied. Actually, the full impact of the statement "Jesus is the Lord," the fundamental statement of Christian faith, cannot be felt without first grasping the reality of his humanity. It is only when one sees Jesus as fully and unequivocally human that his lordship and divinity appears for the staggering mystery that it is. This is the way it will have appeared to his original disciples, who will have known him first as a man, obviously a man, and only afterwards when he rose from the dead, will have perceived his lordship and divinity.

In our culture, by contrast, where Jesus is the archetypal man, the culture hero, it is necessary to move to a position where he can be seen as truly human. To feel the overwhelming mystery of the incarnation in our time it is necessary to pass from the initial stage in which we find ourselves where Jesus is the culture hero, through an intermediate stage in which he becomes fully and unequivocally human for us, to a final stage in which we can appreciate the unending wonder of the statement "Jesus is the Lord."

To reach this intermediate stage where Jesus is fully and unequivocally human for us, we must pass over from the standpoint in which we are subjective and Jesus is objective (as culture hero) to the standpoint in which he is subjective. Luther, for example, attempted to enter into sympathy with Jesus by conceiving the abandonment experienced by Jesus on the cross to have been actual despair. I believe that Luther was wrong on this, that Jesus did not despair, though he said, "My God, my God, why have you forsaken me?", but that he continued to the last to hope in spite of his experience of Godforsakenness—"*Abba,* into your hands I commend my spirit." Still Luther was able, notwithstanding this seeming error in the process, to pass over to the subjective standpoint of Jesus, to grasp the reality of Jesus' humanity and thus to feel the full impact of the gospel that "Jesus is the Lord."

Although we cannot be sure of our grounds, therefore, in passing over to the standpoint of Jesus, it is still supremely worthwhile to make the attempt and to accept the risks involved. For it is only in passing over in this manner, I believe, that the humanity of Jesus becomes real to us and we enter into a position where we can perceive the overpowering significance of the tidings that "God exalted him and gave him the name that is above every name."

IV.

God: Language and Transcendence

DAVID B. BURRELL

REMARKS about the death of God, as those sensitive to language have noted, are in fact observations about contemporary culture. They do not pretend to metaphysical assertions or claim any witness to the event. They rather turn us back upon ourselves, reflecting in one more way our relentless demand for honesty. If most of us are practically pagans most of the time, let's admit it. The statement can assume many accents: a strident boast—we don't need God any more; a cry in the dark—show us his true face, for he cannot be the one we've been told about; or a bland indifference. For the first two, God's death is an event, something one has lived through or is presently experiencing. For the last there is no event, no death; but simply an absence—an absence without any hint of a presence, a bare fact. Simple indifference to transcendence may take the detached Gallican form of Camus' Mersault, or more probably the jerky erratic form of Updike's Rabbit. Yet it remains indifference, with little opening for any voice from within or without.

The strident boast can be absorbed: human needs know many strata. Christianity contains the seeds of liberation from any and all pagan forms of slavish dependence upon God. It has simply taken a good measure of human time to assimilate the message, though authentic Christians have realized it in every age. The *deus ex machina* departed from the scene the day it refused to come to the aid of Jesus and the temple veil was rent. The cry can be comforted and its source dried up. God *has* shown his own

35

face; it is his clerks who have distorted it. "Philip, how long have I been with you and you do not know me. Philip, he who sees me sees the Father." But this sort of transcendence proved insufficiently divine for men. The scandal of God-man had to be removed, and along with it the threat to restore men their freedom. The task of setting it straight again has occupied churchmen from Jesus' time to the present. The world has ever witnessed a kind of complicity between clergy and laity to keep the message under wraps lest men have to face their own humanity in acknowledging the humanity of God. Indeed nothing authenticates the Christian message quite so much as this incapacity of its purveyors to assimilate it.

Observations like these can divert both boast and cry into an honest inquiry into the sources of man's questing after God. And this we shall begin, investigating *transcendence* as the key to man's opening to himself as well as to God. But, first, the indifference. Unlike the other two attitudes, this has to be challenged. Not castigated but challenged, for it seems to be more of a cultural fact than a personal response—since it marks the lack of any response. The roots of this indifference have often been traced to the analytical sophistication of "contemporary man," who has consciously assimilated a scientific world view and consequently has no need of the God-hypothesis. While this may be true of some, it seems too academic to be true of most. For the question of God has seldom posed itself as one to be satisfied by scientific reasoning or proof. It seems rather more germane to questions of the worth and meaning of human life, and few feel that science sheds much light here. I would suggest a more promising and illuminating reading of current indifference as symptomatic of the contemporary democratic man who has quite innocently assimilated a Marxist view of himself and his worth.

The release of energy effected by the scientific revolution has certainly liberated us from any need for superstitious dependence on the vestiges of pagan divinities. But it has not always left us time to pursue the essential question of what is worthwhile. Indeed, the simple lack of leisure in our society is puzzling enough, but the near incapacity for it is baffling. Baffling at least until we recognize that "leisure" is not a simple descriptive term, but stands for an entire complex of attitudes that turn on appreciation and celebration, and these attitudes presume some point of contact with what spells worth and bestows value.

Now the quest for genuine worth, a conscious pursuit of "the Good," has never been expected of everyone. So the social structure envisioned by Plato and embodied (if only in barest outline) until quite recently in aristocratic society bestowed worth on the various positions in society and so granted to each free man—even the lowest—a sense of participation in a communal endeavor. The questions that one felt unable to ponder on his own had been considered and decided by others more eminent. Their decisions wrought the social organization, so each man's humble contribution *was* worthwhile. A convenient arrangement, and most certainly humanizing in its own right, but "man come of age" simply cannot settle for it. We can no longer rest content with a pre-determined worth or even a pre-fabricated respectability. Whether we are impelled to the genuine article or content with its artificial substitute, there is no other route open than the precarious one of achievement.

Now it seems clear that a world given over to achieving can leave no room for leisure. For celebration and joy introduce an air of the gratuitous, of worth bestowed rather than achieved. To the taut psyche required of an achiever, "leisure" can only mean "slack," and not much slack can be tolerated. The same could be said for genuine relations with other persons or a possible encounter with God. For the resolute achiever simply has no room for another—even less the Other—though the blame is often laid elsewhere: God is inimical to the human spirit. To the aggressive spirit, agreed; but how inimical has this same spirit proven to man himself?

Ironically and tragically, however, perhaps God seems inimical as well to the spirit made aggressive by a society where worth must be earned, respectability attained. Perhaps Nietzsche was prophesying the need that post-artistocratic men would have to forcibly eliminate God, and notably the God who showed his face in Jesus, as they would be constrained to forge their own way to recognition, devoid of a tradition to assign them worth and their actions value. (There will certainly be black moments for one chained to achievement. Besides the imminent possibility of failure, respectability itself is often endangered by the very manner in which one had to attain it. But to appeal to God at these points would certainly be reaching out for a crutch. It would be demeaning to the person and insulting to God. Hence despair, whether of a dramatic continental variety or the more diffuse, cynical Anglo-Saxon type, remains one's only *resource*.)

Now to be assigned one's worth was not exactly truthful. But many would probably find it somewhat more comforting than beginning with none—which seems to be the inevitable interpretation of *equality*. One must indeed make himself; no one can be spared the task. That is what rings true about a democratic renunciation of prior social structure. But how? Along what lines? By what model? Here hangs the question of *worth*. No longer a worth assigned but one required nonetheless, yet only available to him who would seek for it. But where can anyone find the time and the atmosphere to seek for it? For seeking of this sort is not achieving. It may mean bracketing the entire achievement process for a space, and is certainly threatening to it—for it explicitly asks whether the whole enterprise is worth it!

Now detours like this are uncomfortable for most when respectability and advancement are at stake, so we tend to settle for an assurance that all is worthwhile. Any assurance that is consonant with the democratic animus against pre-assigned worth, and also convenient and ready at hand, however, is bound to be some variant of Marxism: striving itself is a value and man's worth is measured, indeed created by his achievements. For us, of course, the ideological meat has been blended into a more palatable formula: contributing to the great American dream of universal prosperity. Hence "striving" means carefully shaping one's aspirations to the present model and projecting it into an expansive future.

If the churches will support this myth, they are welcome, for their support enhances its claim to provide a genuine goal for one's life. They may render ritual service to the society and its gods as Christendom once bestowed permanence and sacredness on the arbitrary values assigned by an aristocratic society. But there is no room for God, of course. There cannot be, so long as one eschews the search for value and settles for the ersatz worth of historical process. Add the fact that concentrated striving has indeed transformed the face of the earth and given men many more playthings as well, so that the Socratic cry for reflection, for examining one's life to see if it be *worth* living, often finds but busy minds and distracted ears.

Harsh though they may sound, these things must be said, for there is an easy secularity, as Richard Comstock remarks, which "avoids serious issues and accepts the comforts of urban life with a superficial and thoughtless complacency." It is not without its ghosts, of course. One has only to reflect on the malaise lurking in suburbia, the protest of modern theater, the bitterness with which the conscious student rejects the myth or how he hates himself for subserving it. My sketchy attempt to culturally position this question of God is intended to meet these churnings as well as the stubborn fact of indifference. Whatever its success, none of us can spare himself the attempt, for the question of God was never one for abstract discussion, but ever a quest for what is of worth, an inquiry into the well-springs of our activity, a search for ourselves—now.

Augustine underscored the reflective and personal character of man's search for God when he gave general directions to "turn within." Questions about God do not seem to arise out of intellectual curiosity, but rather in the mind's acceding to more intimate demands of the spirit. Indeed, philosophical and methodological treatment of these questions often finds itself embarrassed at being unable to respond to them with sufficient finesse. I will try to establish their philosophical propriety by highlighting the structural similarity between questions about God and discourse about value. But something else is clearly required, something that can give us all enough confidence to take up Augustine's advice. One idiom could well be the fantasy tale—the Tolkien trilogy or Lewis' Chronicles of Narnia—whose very purpose is simply to provide pastures for the spirit to roam, discover its reaches, come to recognize its own visage.

Literature of this sort seems especially needful today, for spirits whose intensity has been harnessed to achieving. Perhaps the freedom foretasted here can give us courage to begin the search for what is worthwhile. And courage is needed, for a genuine search is bound to be painful as well as threatening: I am not only inquiring into the value of what I do, but wondering about my own worth as well. Perhaps fantasy literature can provide the space each spirit needs to recollect itself from within and renew its resolve not to be distracted from becoming a man.

There is no assurance, of course, that the search for what bestows worth will carry us to God; there is in fact no assurance it will *arrive* anywhere. But it is imperative that we undertake it, and I shall try to show how the inherent demands of this search intertwine with many of the supporting strands of the most sophisticated Judaeo-Christian discourse about God. Hopefully, by establishing an inner affinity between men searching for what is genuine and believers seeking understanding of their God, one can clear the way for a community of sentiment, and a gradual realization that their object may well be identical. More than this I cannot do.

But first a word about the not-so-sophisticated talk about God, which I suspect represents the greater part of it. Theological formulations, however remote and metaphysical they may appear, have a way of settling into clichés. These implant themselves in ordinary educated discourse about the divine, creating a kind of collage that serves as a common referent for "God."

40

Witnessing the now stereotyped polemic of a Sartre or the revulsion of so many who have endured a standard catechesis, anyone religiously sensitive cannot help but feel that the response to the sacred and the demand for authenticity have been unduly estranged by the sedimented obscurities of our theological legacy.

Leslie Dewart (in his *Future of Belief*) speaks accurately of an "underdeveloped theism." Indeed nothing seems so underdeveloped or uncriticized, to believer and unbeliever alike, as our discoursings about God, whether from the pulpit or in the classroom. Or I should say nothing *seemed* so, until we were forced to realize how little of it we took seriously, how little we *could* take and remain humanly or spiritually alive! We have been forced to examine our formulations to ask whether "God" as we have continued to use the word could have any referent or is not, in that sense, dead. Nor can this examination stop short of a re-assessment of the classical theological tradition which has shaped the formulae sedimented in common usage.

The focal point of that tradition is Thomas Aquinas. To summarize his teaching on God here would be preposterous. No serious student can confront it without sheer admiration for the subtle way he presses semantics into serving a keen wit and a deeply honest religious sensibility. Yet we may speak to the *form* of his thought. God must be at once the source of being and the supreme being, if Aquinas is to be faithful to the metaphysical framework he inherited and made his own. That the source of being be beyond being follows from the logic of causal discourse; and once acknowledged, that this source *be* is a matter of strict logic. Yet God must exist in an utterly unique way: as the source of *all that is.* "He is not a substance, but the source of substance," Aquinas will say; he exists but *not* as anything else does. This paradox became domesticated by the schools into a "doctrine of analogy," allowing us to say and not say what he is like.

What is missing in the doctrine, however, and extremely underdeveloped in Aquinas himself is any suspicion that in talking

41

about God we are doing more than speaking of a supreme something out there. Not that one denied the authenticity of religious experience, but the conviction remained that theology had to be able to discourse about God in categories germane to objects if it wanted to be considered a science. He had to be a transcendent object, of course, and this posed severe semantic difficulties, but his transcendence could not remove him from being an object. "Transcendent," then, would only come down to something like "far far away" yet still within the realm of objects. And if religious sensibility intervened to insist that he is totally other than any object we know (as it often did in Aquinas' own reflections) then anything said about him—spoken, that is, in the manner we speak about objects—was condemned to "death by a thousand qualifications."

So logicians must concur that analogy will not work, and that one simply cannot speak in a meaningful way of God, if he must also be a *transcendent* object, agent and the like. It has been the merit of the more logically inclined of the linguistic philosophers to have shown the weaknesses inherent in any attempt to treat God as an object. They have proven far less successful, however, in attempting to show what is really operating in religious discourse. Theirs has proved a useful critique of a theology which shared their assumptions, namely that meaningful discourse must be "about objects," and party to a species of scientific verifiability.

The weakness of traditional theism and the God it has left us to discourse about does not seem to lie so much in the metaphysical categories it employs to conceive the God-object, as in an unexamined use of "transcendent." For whether one thinks of something "far far away" or "deep deep within," he is still ruminating about an *object,* and the religious pressure that insists on God's transcendence tends to push any consideration of him completely out of the realm of objects. Whatever else "transcendence" means, it must place God over against the world and everything that is in it or could be in it. Since "transcendent" is our way of stating what makes God God, religion's primary demand upon

42

theology is that it develop a language in which his transcendence be exhibited. So when one judges a theology of God underdeveloped, he means primarily that it has failed to remain consistently faithful to this demand.

If the tradition seems most vulnerable to us in failing to discover a language of transcendence, then the current neo-Whiteheadian effort seems quite beside the main point. For it challenges the way classical theology conceived the God-object—as *substance*—and then proceeds to substitute another metaphysical notion whose status is every bit as objective and ontological, namely *process*. And whatever the merits of process as an alternative category for conceiving the God-object, neo-Whiteheadians feel constrained to assert transcendence as well, which they tend to do in uncritical, classical terms.

But if his transcendence pushes God out of the realm of objects altogether, what hope can we have of speaking about him at all? Two clues to an alternative program can be gleaned from Aquinas himself. The first is an incidental remark to the effect that the most adequate lead we have to understanding spirit is one's presence to himself in conscious activity. The second is his constant insistence that any predicate used of God represent a *perfection*. Now if Aquinas' insistence is not to be redundant or banal, "perfection" must be an operative term. And to be operative it must be rooted in the fertile soil of human aspiration rather than merely occupy a niche in an ontological hierarchy. Indeed, how else are we to speak of a *perfection* except as that towards which *we* aspire? Unless what is to be valued appears as just that—of value—then we are accepting a valuation imposed from without.

Now we aspire to what is worthwhile, or better, only what is of worth can sustain the demands of human aspiration. In fact, the severe self-criticism built into human aspiration serves to define what will count as worthwhile. And the fact that autocriticism represents an inherent demand and requires an ongoing and reflective process makes this act of defining into something far

43

more active and plenary than a mere tautology: that to which men aspire is what they value or "where one's heart is there his treasure is also."

The language of aspiration, of course, has consistently defied attempts at straightforward analysis on the literal "propositional" mold. But this resistance could only be expected, for the hiatus between notional and real assent is a commonplace of our moral and personal experience. We are always asking of ourselves and of others whether we really stand for the ideals we verbally espouse. How often have we not found ourselves enunciating an insight into a new dimension of moral experience—that friendship, say, demands that I allow the other freedom to grow and be himself—only to realize both in our actions and in later reflections that we had but the barest suspicion *what* we were saying? I am not simply calling attention to the gap between saying and doing, but to the incredibly open and progressive character of moral knowledge. Realizations that we come to about ourselves and others or our relations with others, even when formulated initially in a way which will prove basically accurate, can so grow in clarity and resonance that we often literally wonder whether we understood anything when we first formulated them.

Plato displayed this uncanny human experience in the irony of Socrates and captured it in his adage: "the [truly] wise man is one who realizes he is not wise." What saves the statement from contradiction is the mediating term "realizes," for this interior activity of recollection and self-assessment controls the resulting paradox and allows us to put it to use. Socrates hit upon a logical form for discoursing about anything to which we aspire, anything worth pursuing in its own right. "Justice," "sensitivity," "intelligence," "holiness," all fit the mold: "the (sensitive) man is one who realizes he is not (sensitive)." Trying to live by an ideal, reaching to incorporate it into our conscious activity only serves to open us to yet further reaches, even greater demands. Descriptive terms with evaluative overtones will also fit the mold, though we usually have to add "good" to avoid ambiguity. Thus "the (good) salesman realizes he is not a (good) salesman." But valuations imposed from without—in so far as they are imposed —will not work. We cannot say that a champion runner realizes he is not a champion runner, for he has been judged to be so, and champions are *made* by qualified judges employing predetermined standards.

Being a salesman differs from being just precisely in having to justify selling. Someone could ask "why be a salesman?" but it makes no sense to ask "why be just?" Classically, of course, men tried to grapple with the latter question by showing how intimately justice is linked with other human aspirations and concluding, as Plato did, that one must aspire after it if he would be human. But "human" is not used in a purely descriptive way here. It rather becomes a summary term for everything to which men aspire. And aspiration is built into what is human along with the possibility of turning against our nature, so it is not a simple fact that man must be human. The "must" here is a moral requirement, not a fact of nature; hence we can speak of personal and moral growth as "becoming human" and use "humanism" to describe a set of values. In other words, "human" used in this way will fit Socrates' mold.

This demand for what is worthwhile, coupled with a progressive ability to discriminate between genuine needs (or aspirations) and immediate or compulsive needs has been termed human "transcendence." And aptly so, for talk about the worthwhile gives us a model for discourse about God and releases us from attempting to capture the transcendent as an object in imaginative terms: far far away or deep deep within. Furthermore, the Socratic paradox provides a human way to express and to recognize the essential feature of the *worthwhile* which links it so closely with God and his transcendence. That is what distinguishes what is worthwhile from a simple strategy, values from mere options—namely that what is worthwhile is simply that, worthwhile, and cannot be traded off for something else "above it."

The sign of this fact is not so much that the worthwhile, the authentic, imposes an obvious duty, as that it continues to draw us on. The source of human aspiration is not an imperative but the inexhaustible character of what is truly worthwhile. Though the quest for justice never be realized, our actual achievements are not thereby judged and condemned by some ineluctable standard. These very achievements only serve to renew our faith in what is essential to man—his aspiration to value. Socrates' just man who realizes he is not just does not despair but grasps that much more about himself—as he is and as he must become.

The "transcendence" built into the worthwhile, then, serves to define it and explain why questing after it need not be justified. And the fact that man's purposes need to subserve a value if he is to be free says something about man himself. And these twin facts provide a key to men's questions about God and their discourse about him. For the questions are raised concomitantly with those demanding a direction, a meaning for one's life. And any response which mentions God will speak of him in terms of like logical structure with those of human aspirations. As Ugo Betti put it, "Each of these mysterious needs . . . without which man cannot breathe or survive . . . is one side of a perimeter whose complete figure, when we finally perceive it, has one name: GOD."

Paradox remains the form for grappling with the transcendent, though its tension will be heightened, its grip tighter when used of God. He is present to those who acknowledge his presence, but always in darkness; he is present by an absence. Like Socrates', this paradox is not an outright contradiction. It rather illuminates for us, starkly yet accurately, something of presence as we experience it. Only what remains recessed and in some way absent can ever be present to me. What is transparent or merely puzzling is simply there, over against me but never present to me. Properly religious discourse grows more confident of this presence, and unlike theological talk *about* God, begins to speak more of him as one who is living with him.

46

Since the presence remains an absence, questing is never done with, but the accent shifts from our striving to his initiative. What justifies this shift in accent? Nothing of course but the growing presence-in-absence of God. But we can open ourselves to it by yielding to the unyielding demands of our spirit for what is worthwhile, both in fantasy and in fact. Nothing can assure us that the other side of these transcendent human aspirations is God but God himself. This he has tried to do by showing us his face in the man Jesus.

V.

The God of History

LOUIS DUPRÉ

CHRISTIANS CLAIM that theirs is an historical religion, distinguished from the non-historical, cyclic world view of the Greeks by the definitive, irreversible meaning of temporal events. Yet, no sooner is someone willing to believe this and to consider Christianity as historically determined and historically developing, than believers lose faith in their own assumption that God *can* speak an historical language. Their perplexity in the face of present-day reinterpretations of scriptural texts and ecclesiastical documents shows that they had never accepted evolution and relativity as essential characteristics of the historical, but had simply redefined history so as to fit a purely static concept of religion.

Now, it must be admitted in all fairness to the perplexed believer that religion is much more than an historical process: it is above all a dialogue with the transcendent, initiated by a revelation from a *trans-historical,* divine sphere. Still in the Judaeo-Christian tradition this revelation itself occurs as an historical event. God reveals himself through the history of a particular people and, within this history, in a definitive way through the acts and words of one man. Insofar as the revelation takes on an historical character, it must be received into that dynamic process through which man constantly creates and recreates his values.

Many Christians are not willing to draw this conclusion and hold strongly anti-historical views on scripture and tradition.

48

They refuse to accept the fact that the books of the scripture remain intrinsically dependent on the civilization in which they were written. Of course, we no longer use the bible as a test for judging geological and biological theories. But in more sensitive matters *concordism* is far from dead. Many still find it difficult to accept the idea of *moral* progress since the New Testament and, even more, that of *religious* development. Yet such progress is inevitable if the revelation is truly historical.

The sacred writers themselves seem to have been more aware of the fully human (and, therefore, historical) manner in which God's message is communicated to man. The author of 2 Machabees presents his book to the public with a slightly apologetic justification for his one-volume abridgment of another author's five-volume history. "The thing is not easy, and takes sweat and midnight oil" (2 Mc. 2:26-27). God's transhistorical message here is communicated through the unimaginative and pedantic mind of a hellenized Jew who may not have known that he was writing a holy scripture but who certainly knew how to sell a book.

Even the evangelists, who were fully aware of the unique religious import of the words and events they reported, realized that their writings would capture only as much of the divine revelation as their human and personal limitations would allow. The Fourth Gospel concludes with the following declaration: "There is much else that Jesus did. If it were all to be recorded in detail, I suppose the whole world would not hold the books that would be written." And Luke commences his story with a modest evaluation of his own position among the gospel narrators: "Many writers have undertaken to draw up an account of the events that have happened among us. . . . And so in my turn, your Excellency, as one who has gone over the whole course of these events in detail, I have decided to write a connected narrative for you, so as to give you authentic knowledge about the matters of which you have been informed."

If the divine message is to make sense at all it cannot be a

49

meteoric block "hurled at the world," but it must be actively received within a particular universe of discourse that will restrict it by its own limitations. There is no such thing as a purely passive reception of truth. Man alone can make truth, even though he must be divinely inspired to make *revealed* truth. But if this is the case, it follows that the *expression* of a revealed truth depends largely on the capacity of the receiving subject and this capacity is always to some extent culturally circumscribed.

Can there be a definitive expression of God's revelation, a final truth about what he has communicated to us? If *definitive* and *final* are understood in the sense of a total adequacy between the expression and the expressed, no single historical expression can ever exhaust God's revelation. Not even divine authority precludes concrete statements concerning man and his values from being subject to further evolution, for man himself continues to develop. On the other hand, the revelation (and the authentic tradition) must be expressed adequately enough to remain authoritative for later generations.

This conclusion applies even to the words of Christ. As a man Christ could not but think and speak *within* the framework of a particular time and culture. It is true enough that *as God* Christ suffered no cultural limitations, but it is equally true that such limitations are essential to human nature as omniscience is to divine nature. Nor is it sufficient to juxtapose Christ's human nature to his divine nature: the two were synthesized in one person. The First Lateran Council (649) used the expression "two wills harmoniously united" (Denz. 263) to establish the full autonomy of Christ's human nature, not to inflict upon the faithful the absurdity of a dual consciousness, ultimately opposed to the Ephesian doctrine on the one person in Christ.

Catholics usually avoid this problem by adopting some pragmatic version of docetism: they restrict the human nature of Christ to the biological functions of his body, while they treat all his other activities as if they were purely divine. But if Christ preserved the specific character of human nature, as the Council of Chalcedon clearly states (Denz. 148), then I do not see how the notion of an omniscient Christ unbound by any cultural limitation can escape contradiction. I also wonder what then the Gospel of Luke means when it states: "As Jesus grew up, he advanced in wisdom" (Lk. 2:52).

Man's relation to God can be expressed only within a particular language, that is, an interpreted set of symbols. This holds true even if the man who expresses this relation is also God. The creation of symbols is essentially a human task. Man alone uses symbols, and symbolic expression is the most distinctive trait of his embodied spiritual nature. This remains true even for divinely inspired scripture. The divine inspiration allows man to view reality in a special religious way and to express this insight adequately. It can never dispense him from creating the symbols himself. Only man can speak the language of man.

Through the incarnation God is able to speak to man from person to person, but the language is human and bears the mark of a particular person who lived in a particular culture. One does not improve the mystery of revelation by eliminating or minimizing this human element, for on this element depends the entire meaning. Some of Christ's followers in later ages may have brought out aspects of his message which could neither have been conceived nor expressed during his lifetime. The hypostatic union does not necessarily imply that the man Jesus was able to understand and express this union in all its inexhaustible fullness. Christ is absolutely authoritative in *what* he expressed and in that it was *he,* the God-man, who expressed it. But his particular way of expressing it is, as all expression, co-determined by individual and cultural characteristics.

The same is even more true of the reports of Jesus' words and deeds in the gospels. The gospels possess a unique authority not because of their historical accuracy or their depth of theological insight but because their vision of Jesus' teachings and doings is an inspired expression of the faith of the original Christian community. Whether all the details are historical or not, whether

51

the theological insight is profound or not, is irrelevant. The story of the second coming in Matthew 24 shows that even at the time of writing the evangelists were still very confused on some parts of Christ's message. However, the authority of the gospels is not based on historical or theological qualities but on the faith of those who read it as an authentic expression of God's revelation in Christ.

Historical determinations also restrict the proclamations of the Church's magisterium. Each dogma shows the mark of the cultural conditions in which it was formulated. Often no correct interpretation of an authoritative document can be given without a good deal of information on the historical—and very contingent!—circumstances in which it was issued. The Council of Vienne (1311-1312) condemned Peter John Olivi's doctrine that "the substance of the rational, intellectual soul is not truly and by its own nature the form of the human body" (Denz. 481). To an uninitiated reader this must appear to canonize Aristotle's hylomorphic psychology or, at the very least, to condemn a plurality of psychological "forms." Historical research alone reveals that the issue at stake was not Aristotle or the unity of the psychological form (both rejected by many of the participating fathers) but the substantial unity of the person of Christ, which Olivi's loose concept of the unity of man might jeopardize.

In other documents the response lies so much buried in the particular controversy which provoked it that even historical research does not enable us to determine its exact import. The Fourth Lateran Council states that God created the world "from the very beginning of time" (Denz. 428). Does this mean that the universe has existed only for a finite number of years or is it merely a rejection of the Albigensian doctrine that the "creation" of the world was preceded by centuries of an "uncreated" (which means in their vocabulary, *unredeemed*) existence? Or what is the meaning of the Fourth Constantinopolitan Council's condemnation of Photius' "error" that man has two souls, when all we know about him is that he explicitly adopts the opposite thesis in his work (Denz. 338)?

The words of Christ and the basic directions of his Church guide man authoritatively in his relations with God. To question their way of viewing this relation would be tantamount to rejecting the entire message of Christ. But the symbols in which this view or, in phenomenological terms, this *intentionality* is expressed are, as all human symbols, determined by a cultural tradition. This is not to say that they are false or even inadequate. If a revelation is to take place at all, the symbols in which it is expressed must have at least that minimum adequacy which enables them to transmit the message effectively to later generations. But beyond that, every generation has the task of capturing the message of the revelation anew.

The difficulty, however, is to distinguish intentionality from expression. A symbolic expression is not a disposable form wrapped indifferently around a content. Man *thinks* in symbols and, as Cassirer and his followers have shown, the content of his conscious activity does not pre-exist its symbolic expression. Without expression there is no intentionality at all. It is, therefore, insufficient to assume that the intentionality of revelation and of authentic magisterium is divinely determined, whereas the expression is not. This over-simplification seems to be inherent to the concept of *demythologization*. If symbolic form and content are so intimately united, it is impossible to separate the "mythical" form of scripture from its content. The concept also seems to suffer under a latent rationalism by pre-supposing that the demythologized expression will be religiously more adequate than the "mythical" one.

Even so, form criticism deserves much credit for having made the first serious attempt to integrate revelation into the evolutionary process of history without abandoning its uniquely religious character. Most Christians avoid the mistakes of form criticism only by ignoring or denying all human autonomy in the

53

symbolization of the bible. They do not seem to realize that the meeting of the divine and the human in one act requires more initiative on man's side than that of a secretary taking a dictation.

In giving expression to God's revelation man is as creative as he is in building the world. A biblical author's individual and cultural qualities and limitations account not only for his literary style but also for the intellectual quality and even the religious depth of his work. Inspiration does not eliminate the creativity (good or bad) of a literary work; it merely guarantees that this work is an authoritative expression of an original religious impulse.

But this intimate mingling of divine inspiration and human creativity makes the question all the more urgent: How must Christianity develop so as not to betray its original message? How can we separate the relative from the absolute? The old theories claim that development consists merely in making explicit what is implicit and that nothing basically new is ever introduced. In his remarkable study *The Future of Belief*, Leslie Dewart convincingly shows how inadequate this explanation is. Yet, I am not sure that his own solution, interesting as it is, is altogether sufficient. He states that truth is achieved *in* conceptualization but not *by means* of any given determinate concept (p. 110). But the difficulty is that Christians have always considered the "conceptualization" (I would prefer the term *symbolization*) of *scripture and authentic tradition* as different from any other conceptualization of a religious experience, even from that of other (non-inspired) religious witnesses of the same original Christian community.

Why, for instance, are the *Shepherd of Hemas* and the *Didache* not authoritative while the *Second Letter of Peter* is, even though it may be later in date and not more religious in content? The question itself proves that inspiration and authority cover not only the factual content but also the phrasing and interpretation of this content. The Christian's faith is based not merely upon the facts reported in the scripture but also upon the scripture's special way of looking at these facts, which alone makes them into *religious* facts. If then the sources of the Christian religion are interpretations of facts rather than mere statements of facts, any further evolution of doctrine must keep in close touch also with the basic *interpretations* of the Christian tradition (starting with the New Testament writings).

To say that "Christianity was a *mission,* not a *message,*" as Dewart does (p. 8), is not entirely correct. Christianity may not have a doctrine (that is, a systematic body of knowledge), but it definitely has a message. Scripture is not merely "the report of an event that happens"; it also provides the authoritative interpretation of that event. A basic question, then, for any theory of a future development of the religion based upon that interpretative report is how far the meaning of the interpretation can be stretched without losing its identity. Until that question is answered we can freely "develop" the message of Christianity (as Hegel did quite successfully), but we will never know whether our development is still Christian.

From a Christian point of view, all speculation preceding that answer remains hypothetical, or, in Kierkegaard's words, "a project of thought" about which one must suspend one's final judgment. The most radical interpreters of the past, like Spinoza, Lessing and Strauss, very much realized the need for a prior evaluation of the basic meaning and authority of the scripture and concentrated most of their efforts toward reinterpretation on these two points.

The relatively small consideration which Dewart gives to the problem of scriptural and traditional authority may be due to the fact that, for him, religious truth (like any other truth) is defined as a conceptualization of *experience.* But is it sufficient to say that "Christian belief is a religious *experience*" (p. 113)? To the believer faith is always considerably more than a religious *experience.* An objective experience is experience *only to the extent that it grasps its object,* whereas the object of the religious act remains mostly transcendent to the experience. This is the very reason why the religious message has to be *revealed*. It is also the reason why the original expression of the message must be more than the "conceptualization of an experience." The symbolization of Christianity and its evolution cannot be determined by the experience alone because it expresses more than a mere experience. Any renewal, then, in the symbolic expression of the religious intentionality must be made in close continuity with its original, determining expression in scripture and early tradition.

However, this must not be understood as a call for traditionalism. The basic fallacy of traditionalism is that it detaches tradition from the living experience in which alone this tradition becomes meaningful. The traditionalist confuses the indispensability of the original expression with an absoluteness that no expression can ever possess. This confusion is caused by the strange idea that the divine eliminates *ipso facto* any sort of relativity. But scripture, even though divinely inspired, is *not* God: human language excludes any possibility of a full manifestation of God. The traditionalist somehow seems to think that the revelation is able to reserve its *absolute* character only by freezing symbols into unnatural, immutable forms. But it is a mistake to expect that an expression will convey the supernatural just because the natural characteristics of expression have been eliminated.

Still, it is easier to criticize traditionalism than to answer the question: How can the symbolic expression ever allow of any real development if the divine inspiration extends to the *wording* itself? The Christian seems to be caught in a dilemma. If he abandons the original symbols, he must also abandon the verbal inspiration which is the very guarantee of religious truth, and if he keeps these symbols immutable, he stifles the living spirit which they are to express.

To handle this problem adequately would require a more fundamental discussion of the nature of religious symbolism than can be given here. I will merely point out that religious symbols are much more flexible than those of scientific or even ordinary language, because their inability to express the fullness of their transcendent content makes the connection between the expression and the expressed less tight. Even compared to its nearest in kin, the aesthetic image, the religious symbol stands in a much looser relationship to its content. The aesthetic image fully, although inexhaustibly, expresses what it symbolizes, while the religious symbol always falls short of what it expresses. This deficiency is not due to an absence of precise meaning. As all other symbols, the religious symbol conveys an immediate, intrinsic meaning, for example, that God is Father, Son and Holy Spirit but, unlike other symbols, it attempts to attain through this obvious meaning a content that cannot be directly expressed.

The religious experience therefore lives in a constant tension with its forms of expression and at its highest moments tends to dismiss these forms altogether as insufficient. This basic ambiguity is what makes religious language so unscientific even when it attempts to be scientific. But it also enables religious symbols to develop organically and to renew themselves from within, while scientific symbols can only be discarded as soon as there is a basic shift in signification.

As early as the second and third centuries, Christians realized this polyvalent nature of the sacred expression and discovered a great variety of "allegorical" interpretations of the bible. It was their simple way of capturing meaning beyond expression. This approach is no longer satisfactory, for it replaces one expressed meaning by another one that is just as clearly expressed. Strangely enough, the Alexandrian commentators did not pause to wonder why the biblical author could not give the second meaning himself if they were able to express it so clearly. The disconcerting use of biblical quotations in medieval scholarship to prove or disprove a thesis is another illustration of the same phenomenon (although the custom antedates Christian times). Even expressions meant to be purely "scientific" gradually obtain this religious flexibility. The concept of *trans-substantiation,* originally intended to explain Christ's presence in the Eucharist by means of scholastic terminology, acquired throughout centuries of Christian tradition a religious meaning which still speaks even to those who long ago stopped thinking in terms of substance and accident.

I therefore think that it would be wrong (granted that it would be possible within the tradition) to abandon a notion that has become a religious symbol more than a scientific concept. Its religious transformation leaves the term so scientifically vague that theologians have sufficient freedom of interpretation, whereas a new definition would simply be another attempt to fix a datum of revelation in precise philosophical terms.

Because of the flexible nature of religious symbols, evolution *can* take place without any abandonment of traditional symbolism. Insofar as the symbols are part of the revelation, they *must* be retained if contact with the original message is to be preserved. However, the traditional character of revealed religion by no means implies that no new symbols ought to be created beside the old ones. Since the *experience* of the transcendent is always expressed in terms of the *self* and the *universe* that is being transcended, modern man's entirely different outlook on both compels him to look for new religious symbols in order to retain or restore the meaning of the old ones. Science, philosophy and theology may help him in this discovery. But the creation of religious symbols is ultimately the task of the religious man himself and of the religious community. The reason why the writings of Teilhard de Chardin have proven so fertile in new religious language is that they express above all a religious experience.

At the end of this argument we must face an objection that could be raised. The problem was how to reconcile two seemingly contradictory theses connected with any theory of divine revelation. On the one hand, all symbolic expression is essentially human and therefore subject to a basic evolution. On the other hand, revelation extends to the expression as well as the content (since both are inseparably united) and therefore the expression must remain authoritative as long as revelation itself.

Against the proposed solution of a development *within* the

revealed (or authoritative) expression, supported by a creation of new symbols, some will object that in this evolution *either* the symbolic expressions expand their meanings but still preserve the original ones (and then we merely have a development from the implicit to the explicit as in all previous theories), *or* the symbolic expression loses its original meanings altogether but preserves the expressive form (and then we develop a radically new form of Christianity behind the façade of the original expression).

I would answer that the second interpretation must definitely be rejected because the basic reason for preserving the original expression is precisely that they capture a *meaning content* which would be lost in a different expression. As to the first interpretation, evolution is much more than explicating the implicit. To interpret the creation myth in Genesis, the story of the magi in Matthew, or the description of Christ's second coming in the synoptics in other than a literal sense is to leap to a new meaning in and through the old one.

Is it possible to go even further, beyond tradition, and to envision the possibility of new *beginnings?* If the last words of revelation were written in the first century or shortly thereafter, then only development of the tradition is possible. But are we willing to accept the conclusion that even for those who will live one million years from now, no new revelation will have occured? Christians know that even now God's Spirit is actively present in the Church, urging its members to explore new horizons. But his light has traditionally been understood to illuminate only a message delivered in times past. Also, the living contact with Christ in the sacraments is always interpreted as referring to the events and words of his life in a historical past: *Hoc facite in meam commemorationem.* Could epiphanies only occur in the past, and has God really spoken his final word in this world? Could there ever be a new Pentecost?

Maybe the early Christians lived too much toward the future. But perhaps it is our self-satisfied aversion to change of the *status quo* that makes us look exclusively to the past. Christ promised that those who have faith in him would do greater things than he had done (Jn. 14, 12). Is all this already behind us? Orthodox Christian tradition has never asked these questions; in fact it has positively discouraged Catholics from asking them (see the decree *Lamentabili,* Denz. 2021). But a reflection upon Christianity as an historical language of God can hardly avoid raising them, for history has a future as well as a past.

VI.

God and the Supernatural

LESLIE DEWART

THE CLASSICAL Christian concept of God has endowed him with transcendence of, and at the same time immanence in, creation. In part this has reflected an essential truth of Christian religious experience. But the specific meaning given to it by classical Christian speculation—transcendence and immanence being so understood that they were conceptually opposed to each other, yet mysteriously reconcilable in God himself—has reflected only a specific, contingent conceptualization of the Christian faith in the cultural forms of a specific, contingent historical situation.

In St. Thomas' metaphysical (hence, hellenistic) philosophy, for instance, this opposition was implicit in the twofold doctrine that although "what the intellect first conceives is being and being-ness (*essentia*)," Being, He Who is, "is the most proper" name of God. God is so truly being that he is Being Itself—and yet we learn the "name" being not in any way from God but from creatures. The doctrine of analogy tries to rationalize this with the assertion that, in effect, "names" learnt only from creatures are truly applicable to God if only we confess, as we apply them to God, that they are not actually applicable to God. But the attempt scarcely succeeds: we know that God is Being—yet we do not know what God is. This ancient contradiction has not been resolved by the claim of some neo-Thomists (both absurd and quite un-Thomistic, as Maritain has shown), that God has no whatness—that is, no essence, no being-ness—though he truly *is* Being.

61

But the real difficulty with this doctrine is hardly that it has created insoluble academic problems; it has rather to do with the growing inadequacies of the classical concept of God for the real-life needs of the Church. For despite original advantages this understanding of God has shared the fate of all conceptualizations of the Christian faith: its deficiencies have become increasingly apparent and, in the end, intolerable. Western Christendom's division against itself, its schizophrenic apostasy (so well described by Toynbee) from its own religion, the paradox that Western Christendom no longer professes as a whole the belief that even today continues to animate it culturally and to describe it historically—this is the best illustration of how the mere inadequacies of an originally adequate concept of God have been allowed, through lack of suitable redevelopment, to degenerate to a scandalous point.

Apologists may suggest, of course, that the unbelief of the modern Christian world has to do not with the inadequacies of Christian concepts but with the world's moral degeneration. There may well be some truth in the second part of the claim. But to suppose that modern unbelief is wholly attributable to moral failure is not self-evident—and we must be careful not to argue circularly that the modern world's unbelief proves its immoral character. Nor does this opinion take account of the increased moral sensibility of man as he has developed culturally —whether or not he has actually abided by the morality of which he has become increasingly conscious as he has become more civilized. Nor is this view easily reconciled with the largely intellectual character of some of the causes of unbelief—for instance, the typical scientific attitudes. Nor does this apology recognize that *some* of the world's moral reasons for disbelief in the Christian God are at least partly valid in concrete cases —for instance, among those of rebellion against inhumanities perpetrated, with utter sincerity, in behalf of God.

In any event, the inadequacies of the classical concept of God are borne out not so much by that part of Christendom that has ceased to believe, as by that which continues to do so. For the believing remnant of Christendom too, has schizophrenically divided itself against itself. It has managed to preserve orthodoxy, but only at the cost of severing faith from ordinary, everyday life. Thus, we *confess* the true God, both immanent and transcendent. But in real life we find it very difficult—often impossible—to *live* the contradiction, to "hold on to both ends of the chain, confident that the two are joined, out of our sight, in God himself." Impaled on a dilemma whose nature and reality we do not always recognize, we instinctively opt for the "safer" extreme. And so, our contemporary belief typically bears, in effect, only upon a transcendent God. We continue to believe in an immanent God, to be sure, and to do so sincerely—but only ineffectively. We confess it, but we do not *mean* what we confess.

This does *not* mean that by sin we deny practically our belief in God, or that we fail to live up to the moral requirements of what we actually believe. It means that there is a gap between what we simply *admit* to be true, and the truth we spontaneously *engraft* into our experience, our creativity and our collective life. The existence of this gap, I believe, is the only possible conclusion to be drawn from the history of the Church since the beginning of the modern world—and particularly from the Church's abdication of its responsibility to provide *effective* leadership to a mankind but recently embarked upon the task of consciously creating its own history (an abdication, I happily add, in some indeterminate measure withdrawn since Vatican II). For each different way—and there have been many—in which Christians have held the world in contempt, distinctively constitutes a living rejection of the immanence of God. Not only our readiness to convict the world of sin, sometimes prematurely and usually with indecent haste, but also our consignment of the world to perdition on account of whatever true, real and unrepented sin it may bear: what does this amount to, but to a living act of faith in the absolute absence of God from the world? What does it mean but that Christians have, in effect, believed that when man kills God, God does not rise again?

The classical concept of God has become *unviable*. It can no longer enter fully and integrally into the life of believers themselves. It is cold comfort to warm ourselves with the thought that we have avoided every naturalism, every scientism, rationalism and pantheism, if we have not effectively avoided every supernaturalism. Indeed, we have not even feared it as a grave danger: we have tended to assume that it is impossible to err in this direction. But the contemporary difficulties of the Christian faith suggest otherwise. Let us attempt to trace the difficulty to its root.

The heart of the Christian gospel was Jesus' proclamation that Israel's messianic hope had been realized in him: he, Jesus, was the Christ. But Jesus maintained that his advent had not merely reaized the Jewish hope; it had in a sense also transcended it. He was indeed the expected king. But his kingship was not quite of the sort that had been expected: it was "not of this world," or of Israel alone. It was a spiritual and catholic kingship. Therefore, the *Christian* kingdom of God had a distinctive character: it was not merely the morally ideal way of life anticipated by Judaism, but a new way of life not previously available to man. It was not simply a *better* way in which ordinary human existence could be exercised: it was a *new* way to be. This is why the gospel proclaimed a new covenant, a new age in man's relations with God. In this new age God offered to man the possibility of existing at a level of existence other (and indeed nobler and more perfect) than that which man *already* had. Hence, the "spiritual" kingdom of God was no mere continuation of "fleshly" human life with but its evils and imperfections removed. It was literally a "new life." To have entered into it was truly to have been "born again." By baptism into the new Israel the Christian became a "new man," one who had "died" to the "flesh" and "risen with Christ" to the "spiritual life." Like St.

Paul, every Christian could say: "with Christ I am nailed to the cross. And I live, now not I; but Christ liveth in me."

But it must be remarked that the "new life" was offered to man only through the saving events, the "mysteries" of the incarnation and redemption. The Christian gospel of the "new life" supposed, in the first place, that the kingdom instituted by the Christ Jesus differed from that expected by Israel only because the Christ of the gospel was *not merely* a Christ. Jesus was no mere champion sent by God; he was the epiphany of God himself. Clearly, then, the gospel implied a new self-revelation of God. In the New Testament God was not only the creator and protector of man but, more fundamentally, self-gift or self-communication: *Deus caritas est.* The incarnation and the redemption meant that God had *literally* given himself to man.

This affirmation had a twofold weight. In the first place, it is literally true that God *gives* himself to us. But it is also literally true that he gives *himself* to us. If so, when God, by manifesting himself to us in Jesus, reveals himself to us as self-communication, he reveals not simply what he is *for us,* but also what he is *for himself.* (Thus, the doctrine of the incarnation and redemption implied the doctrine of the Trinity: the different ways or "modes" in which God relates himself *to us* are the truly distinct —and even, in hellenic terms, separately "subsistent"—ways in which he is related *to himself.* This must be true if the God who comes to man in the Incarnation is "true God," with no part of his divinity held back from man—that is, there are *only* three "persons" in the one divine nature of God). In brief, God's gift of himself to us is identical with his offer of the possibility of a "*new* life" over and beyond the life we *already* had. But why is it the possibility of a "new *life?*"

The existence every man *already* has when he is called by the gospel is in a very real sense a gift *from* God. In fact, for the Christian, existence *means* most fundamentally this: God's original and gratuitous gift of being to being, God's uncaused gift to being of *itself.* But this gift from God is not God himself: it is being, existence. It is God's gift of being, not God's gift of himself. The difference between the "new life" and the "old" is not that only the first is a gift from God: existence means gift from God, and gift from God means existence. On the other hand, there is a difference between the "new life" and the "old": the "old" life is *already* had when the "new" is given. This is precisely what opens up the possibility that the "new life" be not merely a gift from God, but God's yet more gratuitous gift of himself to man is of the order of existence: it means that henceforth God lives within man. Therefore, when man *receives* God within himself he accepts God's offer to participate in the life of God himself.

Evidently, God cannot create a being without giving it being. Nothing forbids it: it is simply that to create being and to *give* being are the same. Thus, God need not create being—but if he does create being, *ipso facto* he gives it being. For instance, if man is a being, he *already* exists. But to be already existing is to *have* existence—which is not the same as to *have received*, that is, *accepted*, existence. The gift of that sort of existence which man already has when he is called by the gospel, is a gift from God that can only be given: it cannot be received. This means that God can create man without giving him more than being: God need not give himself to man, even after man already exists. But if, on the other hand, God *does* give himself to man, then the gift is, in a true sense, the gift of a new mode of existence —but because man already exists, this mode of existence must be received, accepted, or else God cannot give himself to man.

In the idea that the root meaning of all existence is that of a gift from God, that there is no meaning to existence except that of being a gift from God, but that the existence man already has when called by the gospel is (though truly given) a gift that cannot be actually received, for being does not already exist before it is given existence—in this idea we find the reason why, to the Christian faith, being as such does not acquire a necessary relation to God through creation, but remains always, even after

66

it exists, totally contingent and historically factual. And even man, who is conscious of existence, who is existence aware of itself, cannot, simply as conscious being, *receive* existence from God unless God gives himself to him. But because he is present to himself man can *recognize* that existence is a gift he holds from God: this recognition is, by another name, the experience of the contingency of being *as such*. It is man's recognition that he holds existence gratuitously, without reason—"superfluously," if you wish—and that he truly holds it having never had the opportunity to turn it down before it was given.

To sum up: if *existence* is essentially the same as *gift from God,* the gift offered by God to a conscious being which already exists, is literally, not metaphorically, the offer of a new, additional level of existence. Conversely, this new mode of existence is, precisely as "new," as obtaining over and beyond the mode of existence already held by man, definable as participation in the life of God himself. This is possibly only because God gives himself to us in his true reality: the "new man" lives, as such, by the life of God himself, a life gratuitously communicated to him by God himself. And since the "new man" lives, as such by the life of *Another* living in him, his "new life" is *not a substitute* for the "old" life—except in one most important respect. For it is clear that as to moral effects, the "new life" must indeed replace the old. Hence, the Christian loves—or should love—his neighbor for the love of God. This does not mean that he must love his neighbor in order to deserve God's love. It means that God's self-gift to man creates the *obligation,* and confers the efficient *power,* for man to rise to the historical occasion created by the events of the incarnation and redemption: the vocation to imitate God through his free decision to define himself, to reveal himself to himself in actual, conscious existence as self-communication, self-gift.

Needless to say, the Christian faith I have rendered above, as I hope, in fidelity to the spirit of the gospel but in concepts which reflect contemporary experience, could have been rendered during the formative centuries of Christian dogma, or even during the scholastic period, only in a hellenic conceptual form. This was, of course, not only legitimate (and, in any event, unavoidable) but also most advantageous for the Christian faith. (For instance, the Trinitarian formulation of the novel Christian belief in God was made possible by the adoption—and, to be sure, the adaptation—of hellenic philosophical categories.) But this historical development also contained potential difficulties which, as they appeared, should have been disarmed. Unfortunately, circumstances conspired. In the end, they were compounded instead.

As has been implied above, every conceptualization of the Christian belief in the "new life" must be relative to a prior conceptualization of the "old." Gentile Christianity, which as a whole was culturally hellenistic, could not have conceived the "old" existence, the life that man already has when he is called to "conversion" and "rebirth," except as a *natural* one. And this, of course, had corresponding consequences for its understanding of the nature of the "new life."

To the Greek mind nature accounted intelligibly for the actions of a natural being only in terms of an inner necessitation. For every being acts strictly in accordance with what it is—and a being is what its essence determines it to be. But what a being is essentially, is that which it is necessarily in order to be intelligible—on the assumption, following Parmenides, that intelligibility was the condition of the possibility of existence. (Indeed, it was identical with that possibility: "that which can be and that which can be thought are the same.") Nature, therefore, accounted *exhaustively* for a being's operations, since a being's essence accounted for what it was necessarily as intelligible and, therefore, as being. Free human actions, for instance, were both intelligible and possible only because they were *natural* operations. They were free not because they were unnecessitated (which would have made them unintelligible and hence impossible), but because they were *self*-necessitated. But this implied that free

68

human actions could proceed *only* from human nature: they could be attributed only to that which (by definition) could be the only intrinsic principle of human operations—namely, human nature. Conversely, any principle other than nature could be the source of human operations only as an extrinsic principle of necessitation—and this was (by definition) a source of *violence*. In short, human behavior was either necessitated naturally —in which case it was free—or else it was necessitated from without—in which case it was coerced.

It is instructive to note that the problem of grace and freedom was preceded by a period during which Christian speculation was bent upon maintaining a truer and more radical idea of human freedom than that of contemporary philosophy—and that this was conceptualized, however, in terms of maintaining the autonomy of nature. Christian thought easily apprehended its fundamental opposition to the Greek philosophical attitude towards the human situation, particularly that of the Stoics and Epicureans. Hence, it was bound to emphasize the utter reality and puissance of man's freedom, and the benevolence of a God who did not subject man to Fate. Christians admitted that there was a Providence, quite as the Stoics said. But Pro-vidence was not the fore-seeing power that frustrated man's freedom; it was not the supreme principle of natural necessitation, indifferent to man and human striving, to which man must, however unhappily, intelligently submit under pain of greater unhappiness still. Providence was rather God's wise, benevolent, loving and helpful guidance of creation towards its final achievement. But when this doctrine, not illogically, issued in the conclusions of Pelagius, it was necessary on the contrary to emphasize that the life of grace (implying, for instance, a call to an end that man could not merit or achieve by nature) could not be brought about by the efficiency of the operations posited by human nature as such. Otherwise the life of grace would have been indistinguishable from the state of human perfection to which Stoic and Epicurean philosophy naturally led through intellectual and moral *askesis*.

But to emphasize this, once the Greek conception of nature was assumed, was in effect to emphasize that in a very real sense Providence *was* a sort of Fate. Man, therefore, was in a sense truly fated or predestined. Having accepted the terms in which the problem naturally posed itself to Christianity's hellenic mind, Christian thought doomed itself to assert thereafter that *somehow* man was both free and predestined, that God was *somehow* the cause of Fate and nevertheless the friend of man.

The *somehow* has never been satisfactorily explained. This would not have been too unfortunate if it had been actually possible for Christian thought to "hold on with equal firmness to both ends of the chain." And the process was far from complete when St. Augustine wrote his last anti-Pelagian word. If, to repeat, one can understand the "new life" of Christian belief only in relation to one's prior understanding of the "old," then the assumption that the "old" life was a "natural" one potentially contained more than the foregoing problem of the opposition between grace and freedom. It also implied that any reconciliation of the two should be based upon an understanding of the "new life" as functioning in essentially the same way as nature did, albeit without actually being an integral part of nature. The "new life" was not a substitute for nature—on the other hand, it was not unnatural. Conversely, it was non-natural —but nonetheless it was somewhat like nature. Its nature, as it were, was that of a nature which was not natural. Hence, it was a sort of second nature, a nature over and above human nature. It was, in the scholastic expression devised *ad hoc,* man's *super-nature.* The "new life" communicated by God was a *super-natural* life.

The supernatural life of grace was, therefore, truly a sort of nature. It was, to be sure, a *super*-nature. It was, nonetheless, a (super) *nature.* Therefore, to the extent that the life of grace became a super-*natural* life, it was no longer identical with man's participation in the life of God living within him. It would have been unthinkable, of course, actually to deny that man did so

70

participate. But the "new life" was not itself such participation: it was the *means* whereby such participation could obtain. Thus, a distinction obviously suggested itself: on the one hand, un-created grace, which was the life of God himself insofar as it included the act by which he gave himself to man; on the other, created grace, which was a created reality, a second nature (both in the sense that it presupposed nature, and in the sense that it was a "habit" rather than a substantial nature), a super-nature which so modified man's substantial nature that he could achieve, through its efficiency, what he could not achieve by nature alone.

The traditional belief that by grace man participated in the divine nature was thus retained, but considerably weakened. In his meaningful religious experience the Christian no longer sought God himself—at least not in this life. He sought grace, an insubstantial ectoplasm flowing from above, a spiritual coin issued by God *ex opere operato* and certified as legal moral ten-der by the decrees of Providence. Man's acceptance of super-natural life no longer meant literally that "I live, no not I; but Christ liveth in me." It did not convey that man had risen to a new level of *existence*. It simply meant that a certain quality—given from God, but not itself God—now qualified inwardly (but proceeding from without) the powers of nature with a per-fection which was not due to nature but which enabled nature, precisely as supernaturally perfected, to attain a supernatural end.

Moreover, since it occurred only through the *means* of grace, participation in the life of God now referred to a God who was not immediately present to man. (It was also thought that an immediate participation would be dangerously near to panthe-ism—as it would indeed be, on the continued assumption of the hellenic concepts of nature and being.) In fact, God was not *effectively* present to man, immediately or otherwise: the pres-ence of God was still affirmed, but it did not necessarily have a meaningful role in Christian religious experience. The operative note became God's transcendence. But, of course, transcendence was no longer understood as an attribute of God's immanence, his incommensurability with the being in which he lives and to which he is present. It was rather the incommensurability of creator and creature, the infinite distance between created being and uncreated Being. God's immanence was confessed, but no longer effectively believed in.

As Christianity's sense of God's immanence became dulled, as the Christian God receded into the infinity beyond, and as the experience of his presence was no longer facilitated by the immediately meaningful teaching of the Church or by the everyday institutions and practices of believers—and it should be noted that even the sacrament most directly concerned with the Real Presence tended to give less emphasis to the presence itself than to the metaphysical mechanism whereby that presence could be harmonized with a *hellenic* understanding of nature—as these things came to pass the Christian God became increasingly unbelievable. For, at the limiting case, a strictly transcendent God is both utterly unreasonable and thoroughly immoral; whereas, at the other extreme, a strictly immanent God may amount to no Christian God at all, but is not positively absurd and is at least superficially moral. In this way, to most science and philosophy, belief in the Christian God became synonymous with superstitious credulity; and to many of the dispossessed, institutional religion became the opium of the people. No doubt, these and like judgments of the modern world have been precipitate and undiscriminating. But it may be equally precipitate and undiscriminating to suppose that they have been altogether wrong.

Yet, if nature is not that which determines a being to act in accordance with its inner, immutable, constitutive principle of intelligibility but, on the contrary, that which emerges from the contingent history it undergoes (or the contingent history it creates, in the case of man), the level of existence to which man is called by the gospel need no longer be super-natural. If so, the Christian God need not have a super-natural character which alienates him from man, and the Christian faith may again become directly relevant to real, everyday, present life.

The level of existence of fellowship with God to which the gospel calls is not superimposed upon an independently evolving history of creation: it is the same level of existence as that in which as a matter of fact creation evolves historically, but under the concrete, contingent, historical condition brought about by God's free decision to be present to creation and to take part in its history by making its history his home. Grace is, then, a historical fact: the irruption of God into man's history, a definitive and actual event within a merely possible event.

But this means that God does not reconcile in his private life the opposed transcendence and immanence of his cryptic public announcements. Therefore, he must be conceived as that which, though other than being, is revealed by and within being only because he is present to being. For the historicity of grace means that the "natural" order does not, as such, actually exist. But if, having reached this point by transcending the hellenic idea of nature, we were to proceed without transcending the hellenic idea of being, the conclusion would be inevitably reached that nothing which exists in reality is other than God.

Being exists—but God is present to it. God creates being—but he creates it in his presence. And, moreover, within the totality of being he brings forth the being to which he gives the power effectively to define itself, the power indeed truly to create itself —for this being is no longer simply being in relation to another, whether God or man, but being which is present to itself and, hence, being which exists in and for itself. To this being, God is freely present in a correlative way, namely, by giving himself, in his very reality, to it—hence, by offering himself to man so utterly gratuitously that he actually creates the possibility of being unaccepted, positively rejected by man.

Correspondingly, then, God is found *in* being, but only as that which is *other than* being. And it is indeed his presence *in* being that leads us *beyond* being. There is, thus, no infinite gap separating God from man—but there is an openness to being, and in this opening God stands. There is no distance between God and man: on the contrary, the God of the gospel has come into the world in his true and utter reality, leaving nothing behind and, evidently, planning to stay. The Christian God is not elsewhere: he is always *here* and, therefore, he is always faithful, always he who abides, always *Yahweh,* he who remains present here and now with us. To sum up, the transcendence of the genuinely immanent God means this: if the God whom we find always *here* is not to vanish into thin air, if he is not to become an idol, if he is not to be reduced to the totality of being, and if he is not to be explained away as the becoming of the world or the projection of man—in a word, if the God who is actually *here* within being is the God of Christian tradition, it follows that he is not to be conceived as being.

To be sure, a whole *problematick* issues from this. But if the foregoing observations are correct this affirmation is not itself problematic; it is an empirically derived principle of investigation. This means: the history of Christian speculation about God suggests that henceforth the starting point of its quest should be, not the idea that although we do not experience God he must be nonetheless Being, but the observation that we do experience God, although evidently we do not experience him as being.

VII.

God and Contemporary Philosophy

JAMES COLLINS

No PHILOSOPHICAL DISCIPLINE can stand still and yet claim to live. The requirement of keeping responsive to developments in the broader human setting and in the current level of philosophical thought is appropriately made upon the theory of God. As far as this part of philosophy is concerned, the most relevant part of its human setting has always been the trend of intellectual discussion among believers at a given time. Thus the philosophical theory of God is deeply affected by its twofold context, furnished both by the prevailing conditions in philosophical inquiry and by the reflections of theistic believers. I would like to consider here a curious phenomenon marking the relationship between these two components in the present American environment for the theory of God.

At least as viewed from my limited and corrigible perspective, there is a lack of full communication between the two conditioning factors just mentioned. On the one hand, philosophers have not yet had time to digest and evaluate the many efforts of inquiring believers to rethink their conceptions of God. The scope and significance of recent shifts in the attitude of theologians toward the problem of God are not yet fully realized and reflected in philosophical discussions of the issue. And yet there is a consistent tendency, on the part of many inquiring believers, to over-evaluate the philosophical impact of what they have done to date on the God problem. Here, there is a failure to realize that reorientations within the believing community itself are only a

75

preliminary step toward contributing something significant to the general trend of philosophical speculation on God. I intend to concentrate upon this discrepancy in the mutual appraisal of the two components, because it affects the entire concrete effort today to philosophize about God. This is part of the real starting point for refounding a philosophical theology.

Philosophers seldom accept at face value the claims of other investigators concerning the philosophical implications of their work. A methodological pause is usually instituted in the face of any call by a physicist, a psychologist, or an anthropologist for a complete renovation of philosophy on the basis of some work he is doing. And a similar critical interval is quite properly interposed between philosophical discussion of God and all current religious recommendations of a new concrete theism. The reflective believer may well maintain that his position draws out the furthest implications of an acknowledged philosophical method or that it expresses a meaning of reality destined to overcome and transform all previous philosophical outlooks. But he must be prepared to have his statement treated, for quite a while, as a self-evaluatory act. Like other such acts in the several fields of research, it has to be estimated not just by its performance but primarily by the grounds adduced to support what it asserts. Only after these grounds are inspected, can the new proposals about theism begin to function effectively within the philosophical community.

Of course, there are reflective believers whose task is to philosophize about God, and it is this condition of partial interpenetration of interests which permits the comparison to be made and to have some larger significance for mankind. But one of the consequences of the maturation of philosophy in the modern world is that it follows its own tempo of response to challenges. Fresh variations on the theme of God which are quite decisive for the believing mind, including the believing philosopher, may be considerable, but it cannot be achieved by exaggerating the present impact of the theistic inquiries conducted in theological circles. The themes of the biblical God of history or the death of God may well have important relevance for philosophical approaches to God, but the bearing will have to be shown in detailed argument and not presumed. To accept this requirement is one way of taking seriously the modern fact of the distinctive structure and growth patterns in philosophy.

There is an understandable personal, educational, and pastoral impatience to have the reforming suggestions of believers count a good deal in contemporary philosophizing on God. Yet to do so, these ideas must submit to the common conditions of scrutiny, the results of which cannot be easily summed up in textbooks for philosophy classes. This follows from the nature of the situation. Any proposed meaning of theism, especially as implying a religious response in the practical order, is bound to be very complex and difficult to analyze. It must be submitted to several diverse methods of analysis and judgment, theoretical and historical, leading inevitably to diversity of interpretation and evaluation. There is nothing peculiar about this pattern of investigation, since it is the prevailing method for reaching philosophical positions on any major topic. Furthermore, philosophers are still seeking to determine the logical theory and implications of biological and cultural evolution, with which the new theological views on God's presence in an evolving universe are intimately connected. The vast complexity of the philosophical effort to understand evolution will now be communicated to the proposal of correlating the meaning of God and divine presence in the world with evolutionary theory.

As searchers after God, we can orient ourselves more closely on the present faith-and-philosophy relationship, if we will examine three areas where the energies of theistic believers are being expended, and yet where the philosophical outcome of the work is still cloudy. Much of the actual research centers around: the problem of atheism, the clarification of discourse and intentional meaning concerning God, and the theme of a creative divine purpose in evolution. I will consider these three endeavors at the general level of the progress they are making toward modifying the philosophical discussion of God, and the distance that still remains before they can become fully functional in philosophy. On this basis, there can be drawn a brief conclusion on the need to tighten the relationship between experience and inference in the theory of God.

The main thrust of recent studies of atheism centers around making the atheistic attitude understandable to believers. This is a step forward from the previous custom of concentrating upon the quite abstract issue of the possibility or impossibility of atheism, an approach dictated more by an interest in the question of imputability for one's view of God than by a direct concern with the actual testimony of atheistic thinkers. The strength of the newer treatment lies in the order of psychology, sociology, and the history of religious ideas. The structure of the atheistic attitude is better understood in the light of the discontents in psyche and society, to which atheism is now seen to be a creative human response. Especially in its nineteenth-century varieties, it is regarded as one member of a social and intellectual situation correlated with the historical forms of theology and church life in the same age.

In the light of the notion of a definite correlativity between the theologies and the atheologies, believing investigators are inclined to revise their view of atheism along three lines. First, there is an admission of responsibility, at all levels of thought and social life, for the inadequate expressions of theism and the oppressive social conditions that have generated the atheistic response. Atheism is now regarded, not as an alien intrusion upon the sphere of Christian belief and sociality, but as an internally generated counterpart and corrective judgment.

From this conviction of sharing a common destiny flows a second aspect in the self-transformation of contemporary theism: a recognition of the human strength and rightness contained in a correlative atheism, with which the honest believer now finds a greater affinity than with the forms of theism and ecclesiology

78

which were brought to judgment. Often this sense of complication and coeducation translates itself into a call for intellectual and social dialogue between Marxism and Christianity, a call responded to by Garaudy and other sensitive atheists. The participants are not regarded as antagonistic spokesmen for complete and exclusive systems, but somehow as joint seekers looking for the meaning of the human, in relation to a possible divine perspective.

A third strain in the contemporary believer's dynamism is a resolve to transcend the shortcomings in the previous theistic and atheistic interpretations of reality. In this task, a clue is taken from Nietzsche, whose greatness is seen more and more clearly to lie in his lifelong engagement with the symbiotic relationship between the theisms and atheisms of his century. Even apart from the symbolic role assigned to Nietzsche in the development of the death-of-God theme among theologians, his significance for our thinking about God arises from his suggestion that no radical renovation of our thinking about God is possible without basing itself upon a comprehensive questioning of the whole tradition of Western conceptions of being, knowing, and moral values. Theists are currently testing out, in a free and experimental manner, various ways of transforming these basal conceptions in metaphysics, epistemology, and moral philosophy. So far, the revaluations remain in the form of programmatic sketches of work that still remain to be executed in argumentative detail.

All these stirrings pivoted around a revised estimate of atheism are leading to observable modifications in the Christian awareness of this world and its ambivalences, in the appreciation of psychiatric and sociological research on the springs of belief and unbelief, and in more flexible alternatives in the social and political realms. As yet, however, these changes do not add up to a noticeable difference in the philosophical treatment of atheism by American philosophers. There is a potentiality for making a difference in philosophical thinking, but the gap is not yet bridged between transformations in the religious attitude and a new direction of philosophical argumentation. Until the religious transformation is able to restate its evidence in terms of the methods and arguments actually used in philosophy, there will be no change in the shape of the theory of God.

To remove the alien quality of much of the theological talk about atheism, it would be helpful to shift the focus of attention now from the dramatic atheistic attitude embodied in a Nietzsche or a Camus to the more undramatic forms of atheism found in many naturalistic and analytic philosophers. Their approach does not conform with the pattern of an anti-Christian anti-theism, but rather depends on the use of methods leading to the unemphatic judgment that the divine reality, presumably signified by even a revised conception of God, is inevident to the ordinary inquirer. From such a perspective, none of the theistic analyses of the psychic, social, and theological conditions breeding a strongly felt atheistic attitude have altered the methodological and epistemological considerations confining our minds to the study of experienced nature and human society. A revision of the story about the genesis of theistic and atheistic outlooks does not add anything to the positive evidence, presentable in philosophical form, for maintaining the truth of affirmations about the reality of God.

Perhaps in order to meet this situation, theistic believers are taking a second look at the philosophy of John Dewey, on whom most of the naturalists are dependent. A sympathetic, and at times even a rhapsodic, reinterpretation is made of his general account of natural process and the generic traits of reality. Attention is centered upon his insight concerning man's actively evolving relationships with the living environment, as well as upon his reverent response to natural reality in all its modes. This is one philosophical locus where it is indeed possible to sharpen the problem of theism. As Dewey formulates it, the crucial question is whether all the values formerly enshrined in the affirmation of God can be transformed, without human loss, into a religious affirmation of nature and human development. Man's religious attitude can be redirected toward the complex values of experienced natural reality, and the meaning of the divine can be wholly interpreted in terms of this affirmation.

This is not simply a recognition of the values of mundanity and natural reality, within which human life joyfully develops. It is also a proposal that our religious response to reality can now sustain itself without including any theistic overtones, any affirmation of God as somehow distinct from experienced natural process. The discovery of natural temporal values on the part of the theistic humanist does not alter the point at issue. Dewey asks whether any good reasons can be furnished for accepting anything more than a religious suffusion of man's inquiring and appreciative intercourse with the rest of nature. Dialogue with him involves showing eventually that religious experience has a more determinate sense than that expressed in our striving with, and enjoyment of, this complexus of man in nature.

One way to meet this challenge is to suggest that, just as the naturalist is engaged in broadening his view of human values to include the religious quality of life, so the theist must engage in rethinking the meaning of God to include its human context. The urgency of discovering a more adequate philosophical conception of God is not based on a purely abstract debate but upon two pressing historical considerations. First, there is the exhibited incapacity of any theism-correlated-with-atheism to satisfy the religious searching and responses of humanity: to surpass these correlates is to look for fresh significance of the divine in human life. Secondly, the general philosophical situation has no more stayed frozen during our century than has that of belief and theology. But one responsibility of the theistic philosopher is to bring out the implications of new philosophical problems and methods for the theory of God. Whenever major advances are made in philosophical inquiry as a whole, they supply the opportunity and the means for attaining a corrected and deepened understading of God's presence in human experience.

Since the aim of believing philosophers is to do their exploring

81

with the resources of the centrally shaping philosophies of our time, they are making primary use of the analytic and phenomenological approaches. Just by itself, the deliberate experiment of trying to determine the theistic implications of these philosophies is a useful contribution. Neither the analytic nor the phenomenological method is inherently restricted to the development of but one conception of God. There is ample room in phenomenology for both Sartre and Scheler, and room in analytic circles for Flew and Ramsey. Yet the theistic possibilities are never automatically explicated, but require constant innovation by many minds. For a good while to come, it is likely that the reminting of the meaning of God will be conducted through diverse and well restricted lines of inquiry. It is premature to expect a fully articulated philosophical synthesis of theism to fill the present scene, whatever the theological and practical voices calling for it to come.

Nevertheless, some of the lines of investigation are being more firmly drawn. Analytic theists are making discernible a definite pattern and orientation in the religious use of ordinary language. They find that speakers imbued with the bible and the life of faith make an extraordinary use of our everyday words and syntax, in order to express a distinctive relationship of the human self to the divine reality. The discriminate theistic talker is careful to distinguish the divine from every particular thing within sensible range, and yet to evoke an intimate, personal, and morally concerned presence of the divine among men. Discourse about God takes the form of a dramatic story, so that the theist may make a symbolic, pointing use of daily language and may suggest another level of interpretation for the happenings in history. God-talk properly tends to become halting and troubled in the face of powerful evil and suffering visited upon the innocent. Yet it always displays a leading and analogical quality, orienting the speaking and listening community toward hope in a God who is a caring friend. Whatever new meanings of God are to be forged, they must give primary consideration to these traits in our actual statements of theistic belief.

Emphasizing the intentional acts in which human reality develops itself, the phenomenological theists seek the foundation of this conception of God within human history. The growing convergence of analytic and phenomenological philosophies in general can be expected to strengthen their regional convergence upon a common significance of God. For just as the analysts are becoming more sensitive to the personal springs of discourse about God, so are the phenomenologists becoming increasingly interested in the theistic word, the linguistic actuation of human striving for the divine. Furthermore, both groups regard their findings as being reformative of our thinking about God and not just descriptive of it. In the degree that earlier conceptions of God did not somehow primarily correlate the divine reality with the interpersonal and historical community of men, they must be transformed by a meaning that does convey this emphasis and hence that is less unworthy of God.

It seems to me, however, that the philosophical status of such analytic and phenomenological studies of theism is still incomplete. They are philosophical in one sense, namely, that they submit the content of theistic belief and the biblical message on God to interpretation through two recognized philosophical methodologies. This is a genuine contribution to the state of discussion about God, since it overturns the assumption that the testimony of faith and the bible is irrelevant to the philosophical theory of God and cannot be brought within the philosopher's range. But in addition to showing that theistic belief is quite susceptible of contemporary reinterpretation, a philosophical approach to God must also ask about the evidential backing and humanly ascertainable truth of the conviction thus reformulated. The problem is not only that of determining an adequate meaning but also that of determining whether, on humanly inspected grounds, we must accept the truth claim made for the divine reality intended by the reformed meaning of theism. A thoroughly philosophical approach to God must show that the theistic conviction is both expressive of the personal and social life of man, regarded in his intentional acts and linguistic patterns, and also judgmentally well founded in its affirmation of the divine reality itself.

The analytic and phenomenological approaches to theism are not yet fully philosophical in character, insofar as they are reluctant to make the passage from a study of meaning to that of the ordinarily accessible bases for the judgment affirming the divine reality. Hence the distinction between a descriptive and a reformative function for their conception of God has a narrower import than might be supposed. The historical and interpersonal view of God does have a reformative role within the believing community's own patterns of thought and speech, but it does not yet furnish a broader reforming norm for determining the judgment of philosophers about the reality of God. From the standpoint of the philosophical community at large, this revised conception of God still remains in the descriptive order of particular meanings for the divine, and settles nothing about the validity of maintaining the reality of God himself. To deal with the question of valid judgment in respect to the divine reality, a metaphysical basis of our conception of God and our truth assertions about his actuality is required. Should biblical theologians employ only the analytico-phenomenological approach to a theory of God, they would seriously underestimate the radical nature of contemporary philosophical questioning about God and the need to make a thorough metaphysical reconstruction of theism.

Sometimes, a quick detour is attempted around the tedious metaphysical argumentation by employing what we can call Heidegger's new-era strategy. This consists in making a drastic simplification and solidification of all philosophical procedures and principles, historically developed for the theory of God. They are all treated as so many variations upon the one defective way of conceiving knowledge, activity, and reality after the model of a dichotomy between subject and object, self and the world of things. A wholesale contrast is then drawn between the entire history of speculation on God and one's own favored conception of reality and the divine. The latter view is then designated as the radical principle of a new era of thinking, and every critical alternative on God is thereby relegated to the already overcome framework of the past.

Although this strategy seems to spike all the guns, it does not carry much conviction among philosophical workers. For it does considerable violence to the plural traditions in philosophical thought, as well as to that whole process of making careful distinctions in which the life of philosophy consists. Hence the new-era verdict represents a disruption of the fabric of philosophical work, rather than its future hope. The questions about the evidential basis for making assertions about the divine reality remain in force, and the theory of God moves effectively in other directions.

The Teilhardian and other varieties of evolutionary theism are attractive to many believers today, precisely because they bring some independent confirmation and can be related to scientific work that is actually going on. The conviction about a creative divine purpose enables theists to regard their belief not only as an elucidation of the bible story but also as a powerful instrument for unifying and orienting the scientific accounts of the world. At the same time, evolutionary theism admittedly suffers from the nebulous condition of its doctrinal content and from a lack of reflection upon scientific methodology and theory formation, such as would permit it to determine the nature and limits of the collaboration between belief and evolutionary research.

The precise relationship between evolutionary theism and philosophy can be clarified, if two questions of definite contemporary interest will be considered. One of these concerns the epistemological nature of any general assertion of purpose in the evolving universe. Even after the rift is closed between phenomena and noumena and after the unified reality of nature is seen to be thoroughly evolutionary, the Kantian problem of purposive judgment remains relevant. It does not concern any fixed ends, laid down in a celestial decree and unfurled through the printed book of time. Bergson and Dewey have sufficiently criticized this conception of ends as being incompatible both with an evolutionary universe and with human dignity.

Rather, the problem is that of determing the meaning and range of purposive models of thought about nature, as well as of inquiring whether any implications can be drawn about the world itself and a divine agency therein.

A very wide range of positions is being maintained on this issue, reaching from a quite restricted use of telic models in some parts of biology and sociology to general proposals about teleonomy as a way of interpreting all the scientific and social findings. To become more reflective and philosophically interesting, evolutionary theism will have to relate its position to some pertinent alternative explanations. Is the notion of a divine purpose operating in the evolving universe anything more than a faith-generated extrapolation, made from the restricted model used to study the internal structure of a theistic moral and religious community of men? Does this concept serve well enough for human thinking about the vast transitions from energy to life to culture, but yet confuse our minds when it is converted into an ontological principle shaping the heart of reality? Or should we say, with the idealist philosophers Findlay and Harris, that the meaning of evolutionary purpose is indeed ontological and not solely hermeneutic, but that the reality in which the telic striving culminates is scientific and social mind as the reflective totalization of experience, and as being divine in no other sense? Only when theistic evolutionism allows itself to feel the bite of these specific questions, will it sharpen its own significance and achieve entrance into the philosophical world.

That process can be hastened by engaging in a second line of discussion, centering around Whitehead's proposals for the consistent application of evolutionary concepts to the divine consequent nature. Many theologians today are rediscovering the need for a metaphysically regulated natural theology, through the promptings of Whitehead on how to make theistic belief functional in an evolutionary and history-minded age. The issue concerns whether every instance of evolutionary theism must agree with his contention that becoming must be found in some real sense within God's own nature, if he is the supreme exemplification of the principles of reality and not a dubious exception to them. In the intimacy and mutuality of His relationship with the universe, God's consequent nature must involve finitude, care, and growth, so that the course of our tragic universe can make a difference in the divine life.

All this can be retranslated into biblical language, but the pertinent question is whether the message of theistic belief and the bible can be given any other philosophically significant rendering than the one proposed by Whitehead. Such a question cannot be handled simply by returning to the polarity between the bible and theistic faith, or simply by pointing to something established or suggested in evolutionary sciences. It forces the theist to engage in independent metaphysical speculation, and thus it encourages the wider philosophical examination of evolutionary theism in all its modalities.

All the indications are that philosophy is operating today to nudge theistic belief from the mode of religious witness and biblical exegesis into that of argument and inference concerning human experience. This persistent nudging—sometimes done gently and sometimes quite harshly—is indispensable to overcome the tendency of theistic believers to identify their convictions simply with those of humanity. Here is a striking instance of what Dewey identified as the inveterate habit of converting a desired ideal into a present actuality. Theists would like all men to share the belief in God and the acceptance of the bible, but in fact the discussion of theism goes on in a world where the truth basis of theism must still be discussed and established in function of ordinary human inquiry.

Among theistic believers, a twofold clarification is needed in order to achieve full philosophical modalization for the theory of God. First, it should be realized that although criticism of "proofs of God's existence" and of the proving attitude toward God-as-an-object has had a salutary effect upon vaunting claims to know God in a mystery-dispelling manner, it has not removed the philosophical requirement for some argument and inference to back up assertions about the divine reality. After all the personalist refinements have been introduced, a philosophically regulated inference must still be made in support of an affirmation of God's reality, if that affirmation is intended to arouse a similar conviction on the part of other men engaged in inquiring about God. In so far as the human search after God is something more than a domestic clarification of intended meaning on the part of theistic believers, the burden of supplying a sound inferential use of our common human experience must be accepted.

And secondly, theists who are presently adapting the pioneer research of Maréchal, D'Arcy, and Lonergan, cannot avoid the use of inference and the justification for such reasoning. To show that the experience of knowing implies an affirmation of the divine or that the experience of intending the divine is correlated with a distinctive growth in selfhood, general principles of analogy and causality must be used, and an argumentative study made of the theistic implications which human experience sustains. These two points can be combined in a recognition of the continued need for metaphysics, considered both as a direct inspection of our experience and as a disciplined effort at making controlled inferences supporting the truth of judgments about God's reality. And the mutual relations between the metaphysical theory of God and the philosophy of religion have to be explored in detail.

In sum, the presence of unresolved problems and conflicting interpretations will continue to characterize the theory of God as well as every part of philosophy. Every effort to minimize the problematic aspect, or to bypass it for purposes of education and edification, is bound to spoil the philosophical nature of the surviving theory of God. In contradistinction to all forms of theistic revivalism, a philosophic approach to God demands unremitting clarification of one's meaning of God, as well as unsparing criticism of one's interpretative inferences concerning the relation between human experience and the divine reality.

PART TWO

Jesus

I.

Jesus of History and Christ of Faith

AVERY DULLES

THE PROBLEM with which this article deals is not new. Already in 1865 the radical Hegelian, David Friedrich Strauss, wrote a book, *The Christ of Faith and the Jesus of History,* in which he undertook to refute Schleiermacher's *Life of Jesus,* posthumously published the year before. In the intervening century the controversy has continued to rage. What relationship can be found between the earthly Jesus, as a figure accessible to scientific historical knowledge, and the heavenly Christ, as proclaimed in the Easter kerygma of the early Church? The fact that the key terms in the discussion—history and faith, Jesus and Christ, gospel and kerygma—are differently understood by different authors, and have themselves become matters of controversy, makes it hard for anyone to say a fresh and luminous word today. Yet the printing presses of Europe and America continue to belch forth bulky tomes and flimsy paperbacks on the subject, as liberals and orthodox, neo-liberals and neo-orthodox, Bultmannians and post-Bultmannians, capture the public eye in dizzying succession.

Roman Catholic theologians, operating within a rather well defined tradition, and sometimes under the eye of vigilant ecclesiastical censorship, have as yet made no conspicuous contribution to the discussion. Indeed it might seem rash for a Catholic to venture onto this mine-strewn soil. But the 1964 Instruction of the Biblical Commission, "The Historical Truth of the Gospels," assures a large area of freedom for Catholics seeking to trace the process by which the gospel message passed from the first eyewitnesses through a generation of oral tradition before it was eventually set down in written form with further adaptations to the needs of various communities and according to the literary aims of the evangelists themselves. Vatican II in its *Constitution on Divine Revelation* (n. 19) gave the fullest approval to the liberal approach embodied in the 1964 Instruction. Yet it must also be noted that the conservative minority prevailed on the pope to insert in the very last draft of the conciliar text a statement to the effect that the Church "unhesitatingly asserts" the "historical character" of the four gospels. It was not specified, however, what kind of historicity is here involved; and this, as we shall see, is the whole issue under discussion.

From the early years of the present century until about a decade ago most Catholic scholars would have felt obliged to hold that there was no real difference between the Jesus of history and the Christ of faith. History and faith were two roads leading to the same point. For apologetical reasons, Catholics thought it expedient to accept the Liberal Protestant contention that it was possible to construct from a critical analysis of the four gospels, by the exacting methods of scientific historiography, an unambiguous and convincing portrait of the real Jesus. The results of the Liberal Protestant investigation were exemplified at their best in Adolf von Harnack's *What is Christianity?*. This classic synthesis, published in 1900, provided the scholars of the next generation with an impressive target to shoot at.

Catholic apologetics, then, set about the task of producing a "historical Jesus" which would coincide with the Christ of the Church's dogma, thus hoisting the Liberals with their own petard. The standard argument, as given in the polemical works of Hilarin Felder and a host of others, proceeded in two steps. First it attempted to establish that the four gospels were excellent historical sources, embodying impartial first-hand accounts of Jesus' words and deeds. Then in a second stage it sought to prove that the evangelists attributed to Jesus the very traits of the God-man of Christian dogma. From these two premises the divinity of Jesus was inferred with a resounding "Q.E.D."

The argument, as we now know, was invalid on many counts. The gospels as a whole cannot be treated as eyewitness reports, nor were they intended to be historical documents in the sense of the historico-critical school, nor were they concerned with the precise problems which the Church later resolved by the great Christological dogmas. While the testimony of the evangelists undoubtedly has great historical and dogmatic weight, the simplistic methods of historicist apologetics were unsound.

By the time Catholics had concocted their own historical Jesus to offset the gains of Liberal Protestantism, Protestant scholarship had become disillusioned with the historical quest. In the first decade of the twentieth century the Modernists were able to point out how Harnack, wishing to peer through the nineteen centuries of Catholic darkness, had succeeded only in finding the "reflection of a Liberal Protestant face seen at the bottom of a deep well" (Tyrrell). Dissatisfied with this Victorian Jesus, scholars such as J. Weiss, W. Wrede, A. Schweitzer, and R. Eisler presented their own mutually divergent constructions of the historical Jesus, while several hardy skeptics maintained that there had never been any Jesus of history but only a Christ-myth presented in historical form.

Amid this welter of contrasting opinions, the conservative Lutheran scholar, Martin Kähler, argued with some plausibility that modern historical scholarship could not hope to recover any "Jesus of history" behind the "historic Christ" of the biblical proclamation. The gospels, he maintained, having been written "from faith to faith," were not suitable sources for a life of Jesus according to the standards of contemporary historical science. In the title of his work, *The So-Called Historical Jesus and the Historic, Biblical Christ,* Kähler introduced the now classic distinction between what is "historical" (*historisch*) in the sense of lying within the range of critical historiography and what is "historic" (*geschichtlich*) in the sense of being a presently important past reality. To Kähler the Christ of faith, but not the Jesus of historical reconstruction, was both real and important.

Inspired by Kierkegaard and Kähler, many of the leading Protestant theologians of the period after World War I took the position that faith is its own guarantee, and is not dependent on the results of critical scholarship. Karl Barth, Emil Brunner, and Rudolf Bultmann sang in chorus that faith would only destroy itself if it sought to rely on proofs, whether philosophical or historical. The more ambiguous and obscure the historical evidences seemed to become, the more delightedly they reveled in the "miraculous" certainty of unsupported faith. Convinced that faith in no way rests on the results of historical scholarship, Bultmann felt free to dissect the gospel traditions quite mercilessly with the newly invented scalpel of form criticism.

Probing the origins of the synoptic tradition, Bultmann came to the conclusion that nearly all the dogmatically important statements about Jesus in the gospels were creations of the early Church and could not be plausibly dated back to the pre-resurrection situation. Following Kähler, Bultmann held that it was impossible to reconstruct the personality and career of Jesus "since the early Christian sources show no interest in either, are moreover fragmentary and often legendary; and other sources about Jesus do not exist" (*Jesus and the Word*, p. 8). But despite this disclaimer Bultmann went on to offer a rough and tentative sketch. His Jesus turns out to be a prophet and ethical teacher who apparently laid no claim to Messianic status, who was convinced that God was about to inaugurate his Kingdom by bringing the world to a cataclysmic end, who energetically warned men to prepare themselves by repentance and obedience.

In Bultmann's theology the decisive event which inaugurates the Christian era is not the preaching of Jesus but the Easter event. Even this event, he holds, cannot be reconstructed in its outward details, since the New Testament accounts are shot through with myth and legend. We must even reckon with hallucinations which would lend themselves to a perfectly natural explanation on the psychological plane. But the Easter event, as understood by theology, retains its salvific value. For the Paschal message, in the Church's proclamation, enables us to achieve authentic existence. The saving occurrence of Easter is reenacted whenever men, hearing the preaching about the cross of Jesus, are liberated from care and anxiety and empowered to face the future with courage, hope, and trust in God.

The Christ of faith, for Bultmann, is far different from the Jesus of history. He exists in the proclamation of the Church and in the faith of believers. The Jesus of history is the real Jesus who lived in Palestine and was crucified. His life and personality may be of interest to the research historian but are, in Bultmann's opinion, religiously irrelevant. Bultmann takes over Kähler's preference for the preached Christ over the Jesus of history. But his doctrine is not the same as Kähler's because he has changed the meaning of the terms. The "historic" (*geschichtlich*) in Bultmann's theology no longer refers directly to the reality of the past occurrence but only to the present call for decision.

While some of Bultmann's positions are extreme and unacceptable, he has made a number of valid points. Particularly helpful is his insistence on the Easter event as a new beginning and his subordination of the earthly life of Jesus to this climactic occurrence. By working backward from the early Church to the historical Jesus he recaptures the movement by which the Christian tradition was formed and makes room for a more dynamic Christology than we have been accustomed to. By giving full recognition to the "change of eons" which occurred at Easter the theology of salvation history can be greatly enriched.

In speaking of the Easter event, Bultmann seems to reduce it to Jesus' acquisition of new life in the faith and preaching of the Church. Although there is a sense in which it is legitimate and necessary to "demythologize" the New Testament affirmations about the heavenly exaltation of Jesus, one may properly complain that Bultmann does not sufficiently respect the obvious intention of the doctrine, which refers in the first instance to what happened to Jesus himself, and only secondarily to the vivification of the community. But Bultmann is not as minimalist as some of his statements might seem to suggest. He takes the "real presence" of Jesus in the kerygma very seriously. For him this is far more than a mere survival in memory, such as occurs when a deceased man is remembered by his friends. Rather than complain about Bultmann's shortcomings, it would be better to ask what we ourselves make of the traditional doctrine that Jesus is really present and active in the preaching and sacraments of the Church and in the hearts of true believers. Is Jesus truly active in our midst or only in some "other" place, called heaven?

Unlike many earlier theologians, Bultmann is able to give full value to those New Testament texts which stress that only after death did Jesus become "Lord and Christ" (Acts 2:36) or, as Paul says, "Son of God in power" (Rom. 1:4; cf. Acts 13:33). No doubt the fact of this glorification at Easter can be used, against Bultmann, as the basis for certain inferences about what Jesus already was in his earthly life; even the New Testament authors made such inferences. Nevertheless Bultmann is to be thanked for having taught us not to seek in the Jesus of the public ministry the identical attributes which distinguish the Christ of the Easter kerygma. Although the earthly Jesus—as we shall see—spoke and acted with sovereign majesty, it would scarcely seem appropriate to place on his lips, before the resurrection, unequivocal statements such as, "All power in heaven and on earth has been given to me" (Mt. 28:18).

In holding that Jesus first became the Christ in the Easter faith of the Church, Bultmann raises very sharply the question whether the earthly Jesus was already in any sense the Messiah. Most scripture scholars today agree that the earthly Jesus probably did not designate himself by clearly Messianic titles such as "Christ (Messiah)" and "Son of God." Apparently he did not even accept such titles without reservation. This may have been because the Jews would not have understood these titles correctly, but there is no reason to deny the possibility of a certain development in Jesus' understanding of his own person and mission, which may have reached its consummation only after his glorification. Our theology of the earthly career of Jesus is still in its infancy. In the coming decades much work will probably be done to clarify the status of Jesus before his Crucifixion.

Bultmann is no doubt too negative in his assessment of the historical value of the gospel tradition. But he has done well to stress that that tradition was compiled in the light of the Church's Easter faith, and that many incidents, as reported in the gospels, are viewed in the reflected light of Jesus' glorification. According to Bultmann, the Christian community, in the first decades in Palestine, was so taken up with the thought of the risen, glorious Christ and his expected return in majesty that there was as yet no historical interest in the traditions about the earthly ministry. It would be pointless to deny that the infant Church was more interested in the present and future than in the past. Indeed, our own Christianity might be more vital if we could recapture something of this orientation. Nevertheless it should be added that not even the first Christians, for all their eschatological expectations, totally neglected the past. The New Testament provides clear indications that already in Palestine in the first generation the words and deeds of Jesus were being solicitously compiled. Paul himself, though he rarely refers to Jesus' public life, was undoubtedly familiar with many sayings of the Lord, and took it for granted that his readers were acquainted with the same tradition.

Largely as a result of Bultmann's influence, the contemporary scholar has learned to proceed with the utmost caution in treating confessionally colored statements in the gospels as strict historical reminiscences. Shocking as it may seem to the faithful who have not been following recent trends in biblical criticism, we have very little secure knowledge about the precise words and deeds of Jesus. The accounts of his infancy and risen life can scarcely be regarded as historical sources in the modern sense.

97

Even for the public life, there are immense critical problems surrounding the authenticity of many parables, aphorisms, and miracle stories.

It is most difficult to achieve certitude about the way in which Jesus thought of his person and mission. Did he conceive of himself as Messiah and Son of God? Did he foresee his own early and violent death, and regard it as redemptive? Did he predict the fall of Jerusalem, the destruction of the Temple, or his own resurrection? Did he intend to found a Church which would endure for centuries to come? Did he preach that this world would end in a sudden cataclysm, and that the end was already at hand? The most prudent and skillful exegetes, both Protestant and Catholic, admit that these are truly difficult questions, to which no final answer can presently be given on purely exegetical grounds.

And yet it will not do to say, as Bultmann does, that the earthly Jesus is devoid of interest for Christian faith. Believers have always sought guidance and inspiration from his teaching and example, and have felt that their salvation depends on what he did for mankind. It is not surprising that many Christians should feel distressed that we cannot know nearly as much about Jesus as we should like to know. But the gospels do provide what is most necessary to nourish the life of faith. Even on points where they do not give strictly factual history, they furnish an inspired record of the faith of the early Church concerning its Lord and founder.

Widely influential though Bultmann's system has been, it has failed to win full acceptance even among his own disciples. In particular, many of them reject his dichotomy between the Jesus of history and the Christ of faith. About a decade ago, some of the most prominent among them—including Günther Bornkamm, Ernst Käsemann and Ernst Fuchs—became associated in what is popularly known as the "post-Bultmannian" movement. These theologians agree with Bultmann that the nineteenth-century quest for the historical Jesus ended in failure and that

Schweitzer's masterful account was its tombstone. They deem it impossible, even with the finer tools of analysis which modern archaeology and form criticism have put at our disposal, to construct a scientifically assured portrait of Jesus' inner life or a biography that would detail the chronology of his career. But these scholars insist that we are in a position to dig down to the bedrock of the gospel tradition and to recapture in substance the impression made by Jesus on those who were with him in his earthly ministry. Bultmann was too hasty in writing off the majority of the reported sayings and actions of Jesus as free creations of the believing community. Many of them could not possibly be such creations because they do not correspond with the way Christians would have spoken after Easter.

Using Bultmann's own form-critical methods, the post-Bultmannians contend that the most primitive strata of the tradition yield an image of Jesus so striking and original, and at the same time so clearly distinct from the Christ of the Easter Kerygma, that we may regard it as authentic. They have dared to present a new "historical Jesus," more fragmentary and impressionistic than that of the old biographies, but still most impressive and, for the most part, convincing.

Günther Bornkamm, in his *Jesus of Nazareth,* paints the most complete and compelling portrait that has yet emerged from this school. Jesus, he holds, proclaimed God's kingdom and its nature as much by the style as by the content of his preaching. He directed his parables and beatitudes, as well as his healing presence and power, not primarily to the devout and observant but rather to publicans and sinners, to those who had been "driven to the very end of the world and its possibilities." He summoned about him, as the "visible symbol of his call," not the intellectual and cultured but the rough and unlettered.

Jesus' early preaching, according to Bornkamm, closely echoed that of John the Baptist. He called on men to "repent, for the kingdom of God is at hand." But on his lips the call assumed a new power. Without making any human preparation the condition for response, Jesus demanded that his hearers should stand before the Creator in all their impoverished dependence. His word seized men as they were and made it impossible for them to stand aside as neutral spectators. By giving the instant and total response for which he called, they were released from the domination of the past and from anxiety concerning the future. Faithful obedience opened up for them the path to freedom, trust, and love.

According to the post-Bultmannians, the eschatology of Jesus carried a unique note of urgency. "If it is by the finger of God that I cast out demons, then the kingdom of God has come upon you" (Lk. 11:20). In popular language, the parables of the sower and of the mustard seed teach not the inexorable growth of what is already alive but the hidden dawn of the kingdom. Whoever comes upon his treasure will be prepared to sell all that he has to buy it. Like Jesus' eschatology, so also his authoritative ethics presents the will of God with startling transcendence and immediacy. The man who hears the Sermon on the Mount is in no position to delay or question the possibility of its fulfillment; he must simply confess that here God has spoken, and that the time for action is now.

The post-Bultmannians detect throughout these early layers of the gospel tradition an indirect, or hidden, Christology. For Ernst Fuchs, Jesus' attitude is "that of a man who dares to act in God's place"; his conduct is "the real context of his preaching." What is remarkable, says Ernst Käsemann, is that he "did what was necessary for the present" and thus made it clear that in him "God has drawn near in grace and requirement." For these theologians it is in the words and actions of Jesus, in his authoritative yet vulnerable appearance on the Jewish scene, that the nearness of God is truly realized.

A Christology is here implied, for the words and actions of Jesus embody an interpretation of history's central theme. He is the man of "unmistakable otherness," before whom "the world comes alive," who does not make a proclamation about God's reign but by his proclamation confronts men here and now with the reality of that reign. By identifying his coming with that of the kingdom he awakens the strongest Messianic expectations.

Yet the Christology of the earthly Jesus is only indirect. Jesus' understanding of himself, says Gänther Bornkamm, "is not a separate or prevailing theme in his preaching to which everything else is subordinated. He certainly does not make it the condition for the understanding of his message and actions. The very nature of his teaching and actions, so vulnerable, so open to controversy and yet so direct and matter of fact, doom to failure any attempt to raise his Messiahship into a system of dogma through which his preaching, his actions and his history would receive their meaning."

For all its merits, the post-Bultmannian approach is marred by some regrettable imbalance. In their neglect of conventional historiography, including archaeological aids, these scholars tend to overlook the nucleus of solid fact that has been established, with fair claim to reliability, by such cautious exegetes as Vincent Taylor and Joachim Jeremias. With the exception of Fuchs, whose language tends to be excessively obscure, the theologians of this school concentrate too exclusively on the words of Jesus and are overly shy of the significant deeds by which he put his message across. They have not as yet come to terms with the abundant testimonies to the miraculous in the life of Jesus. Even their theology of the Word, moreover, is one-sided, since they focus on address and encounter almost to the exclusion of meaning. In their existential concern, these writers are too ready, as H. E. W. Turner complains, to "leave our Lord baldly as a figure of impact," and thus "to deny to our Lord any significant categories for deploying his conception of his Person and Work." While we may concede that the Christology of Jesus was chiefly indirect, "it would be difficult to believe that our Lord never sought to crystallize his intention in Biblical terms." Contrary to the post-Bultmannians, Turner holds that Jesus identified himself with the coming Son of Man. This term, which suggests so much

more than it defines, could most plausibly have been used by
Jesus himself in order to confront men with the challenge of his
person and message (*Historicity and the Gospels*).

Bultmann of course challenges the theological legitimacy of
the renewed quest for the Jesus of history. He denies that the
knowledge of Jesus' earthly personality and life, beyond the
bare facticity of his existence and of his cross, has any relevance
for faith. Yet it seems legitimate to reply, as Bornkamm does,
that for Bultmann, "Jesus Christ has become a mere saving fact
and has ceased to be a person. He himself has no longer any
history." Käsemann has reason to object that Bultmann's kerygmatic Christ, so tenuously linked with the realities of history, is
as unsubstantial as a myth. Other theologians complain that
Bultmann's system amounts to a new Gnosticism, in which the
Word would have become not flesh but—word. The kerygma
of the early Church, as enshrined in numerous New Testament
texts, proclaims that the Word has become flesh and has lived on
this earth as man.

The new concern for the historical Jesus does not aim, as
some forms of apologetics do, to prove that the Easter proclamation is true, but to show, as James M. Robinson puts it, that in
encountering Jesus one is confronted with essentially the same
decision that the kerygma presents, and hence that obedience to
the kerygma is effectually the same as obedience to the word of
Jesus himself.

Bultmann objects that his former disciples make Easter un-
necessary by setting up a second avenue of access to Christianity
which by-passes the proclamation of the Church. If some of these
authors give this impression, they are guilty of a distortion opposite to Bultmann's. While Bultmann neglects the continuity between the preaching of Jesus and that of the early Church, some
of the post-Bultmannians tend to overlook the discontinuity.
While Bultmann sees no religious value in the pre-resurrection
kerygma, his former pupils seem to put it on a par with the
Easter message. A balanced approach would distinguish two

stages of Christological faith. First there is a kind of inchoate or implicit faith, demanded by Jesus in his public ministry. Then there is the full and explicitly Christological faith which corresponds to the kerygma of the Church.

It might be thought that now that we have the definitive edition, published after Easter, the earlier Kerygma would be simply out of date. Is it not mere archaism to reconstruct the proclamation appropriate to a bygone stage of salvation history? I believe on the contrary that this earlier version can still have great religious meaning for men of our time. Many who hesitate about accepting the Christ of full-blown Christian dogma, or even the heavenly Lord of the Acts and Epistles, are still powerfully drawn by the subtler and more modest claims made for the earthly Jesus in the synoptic gospels. The preaching of Jesus, as it has been reconstructed by Dibelius, by Bultmann himself, and especially by the post-Bultmannians, is immensely powerful and stirring. By responding interiorly to the call of the earthly Jesus, a man can best dispose himself to accept the claims of the Easter proclamation. Those who are first drawn to Jesus in the humble form of his humanity are most suitably prepared to welcome the good news that God has glorified him.

Even for the convinced Christian, or perhaps especially for him, it is rewarding to consider prayerfully how Jesus must have appeared "in the days of his flesh." The compilers of the gospels were not mistaken in thinking that the image of the man Jesus would be of permanent significance to the Christian community. More than anyone else who has lived on earth, this Jesus expresses what it means to live in this world in union with God and in generous dedication to one's fellow men. Without the concrete image of the flesh-and-blood Jesus, Christians would be in danger of building their lives on doctrinal abstractions. Not even the dogma of the resurrection, separated from the Person of the risen one, can suffice to found an integral Christian life.

In conclusion we should give some attention to the methodological questions underlying the whole discussion of history and faith. What are the limits of history in probing the crucial events of our redemption? Many would say that the goal of historical science is to reconstruct the past in its objectively verifiable (or "factual") aspects, such as could in theory have been registered on a sound-recording camera. While the historian, on this theory, is entitled to arrange facts in some kind of temporal or causal sequence, he would be exceeding his competence if he tried to give any explanation involving value judgments or metaphysical theories. According to the historico-critical school the ideal historian would be a coldly detached research scientist, free from any affections or commitments that might prejudice his objectivity.

Hard on the heels of the von Ranke school, Ernst Troeltsch, the principal theoretician of the history of religions school, sought to spell out the postulates implied in historical method as such. One such postulate, he believed, was the rule of analogy: things of the past were to be explained on the presupposition that they resemble things familiar to us from experience. This would imply that all men are basically alike and that utterly unique events, such as Jesus' resurrection, are to be discredited. A second postulate was that of continuity: history was assumed to be a seamless web in which all events were to be explained by the operation of inner-worldly causes. The historian, therefore, could not allow the possibility of any immediate intervention of God in history. A third postulate was that of relativity. Historical judgments were never final. They were approximate, and subject to revision as the viewpoint of the historian changed. Thus history could not undergird an unqualified faith-commitment to the truth of its own conclusions.

Troeltsch's historiographical theory is of importance for our subject, because Bultmann, on the whole, subscribes to it. An existentialist in theology, he aims at pure objectivity in historical scholarship. When he mounts the pulpit on Sunday, Bultmann is confident that God acts salvifically in the word of Christian preaching. But when he returns to his study on Monday, he flatly rejects the possibility that God's intervention might have any effect on the course of human history. As a historian, then, Bultmann takes it for granted that Jesus must have been a man like any other, that God could not have worked miracles through him or anyone else, and that his body could not have risen from the grave. He presupposes, likewise, that whatever history recovers about Jesus is a tentative reconstruction, and is therefore incapable of commanding the assent of faith. On such a theory of history it is evident that there must be a wide gap between the Jesus of history and the Christ of faith. For Bultmann, the distinction is not a merely formal one between different approaches to the same reality. Rather, as we have seen, the Jesus of history is discontinuous with the Christ of faith. The existence of the former is a mere presupposition for that of the latter.

It might seem that, having excluded the supernatural by postulate, the positivistic historian would have an easy time reducing Jesus to the stature of an ordinary man. But as the development of the Bultmann school makes clear, it has not been easy to explain away the sovereign majesty of Jesus' bearing, his miracles, the empty tomb, and the resurrection appearances. The more assiduously unbelieving historians tried to prove that the gospel tradition was formed on Hellenistic soil by Christians of the second or third generation, the more evident it became that they embody traditions gathered in the first generation on Palestinian soil. The more vociferously the positivists protested that primitive Christianity was infected with pagan mythology, the more conspicuous it became that the allegation was unfounded. Thus conventional historiography, when applied to the gospels, ran up against a dilemma. It could not solve the problem of Jesus without forcing the evidence or abandoning its own postulates.

Hence we must face again the nineteenth-century question whether the historian as such can point the way to Christian faith. If history is an objective science, totally bound to the postulates of Troeltsch, we must obviously answer in the negative; the affirma-

105

tions of faith would be ruled out by postulate. But in our generation we are witnessing an increasing dissatisfaction with this
inflexible concept of history.

In his enlightening treatment of the post-Bultmannian movement, *A New Quest of the Historical Jesus,* James M. Robinson
maintains that the school has affinities with the existential historiography derived from Wilhelm Dilthey. Reacting against the
historico-critical school, Dilthey argued that history ought not to
ape the natural sciences. In his view, history is a science of a
different type—a properly human science (*Geisteswissenschaft*).
Its primary goal is not to recover objective data such as names,
dates, places, which are just the outer shell. The real goal of history, which gives it its specific character, is to discover the distinctively human dimension of past activity—that which evades
the grasp of detached, impersonal science. It aims to encounter
figures of the past in their properly personal stance, as revealed
in their way of meeting situations and in their impact upon others,
both contemporaries and successors. History, then, does not consist
of information compiled to satisfy an idle curiosity. It is a serious
quest in which one's selfhood is confronted and one's most
cherished views are challenged. The student of history must be
open to radically new discoveries; he must be prepared for the
unexpected. Only if he adopts this attitude can he hope to learn
anything important. But if he has this openness, the resulting encounter with the past can break through the narrow limits of
what he previously considered self-evident. History gives man a
new self-understanding and in this way amplifies the possibilities
of one's own existence.

The French Catholic historian, H. I. Marrou, has adopted in
moderate and appealing form this personalist theory of history.
Like love and friendship, he maintains, history makes us go out
of ourselves. "It is necessary to consider the objective of history,"
he writes, "an enlargement of interior experience, of the knowledge of man, by the discovery of the other. What the historian
hopes, and realizes, is not to verify what he already knows, but to

encounter what is new . . . [History] is receptivity, submission to the unexpected, openness to the other, joy of discovery and of astonishment" (*Cross Currents,* Winter 1961). This does not of course justify an abandonment of the critical spirit. One must still be on guard against fraud and deception. But in addition it will be necessary for the historian to have imagination, insight, empathy. Sympathy without criticism is gullible; criticism without sympathy is narrow. The hypercritical researcher will be a poor historian. His carping, quarrelsome attitude prevents him from hearing what the past has to tell him. Too often modern New Testament scholarship has been in the hands of unimaginative scholars who ruled out in advance the idea that God could have done something singular and new in Jesus. For this reason they have been inclined, on the slenderest grounds, to dismiss much of the gospel narrative as fraud, illusion, myth, and legend.

Once history is viewed as an interpersonal event which may call for nothing short of a real conversion in the opening of self to what previously lay beyond the range of expectation, the gospels assume greater historical significance. As "committed documents" they intend to communicate the inner intention of Jesus' life, insofar as this became manifest in his impact on those who knew him best. They are concerned to communicate not so much the cold factual details of his *curriculum vitae* as the quality of his existence and his meaning to believers of future generations. The inspiration which Christians of later centuries have derived from the gospels proves that the evangelists succeeded admirably in their aim. It would be a narrow view of history which would disallow such an interpretative portrait by those who were convinced that in Jesus they had encountered God himself.

Quite obviously, it would not do to pretend that biblical history, while falling short of the standards of von Ranke or Troeltsch, measures up to the ideals of Dilthey or Marrou. The modern historian, no matter what school he belongs to, has a respect for objective facts (names, places, dates, numbers, and the like) which is foreign to the biblical authors. The gospels, like the "historical" books of the Old Testament, are a tantalizing mixture of authentic recollections and midrashic elaborations which we shall probably never succeed in disentangling. For all that, it remains true that the inquirer seeking to encounter the selfhood of Jesus as he communicated it to his followers, and to experience the quality of his call for decisions, will find great satisfaction in passages of the gospels which offer nothing but frustration to the pundit of the historico-critical school.

If the "historical" Jesus is taken to mean the real Jesus as grasped by those who were best situated to grasp the inner intention of his career, it becomes exceedingly difficult to draw a line between the Jesus of history and the Christ of faith. It is scarcely surprising, therefore, that a small but important cluster of younger German theologians, led by Wolfhart Pannenberg, from a point of view somewhat different from that of the post-Bultmannians, are now holding that historical scholarship can arrive at the truth of Christian revelation. The dualism of sacred and profane historiography, says Pannenberg, rests on an outmoded and intolerable view that there are crude, objective facts which must be supplied with meaning by the intervention of human subjectivity. If Christianity is true, he maintains, this must mean that the believer alone has correctly grasped the content of biblical history. Whoever seeks to wrest the data to another meaning, according to Pannenberg, can and should be convicted of error. The resurrection itself, far from being "suprahistorical," is the very center and consummation of history. It is the climactic moment when the kingdom of god, the goal of history, becomes proleptically present within the historical process itself.

Pannenberg does not entirely deny the distinction between fact and interpretation, but he holds that "every interpretation of an event must be justified from the context in which it was experienced or from the context of new experiences which call forth new interpretations" (*Theology as History*). The "justification" which he has in mind evidently presupposes certain moral and spiritual dispositions, and is not restricted to formal inference. Pannenberg, moreover, differentiates between the Christian understanding of the history of Jesus, which remains only probable, and the completeness of trust, or faith, which arises out of that understanding. Hence there is room in his system for the freedom of faith and for the influence of the Holy Spirit.

Accepting Pannenberg's own qualifications and explanations, one may agree with him that there is no theologically neutral "historical Jesus." The event of Jesus must be interpreted either favorably or unfavorably to faith. In the former view he appears as the one whose meaning was fully disclosed by what happened at Easter. In the latter view he must be reduced to the stature of a man like ourselves.

Any portrayal of the historical Jesus involves some interpretation of the gospel materials. If one forces them into the framework of a naturalistic world view, one can construct a "Jesus of history" in opposition to the witness of the gospels themselves. But if one wishes to be receptive to the evangelists' own evaluation of the man about whom they wrote, one will have to adjust the canons of historical method to handle a potentially unique case. It becomes at least an open question whether Jesus might not have spoken and acted in a completely singular way.

Which interpretation of Jesus is finally adopted depends in part on an estimate of the quality of the traditions gathered in the New Testament. Can they responsibly be dismissed as fanatical delusions or irresponsible inventions, or do they exhibit the characteristics of reliable testimony? But there are larger issues which cannot be avoided. The problem of Jesus, in its widest context, is inseparable from the problem of history itself. Does human history have a goal and a meaning, and are these to be found in the movement which begins with the man from Nazareth? If so, the Jesus of history is the Christ of faith.

II.

The Resurrection and Biblical Criticism

RAYMOND E. BROWN

IT IS NO SECRET that in the past twenty years Catholic scripture studies have made a complete turnabout and that Catholic scholars now accept seriously the biblical criticism against which some so long fought. The resultant reexamination of the bible has changed their views on some very important questions of historicity. It is the purpose of this article to report on how a critical approach affects the evaluation of the bodily resurrection of Jesus. Two preliminary observations should be made.

First, in questions of historicity, when we think of biblical criticism, we rightly think of examining the biblical text to determine the original wording that may have suffered from scribes, of tracing the materials that have gone into the composition of a book, of ascertaining the type of literature involved and the author's purpose. But besides all these technical procedures, there is often at work in biblical criticism a philosophical outlook that governs the application of the scientific techniques and greatly influences their results. Questions of historicity are sometimes decided on the basis of an unwritten principle that what happened in biblical times has to be in accord with the laws of nature and science now known to us. If one reads that the sun stood still for Joshua, or that Jonah lived inside a great fish, or that demons took possession of swine, there is a tendency to prejudge (or even deny) the historicity of such events even before the techniques of scholarly investigation are applied.

This approach to history explains much of the skepticism about the biblical accounts of the resurrection. Although the application of technical criticism to the resurrection narratives does uncover serious difficulties, in many cases skepticism does not really result from biblical criticism but has predated it and guided it. Studies of the resurrection of Jesus have been greatly influenced by the fact that in our experience men do not rise from the dead and by the medical observation that with death there begins a complex series of irreversible bodily changes that makes even the concept of a return to physical life most difficult. Now, a certain amount of preconceived skepticism about the unusual is a good thing, for it causes us to examine the bible carefully. (It offsets another philosophy that is often at work, namely, that everything in the bible is history.) But we must beware of systematically reducing what happened in Jesus Christ to the dimensions of the present. If there is any truth to Christianity, then what God accomplished in his Son must be unique in some way.

In an extremely important work, *Resurrection and Historical Reason,* Harvard professor Richard R. Niebuhr has shown how in the last one hundred fifty years almost every critical approach to the resurrection narratives has been dominated by an epistemology wherein historiography is governed by the laws of natural science. A critical scholar himself, he makes an eloquent plea for recognizing that in deciding the reality of the resurrection the key is the apostolic testimony to that event and not an *a priori* application of the laws of medical science. We may examine the apostolic testimony as critically as good method demands, but in the name of scholarship we must be wary of all those who would decide beforehand that bodily resurrection is impossible, even in the instance of God's Son.

More briefly, a second preliminary is that, while we shall be discussing historicity, the major contribution to an understanding of the resurrection that has come from modern Catholic biblical studies lies in another direction. Indeed, it has been by reaction to the exclusivity of apologetic interest in the resurrection that writes like F. X. Durrwell and D. M. Stanley have explored the

111

theological import of the resurrection and have restored the New Testament emphasis on its salvific value. Jesus was raised from the dead *for our justification,* says Paul (Rom. 4:25). And it is with this theological understanding, and not primarily with apologetic intent, that he insists: "If Christ has not been raised, then our preaching is in vain, and your faith in vain" (1 Cor. 15:14).

If we turn now to the question of historicity, we find that the New Testament does not claim that anyone saw the resurrection and makes no attempt to describe it, as does the apocryphal *Gospel of Peter.* Therefore, the fact of the resurrection hinges on two points of evidence, namely, the missing body or empty tomb, and, more important, the validity of the experiences of those who testified that they had seen the risen Jesus. Biblical criticism affects each of these points, but the criticism of today does not follow the paths taken by the criticism of the past. No longer respectable are the crude theories of fraud and error popular in the last century: the apostles were the victims of mass autosuggestion or they invented the stories; they stole the body or misplaced it; the tombs were confused; Jesus was not dead but in a coma from which he revived; etc. Occasionally some new mutation of the "plot" approach will briefly capture the public fancy, but serious scholars pay little attention to these fictional reconstructions.

Nor has enduring success been enjoyed by the approach to the resurrection that grew out of the study of comparative religions, an approach that was popular in the early 1900's. This was the theory that, consciously or unconsciously, the early Christians conformed the story of Jesus to the pagan legends and mystery cults surrounding the dying and rising gods (Attis, Adonis, Osiris, Dionysus). While Jesus may have risen in the spring, his death and resurrection had nothing to do with nature's cycle of winter dormancy and spring flowering that lay behind the suggested parallels. Perhaps a modern variant of this theory is the suggestion, sometimes associated with the names of A. Dupont-Sommer and J. M. Allegro, that Jesus' career had a historical counterpart and forerunner in the career of the Righteous Teacher of the Qumran (Dead Sea Scroll) community who was crucified and whose resurrection was expected by his disciples after his death. The *fact* that there is not the slightest real proof for either of these affirmations about the Teacher has not prevented dissemination on a popular level, but without further evidence the theory is not worthy of scientific discussion.

Modern biblical criticism of the resurrection narratives has centered around three points: (1) the disagreements in the various narratives of the resurrection; (2) the lateness of the story of the empty tomb; (3) an analysis of the psychology of those who claimed to have seen Jesus.

There are six distinguishable accounts in the gospel tradition of the resurrection: Matthew 28, Mark 16:1-8, Luke 24, John 20, John 21, and Mark 16:9-20. It will be noted that we distinguish two accounts in John and two in Mark. It is generally agreed that John 21, while it stems from the Johannine school of writers, is not by the same hand as the rest of the gospel but was added after the gospel was finished (see 20:30-31). Although clauses were inserted to make 21 fit with 20, the account in John 21 really does not presuppose an earlier appearance and is independent of 20. As for Mark, most scholars theorize that the gospel lost its original ending, which narrated the appearance of Jesus to the disciples in Galilee as promised in 16:7. Later there were several attempts to supply a new ending for the gospel, one of which (16:9-20) has been received as canonical. This "Marcan Appendix" seems to be dependent on material found in Luke 24 and in John 20.

When we compare the six accounts they fall into two groups: those that narrate appearances of the risen Jesus to the eleven disciples in Jerusalem (Luke 24, John 20, Mark 16:9-20) and those that narrate appearances to the eleven in Galilee (Matthew

28, John 21, and, by implication, Mark 16:1-8). Neither of these two traditions shows any awareness of appearances in the other locale.

The *Jerusalem accounts* leave little or no room for subsequent appearances in Galilee. According to Luke 24:50-51, Jesus took his final departure from his disciples at Bethany, near Jerusalem, on Easter night. (The story of an ascension after 40 days is peculiar to Acts and is not in harmony with the Lucan gospel.) According to Mark 16:19, Jesus was taken up into heaven after he had appeared to the disciples at table (presumably in Jerusalem on Easter night).

The *Galilean accounts* seem to rule out prior Jerusalem appearances to the eleven. In Mark 16:7 and Matthew 28:7 the angel's directive is that the disciples should go to Galilee to see Jesus—a command that would make little sense if they were to see him first in Jerusalem. When Jesus does appear to the disciples on a mountain in Galilee (Matthew 28:16-17), they express doubt. Or in the Johannine version, when Jesus appears to the disciples on the shore of the Sea of Galilee (21:4), they do not recognize him. All of this would be hard to believe if the authors thought that the disciples had already seen the risen Jesus in Jerusalem.

How could such discrepancy have arisen if we are dealing with historical accounts? The distinguished Protestant scholar, Vincent Taylor, has made an interesting suggestion. The account of the passion and death of Jesus required a certain sequence: arrest had to precede trial; trial had to precede execution; etc. But there was no intrinsic necessity for a sequence in the post-resurrectional narratives. In Paul's primitive preaching of the appearances (1 Cor. 15:5-7), no locale is mentioned but only the fact that Jesus appeared to various witnesses. Each community would tend to preserve the memory of an appearance to apostolic figures known to that community, and so the important Christian communities in Jerusalem and Galilee would retain the memory of appearances with local associations. Thus, each of the gospel accounts is but a partial witness to a larger picture.

But if we press this criticism to its conclusion, we must recognize that the customary sequence that has been imposed on the post-resurrectional appearances is unsatisfactory. It is virtually an untenable thesis that Jesus appeared first to the eleven in Jerusalem for about a week (John 20:26), and that afterwards they went to Galilee (for some inexplicable reason) where he appeared to them on the seashore (John 21) and on the mountain (Matt. 28) and that finally they returned to Jerusalem where Jesus appeared to them before ascending (Acts 1). This sequence does violence to the gospel evidence, as Bishop Descamps, rector of Louvain University, has argued well in an article in the 1959 *Biblica*.

If one must venture beyond the evidence to make a sequence, chronological priority must be granted to the appearances in Galilee. The accounts of Jerusalem appearances in Luke 24 and John 20 are constructions whose chronology has been dictated primarily by theological rather than by historical interest. (In particular, Luke's account where all the appearances take place in one day requires truly extraordinary efforts on the part of the two disciples who were in Emmaus at evening and yet managed to get back to Jerusalem before the disciples had finished supper!) The return of the disciples to Galilee is more intelligible if Jesus had not appeared to them in Jerusalem first. One could posit that subsequently the disciples went back from Galilee to the holy city and that there Jesus appeared to them for the last time.

But the more biblical answer (and certainly the one this writer favors) is to recognize that no sequence can be established with any assurance. Each of the six gospel accounts centers on an all-important appearance to the eleven in which they were commissioned for their future task. Each of the accounts gives the impression that this is the first appearance of Jesus, whence the doubt of the disciples and the need for reassurance. Bishop Descamps is correct in insisting that, *as far as substance and function are concerned,* all six accounts are narrating the same appearance.

That we take these accounts seriously despite our inability to arrange them into a satisfactory sequence is in accord with the modern approach to the historical value of the gospels. The evangelists, who were not eyewitnesses themselves, gathered and gave unity to many traditions that had come down to them from eyewitnesses; yet often they lacked the information to put these traditions into correct chronological order.

Thus far we have spoken of the appearances to the eleven. What about the story of the women at the tomb? Here the divergencies in the narratives are even sharper. Mark 16:8 clearly supposes that there was no appearance of Jesus to the women; nor does Luke 24 show any knowledge of such an appearance. The first part of Matt. 28 mentions no appearance; but almost by afterthought, vv. 9-10 recount an appearance to the women as they return from the tomb to Jerusalem. John 20:1-2 tells of no appearance to Mary Magdalen when she first came to the tomb, but 20:14 reports that Jesus appeared to her when she returned to the tomb a second time. The latest account (Mark 16:9, drawing perhaps on John 20) gives the most prominence to an appearance to Mary Magdalen. The hesitancy among these Gospel witnesses and the fact that Paul (1 Cor. 15:5-7) mentions no appearance to the women suggest that this story belongs to a later stratum of gospel tradition than do the stories of appearances to the eleven. Lateness, of course, does not preclude historicity.

The impression of lateness in the tomb narratives is bolstered by what they report of angelic visions. These visions are marked by great confusion; and it is an extremely interesting exercise to compare the accounts to find out whether there were one or two angels (young men), whether they were outside or inside the tomb, whether they were sitting or standing. To do justice to all the accounts one would have to posit a half dozen angels in various postures inside and outside the tomb. Obviously we are dealing with a popular narrative that has undergone embellishment. This process reaches a climax in Matthew 28:1-5 where the women are present when an angel comes down from heaven and opens the tomb—a presentation totally at variance with the other accounts where the stone is already rolled back when the women arrive.

How does all of this affect the reliability of "the empty tomb" that has been the cornerstone of apologetic argument for the bodily resurrection? On the one hand, we should make clear that the empty tomb is not an object of faith; we believe in the risen Christ. In Germany some of Rudolf Bultmann's conservative opponents, in their desire to stress bodily resurrection, have loudly proclaimed their faith in the empty tomb—a rather empty faith, as Bultmann was quick to point out.

On the other hand, it is one thing to point out the lateness of the story of the women at the tomb and the embellishments that it has undergone; it is something else to jump to the conclusion that the tomb was not empty and that Jesus' body remained in it. There is no statement about the resurrection in the New Testament that would in any way suggest that conclusion. Matthew 28:13 tells of the fabrication of a story that Jesus' body had been stolen. This is a very late element in the gospel traditions (as is Matthew's contention that a guard was placed at the tomb; the other accounts suppose that the women would have free access to the tomb). But it does represent an argument against the resurrection that was being used by anti-Christians in the late first century. There would have been no need for such an argument if there were a tomb with Jesus' body in it.

Wolfhart Pannenberg, the theologian who enjoys great popularity in Germany today, has summed up the situation well in his article in the 1965 *Dialog*: "We have only to try to imagine how Jesus' disciples could proclaim his resurrection if they could constantly be refuted by the evidence of the tomb in which

117

Jesus' corpse lay." Although the earliest preaching may not have narrated a story of the empty tomb, this preaching is almost unintelligible if it did not presuppose an empty tomb. Some scholars have seen a hint of this in Paul's insistence that the Jesus who was raised had been *buried* three days before (1 Cor. 15:4) and in the contrast in Acts 2:29 between Jesus and David who was still in his tomb in Jerusalem.

It is not difficult to understand why this presupposition of an empty tomb may not have been articulated until later. The early preachers were not giving continuous accounts of what happened but were proclaiming the risen Jesus. Only when there was an attempt at a continuous narrative such as we now find in the gospels would it have been necessary to supply the connective between the burial story and that of the first appearance to the eleven. Despite the diversity of their sources for the resurrection narratives, the writers of all four gospels accepted the story of the empty tomb. Evidently even in the pre-Gospel period the story was widely accepted, and this acceptance is hard to explain if it was known to the Christian leaders that the tomb was *not* empty.

In light of the care with which one has to evaluate this material, it is disturbing to hear from Catholics the facile claim: "My faith in the resurrection would not be disturbed if Christ's body were found in Palestine." Much more to the point is the question whether the faith of the eleven would have been shaken by such a discovery. This writer, for one, thinks that it would have been.

In harmony with the view of some that the narratives of the empty tomb are completely fictional, a new explanation of the post-resurrectional appearances is gaining a following. Unlike the older theories mentioned above, it does not suppose fraud or self-deception on the part of those who claimed to have seen Jesus. (Parenthetically we may remark that nowhere in this paper do we intend to raise the question of whether such men were telling the truth. That question remains what it always will remain—a question of faith.) In this theory Jesus really did conquer death, and those who knew him really did experience his victory in faith. But their explanation of this victory was in the terminology of the only anthropology they knew: they explained it as a bodily resurrection even though they had not seen what we would call the body of Jesus. This theory is based on the fact that in Semitic anthropology there was no dualistic concept of body and soul; rather an animated body was the whole man. Therefore, when the concept of survival after death came into Hebrew thought, it came in the form of resurrection of the body, for without a body the person simply would not exist. And so, it is suggested, when the disciples experienced the glorified Jesus, they described this as seeing his resurrected body. There was no other way to express to themselves the truth that they had encountered *him*.

On the whole the biblical anthropology on which this theory is based is correctly presented. But recently the Scottish Old Testament scholar James Barr, who makes a habit of sticking pins into balloons of over-generalization, has wisely pointed out that, in a laudable effort to distinguish between Hebrew and Greek mentality, scholars have sometimes forgotten that first-century Palestine was a melange of both. Certainly before Christ's time Alexandrian Judaism understood about the soul and its immortality (Wisdom 3:1); and Josephus, the Jewish historian (*War.* II 8:11), attributes such a dualism to the Palestinian Essenes. In his book *Old and New in Interpretation,* Barr argues strongly that certain statements in the gospel presuppose some idea of a soul. Therefore, we should at least be cautious about the claim that the experience of the glorified Jesus could be expressed only in terms of the resurrection of the body. The present writer finds it hard to think that any anthropology could be so monolithic that men could not formulate the idea that in some way they had made contact with Jesus after death and that God had glorified him even though his body was still in the tomb—if that is what they really experienced.

But even if the anthropology of New Testament times offered to the disciples no alternative manner of thinking or speaking except that of bodily resurrection, we have still not established that the disciples did not see exactly what they described. The only available expression may have corresponded to the fact. We have already seen above that the preaching of the disciples seems to have implied that the body of Jesus was not in the tomb, but an even stronger objection to the new interpretation of the resurrection arises from the import of the narratives of the appearances. In several accounts incidents have been included precisely to underline that it was Jesus' real body that was seen by the witnesses. He ate with his disciples (Luke 24:41-43; Acts 10:41) and he invited Thomas to touch his wounds (John 20:27). It is quite true that these incidents belong to a late stratum within the development of the tradition of the resurrection and that they were included to refute arguments that the disciples had not really seen the body of Jesus. But, when joined to the story of the empty tomb, they show us how the appearances were being interpreted at the time the gospels were written. The evangelists thought that in the post-resurrectional appearances the disciples had seen the body of Jesus that had been buried in the tomb, and several of them went out of their way to prevent a non-corporeal interpretation. And pushing back the inquiry to an earlier period, one wonders if Paul would have stressed the burial of Jesus if he also were not convinced that the appearances of the risen Jesus narrated in 1 Cor. 15:5ff. were appearances involving the body that had been buried.

The new interpretation of the resurrection is not categorically refuted by the evidence, but it has no real support in the New Testament. It is to a large extent an instance of the phenomenon mentioned at the beginning of our paper, namely, of deciding beforehand on the basis of modern science what could not have happened and then of ingeniously reading the bible so that there is no conflict. For this writer the evidence of the New Testament, even when studied critically, remains firmly on the side of bodily resurrection.

Has, then, the modern attempt to reinterpret the resurrection been a total failure? Not at all, for, when properly evaluated, it should color our understanding of the resurrection. Too often in the past the resurrection of Jesus has been presented as a simple resuscitation, differing little from his own raising of the son of the widow of Nain, the daughter of Jairus, and Lazarus. At times apologists have been so intent on stressing bodily resurrection that they have not read the very important qualifications supplied by scripture itself. Need we recall the debate about whether the blood that Jesus shed on Calvary got back into his body! Above we have stressed the element of *continuity* in the resurrection. It was the Jesus who died and was buried in the tomb that the disciples saw, and we have suggested that this continuity was such that it rules out any explanation whereby his body remained in the tomb. But there is the complementary element of *transformation* that must also be recognized, as Pannenberg has insisted.

All the gospel accounts stress in one way or another that the risen Jesus was different. Those who knew him did not recognize him as he stood before them (Luke 24:16; John 20:14; 21:4); some among the eleven doubted that it was he (Mt. 28:17; Luke 24:41; John 21:12). Mark 16:12 speaks of his appearing "in another form." Thus the gospels speak of no simple resuscitation. The body that had gone into the tomb had been changed, and Jesus did not return to ordinary life. This was a transformation.

Paul expresses the idea eloquently and perhaps as profoundly as it can be phrased. In 1 Cor. 15:12 he calls on Christ's resurrection to answer those who deny the resurrection of the dead. (We note that the whole point of his argument is to prove that there is a resurrection of the body—Paul would be quite confused by modern attempts to use this passage to disprove bodily resurrection.) His opponents object (15:35 and context) that the idea of resurrecting a long-dead body is foolish. What would it look like? (This is almost an ancient form of the argument that there can be no resurrection of the body because with death irreversible changes set in.) Paul answers with a simile that shows that he has

121

no crass idea of physical resurrection. One sows a seed, and what comes up is a stalk of wheat (15:37); the same thing happens in the resurrection of a body that has been buried.

In 15:42ff. Paul uses a series of adjectives to describe the transformation. In the resurrection of the dead, what is sown or goes into the tomb is perishable and physical; what emerges or is raised in glory is imperishable and spiritual. A man of dust has become a man of heaven. Many of the objections to the resurrection flowing from science would not be applicable to such a nuanced theory of resurrection as Paul presents.

Thus, if the element of continuity seems to demand an evaluation of the evidence in terms of Jesus' bodily resurrection from the dead, the element of transformation requires a recognition that the body that was raised is a spiritual and imperishable body, quite different from the body that was placed in the tomb. The body of Jesus is involved; but, in loyalty to Paul, we must maintain that it is a changed body. The modern investigation of the question has served to remind us that, after all, in speaking of the resurrection of the dead and of life after death we are using analogical terms. There is an element of mystery in the resurrection that apologetic interests should not be allowed to destroy.

It seems to this writer that a firm grasp of the two elements of continuity and of transformation that spring from the New Testament itself will prevent our approach to the resurrection from yielding to the two extreme positions that threaten all Catholic theology today: a liberalism that would completely rewrite revelation in terms of contemporary experience, without any real obedience to what has come down to us in the bible; and a fundamentalistic conservatism that lacks historical sensitivity in considering revelation and its formulations.

III.

The Humanity of Jesus

THOMAS E. CLARKE

BEFORE A THEOLOGIAN ventures a single remark about the humanity of Jesus Christ (meaning here the structure, processes and content of his human consciousness prior to his death), he has first to ask himself, "Just how do I come to know anything at all about such things?" The death of the biographical Jesus would seem to be one of the few certain fruits of several decades of discussion of the Jesus of history and the Christ of faith. We are, on the other hand, rightfully cautious about a purely deductive Christology which, with only a slight nod to the gospels, has woven onto the stiff fabric of Chalcedonian dogma an ornate overlay of human perfections scarcely compatible with the Son of God's kenotic plunge into solidarity with us sinners. In the past, at least, this method has tended to turn the God-man into Superman.

One current temptation is to escape sheer agnosticism by recourse to the pneumatic Christ of glory, present in word and sacrament, in Christian community, in the person of the neighbor, and in historical and cosmic process. But, aside from the fact that sacramental presence is presence precisely of the Absent One, who has left (been put out of) the world and has still to come again, there is something faintly docetic in an almost exclusive recourse to the transhistorical condition of him who, after all, saved us by living and dying as a man.

The more immediate and urgent need of a Christology of the humanity of Jesus is not just one more "portrait," to be added

123

to those of Guardini and others, but rather a clear understanding of the conditions under which any kind of "portrait" at all may be possible. The temptation, today no less than in ages past, is to make Jesus more or less what we would like him to be, yesterday the classic hero, today the existentialist or Marxist or secular hero (or non-hero, the "ordinary guy"). He may, indeed, share something with each of these; but we should not be too sanguine about our ability to keep our own moral and psychological biases from interfering with our knowing him as he was. The task is the more difficult for the fact that, as we shall say presently, there is a legitimate role for our own experience of human and Christian life in constituting the total data of Christology. Difficult or not, the effort is imposed on the theologian.

All of which is said in order to prepare the reader for a disappointment. Rather than speak directly, on the basis of scriptural exegesis or logical inference from the Church's doctrine, of the human endowments and limitations of the earthly Jesus, I will be offering some propaedeutic reflections. These will include: a consideration of some of the general conditions of method, stance and climate required for an adequate Christology of the human Jesus; a development of what I would call the principle of divine and human compatibility; and finally a suggestion of how a personal appropriation of our own human and Christian experience can complement, without replacing, the traditional approaches to the mystery of Christ. Those readers whose disappointment is intense or perduring can easily assuage it by reading again the portrait of "The Human God: Jesus" drawn by Fr. John Dunne earlier in this symposium. They might also wish to examine the ample exegetical treatment of what Jesus knew by Fr. Raymond E. Brown in the July 1967 issue of the *Catholic Biblical Quarterly,* and Fr. Karl Rahner's analysis of the human consciousness of Jesus in a long essay in volume 5 of his *Theological Investigations.*

John McIntyre has recently delineated in *The Shape of Christology* the complexity of the Christological "given" and consequently of its method. I take it for granted here that among the primary data are to be included: 1) The New Testament, particularly the gospels, as expressing the apostolic Church's crystallization of its reflective experience of the earthly Jesus and the exalted Lord; 2) the Church's doctrinal affirmations of the mystery of the incarnation (principally the definition of Chalcedon of 451), along with logical inferences from them; 3) philosophical anthropology, in whatever it can discern of the essential structure and functioning of man as spirit in the world; 4) other truths of the faith, which is to say other aspects of the mystery of Christ than the narrowly Christological one, which are drawn into an adequate Christology by what Vatican I called "the articulation of [revealed] truths among themselves." The inclusion of this last kind of given is important for what I will say later about the aesthetic quality to be looked for in an adequate Christology.

But there is another kind of Christological "given" which is all too often neglected. I mean the reflective appropriation of one's own humanity, in both inner and interpersonal aspects, and particularly as one's humanity includes experience of life with the risen Jesus in his indwelling Spirit.

Here we begin to touch the neuralgic point of Christological method. We see better today that no science is simply taking a look at "the already out there now" (Lonergan), and hence that every science verifies to some degree the Marcellian notion of mystery. Nowhere is this involvement of the reflecting subject in his own data so intense as in theology. Viewed in this perspective, the apparently trite formula which envisages theology as the science of faith has explosive implications for the nature of what is being done. The mystery of Christ on which he is reflecting enters into the very constitution of the theologian as human and Christian subject. His faith, indispensable for Christian theology and, in its normal state, impregnated with unitive Trinitarian love, has already drawn him within the mystery which he contemplates.

This is not to say that a true believer or a holy Christian is by that fact a good theologian, or, for that matter, any theologian at all. Nor is it to deny that between authentic and intensive experience of Christ and theological formulation of what is experienced there is room for error, even of a substantive kind. And certainly, by comparison with scriptural or conciliar assertions, this kind of "data" is only minimally capable of verification by fixed and common standards. It remains true, however, as McIntyre has pointed out, that "we must include within the complexity of this given also our own response. *Christology happens only within a believing community, and the given upon which it rests is something which happens only to believers.* This response, in obedience and love, in faith and worship, is therefore a constituent of the initially given." (Italics added.)

It should be obvious, from the extreme diversity of the "data" enumerated (to which others could be added), that the *method* of their integration cannot possibly be by way of simple logical inference, convergence of probabilities, and the like. Such methods do have a place within Christology. But at the point of assembly, or better, formation, the science of theology would seem to verge on art, and what one looks for is primarily a certain aesthetic quality, a harmony among the statements contained in the Christology, the congruity of these statements, singly and together, with the scriptural and conciliar data and with other aspects of the Christian mystery, and also an affinity with Christian experience.

In this search for congruity, Christology is only seeking to be faithful to the pattern of revelation itself, which in a genuine sense is continuing in the life of the Christian. God is faithful, that is, consistent with his own word and promise. He reserves, to be sure, the right to baffle us, and we have to struggle to make sense of what he says and does. But, though Lord of the absurd, he is no absurd Lord. To the extent to which we are in the Spirit and listening from faith, it is not the circumscribed absurdity but the encompassing Meaning which is primary. The apostle Paul is a clear example of how the Christian theologian finds not only truth but beauty in revelation, and seeks to reflect it in his theology.

The preceding insistence that we include in the data of Christology the whole gamut of Christian doctrine as well as our Christian experience has a two-fold point. First, the chief source of dissonance among Christologists today may be not so much in how they read the identical data as in what data they admit and how this data comes together in a comprehensive methodology. It is difficult otherwise to explain how scriptural and conciliar theologians, who are for the most part in agreement on immediate and even penultimate conclusions, part company on the root Christological questions, and do so, for the most part, congruously with the particular Christian tradition in which they have been brought up. There are inescapable presuppositions or at least postures which condition our reading of scripture and the councils. Awareness of these conditioning factors can only help the Christological endeavor.

The second reason for making much of these two sources of Christological data is the contribution they can make to resolving the essential dilemma which hinders access to the humanity of Jesus: if he was the eternal Son of God, how could he be man? If he was really a man, how could he be the eternal Son of God? Patristic and medieval theology formally accepted living with the dilemma, but being more worried about Adoptionism than about Docetism, accepted also various secondary compromises in the sphere of Jesus' human knowledge and affectivity. The Jesus of liberal theology represented a failure of nerve in the opposite direction. What had, above all, to be maintained, was his being a man, and it was simply asking too much to assert that this man was the eternal Son of God.

Today we have inherited the problematic of liberal theology, and are unwilling simply to repeat the patristic and medieval answers, even without their incidental compromises. Yet some of the alternatives being proposed escape with difficulty the suspicion of being unsubstantially modified versions of positions encountered and rejected by the Christian community long centuries ago. While I have no alternative to propose, I am suggesting that reflection on our own Christian existence within the framework of the totality of Christian doctrine may point the way to new possibilities. This is the point of what follows.

A theologian who reflects within the Roman Catholic community and tradition, in which the compatibility of God and man is asserted and stressed right across the doctrinal spectrum (consider what Catholicism has to say of nature and grace, justification and merit, grace and freedom, the active role of sacramental action, the mediational office of Mary and the saints), will be subjectively conditioned to extend this compatibility even as far as hypostatic union. Something similar may be said of the influence of a climate of *spirituality* for which Sartre's "If I am, God is not—if God is, I am not" represents alternatives not reconcilable with the doctrine of creation as a self-communication of total being, or with the biblical insistence that God is essentially invitation to man, not threat, that he is not jealous of human greatness but rather, *"Gloria Dei vivens homo."*

It is this doctrinal and spiritual climate, more than any technical conclusion from scripture or council, which explains the appeal for a Catholic theologian of Karl Rahner's expression of this basic compatibility of God and man: "This is precisely an attribute of his divinity as such and his intrinsic creativity: to be able, by himself and through his *own* act *as such,* to constitute something in being which by the very fact of its being radically dependent (because *wholly* constituted in being), also acquires autonomy, independent reality and truth (precisely because it is constituted in being by the one, unique *God*), and all this precisely with respect to the God who constitutes it in being. God alone can make something which has validity even in his own presence. There lies the mystery of that active creation which is God's alone. Radical dependence upon him increases in direct, and not in inverse proportion with genuine self-coherence before him." (*Theological Investigations,* I)

But it is not only on God's side that this compatibility of God and man even to the point of hypostatic unity has its foundation. While Rahner's statement that the creature is autonomous because of, and not in spite of, total dependence on the creator God, has application throughout creation (thus excluding both deism and occasionalism), it is the uniqueness of man as image of God, *capax infiniti,* which grounds his obediential potency for immediate and personal union.

It is not so difficult for us today to accept a radical capacity for self-transcendence in man. The scientific, technological and cultural explosions of recent times make us wary of setting any fixed limits to his openness. Another age might have looked on Teilhard's projections as sheer fantasy, but we, at the least, are not so sure that they are. A few decades ago, in theological circles, this self-transcendence was conceived as setting man in contrast with Nature, and was taken as ground for the inappropriateness of thinking of him with the category of nature at all. Today, however, we are more inclined to accent his continuity rather than his discontinuity with his milieu, and to view him more as spearhead of a total creational process of which self-transcendence is the hallmark. There is, however, no contradiction between this continuity and the uniqueness of man as alone capable of immediate, personal union with God. Just why the threshold of spirit must be crossed before Spirit can be perfectly immanent in the world need not detain us here.

The point being made in all this is that our instinctive shying away from the mystery of the incarnation of the Son of God fails to acknowledge the limitless horizons not only of God's capacity to give himself but also of man's capacity to receive and, in that reception, to achieve himself. This may appear to be smug, and to be suggesting that the incarnation is something that any reasonable man should be able to accept, once he has the wisdom to accept the analogy of being. Such is not my intention. I would insist that the mind which really comes to rest before this mystery is not in the presence of Christ but of either an absurdity or a banality. The apophatic tradition, found in the same Greek Fathers who gave us our classic conciliar formulations, and well expressed in St. Augustine's *"Si comprehendisti, non est Deus,"* is, unfortunately, rarely carried over to God as he is in Christ. No more do we know what Christ is than we know what God is. We know of Christ rather what he is not than what he is. I would, to be sure, wish to employ this agnosticism of definition against any too facile assertion of the repugnance of the Son of God becoming man. Let him who is assured of knowing what God is and what man is in relation to God make that declaration!

The absence of a full sense of this compatibility of God and man could render sterile the much needed movement in Christology today to reformulate the mystery of Christ in terms other than those employed by Chalcedon (one person, two natures, one and the same is God and man, etc.). This trend should be viewed sympathetically, especially where it is more concerned with formulation than with the underlying affirmations (even though the two cannot be neatly dissected). The possibility, after all these centuries, of a valid and relatively adequate formulation of the mystery in Antiochene, *assumptus homo* terms, rather than in Alexandrian terms, should not be excluded *a priori.* But where the effort is taking place in a climate of either-or, it seems doomed to failure. This is where a general theology and a tradition of spirituality which fully accepts the principle of divine and human compatibility will be reluctant to embrace any compromise of either full divinity or full humanity.

Here also (and this is what I would now like to show) is where a reflective appropriation of one's own human and Christian experience can support this ability to live with Christological tension. Rahner is quite correct in insisting that only a divine

130

person can so radically make his own a distinct finite reality as to invite, not embarrass, the creative freedom of that finite reality. Yet we are not entirely without models which may help to make us receptive to such a possibility. I am referring to our two most basic experiences, of the self in its unity and duality, and of life with another as another kind of unity in duality.

It so happens that both of these experiences, or at least the conceptions derived from them, have been prominent in Christological history. The soul-body relationship is the most favored analogue for the incarnation, especially since its incorporation into the *Quicumque* creed: "As reasoning soul and flesh is one man: so God and man is one Christ." While not specifically Alexandrian, and admitting of various understandings in accordance with different anthropologies, the comparison lends itself more to a stress on the *unity* of Christ, especially today when it is the unity of the human subject, not the transcendence of the spiritual component, that is emphasized. Some theologians, in fact, dislike speaking of man as soul and body at all, just as they dislike speaking of Christ as God and man. But it is difficult to escape a certain duality. Some might prefer a duality of person (in the sense of free self-disposition) and nature (in the sense of the complexus of drives, aspirations, situation, etc. as the material and condition for free self-disposition), or a duality of what one *is* and *has*.

In any case, both the broad philosophical tradition of most schools and common human experience would seem to demand the presence in the one human subject of some kind of basic duality. By whatever name we choose to designate it, and however we translate it into a reflective anthropology, it is inescapably part of our mystery as human beings. We experience it as mystery. We struggle with it without ever mastering it. In its psychological and moral dimensions, it provides the arena for the conquest of the good and human life conceived as self-integration. We feel that to the extent to which we are able to master and direct our spontaneity without rendering it limp, and to sustain opposite tensions within a basic order, we are better and richer human personalities.

The personal appropriation of this duality-in-unity of our lives as human subjects can help us to accept the duality-in-unity of Christ. This appropriation can take place on various levels, the highest of which is the achievement of personal holiness. Progress in holiness, insofar as holiness means self-integration at the deepest level of human existence, thus provides us with a Christological "given" which, while it cannot replace the other givens, and is not homogeneous with them, cannot either be replaced by them. Other things being equal, it is the saint who is best disposed to accept the mystery of Christ, and, given the more technical skills of the theologian, to express it.

But experience of the self as a duality-in-unity is only one part of the basic human and Christian experience. In a sense it is a derivative part, for both genetically and ontologically self-possession as free subject is consequent upon encounter with the world as experienced in other human subjects. This is the second major Christological analogy, formulated principally in the conception of Christ as *assumptus homo*: Jesus is the man, son of Mary, assumed by the Word, God's eternal Son. Like the soul-body formulation, this one was the exclusive property of no single ancient school. Still, its affinity is clearly with Antioch, and with the steady recurrence in Christological history of the Antiochene insistence on duality in Christ. In its most acute form, this tradition would insert an I-thou into the unity of the incarnation: the man Jesus would address a "thou" not merely to God as Father, but to the eternal Word.

I find it difficult to see how, within the limits of the essential Christian tradition, this interpersonal model can be thus employed in a proper analogy. It can serve, however, as a corrective and complement for the soul-body model, which suffers as a model in that only one of the terms is endowed with intelligence and freedom. However limited its contribution, then, the appropriation of our interpersonal life as a duality-in-unity would seem to be a further source for understanding the mystery of Christ. The transcendence of division, the interpenetration of person and person which takes place in a knowing and loving relationship, surely pertains to the realm of human mystery. *That* true lovers are somehow one, and one *in their very duality,* without mutual absorption or reduction, is clear to whoever has experienced or witnessed such a relationship; *how* the oneness is achieved without destruction of the uniqueness of the other, and in fact in the very act of constituting that uniqueness, escapes us.

As in the case of the soul-body model, the appropriation of the I-thou model can take place on various levels, the highest of which is, once again, Christian holiness, now in its outreaching, horizontal dimension. Let him who would have some dim inkling of how it is possible, or at least not impossible, for one and the same to be God and man lay hold of and reflect on the mystery of human charity. And, since the mystery of Christ is a unity of qualitative unequals, in which the reality of the lesser is, without the slightest detriment to itself, already, though in totally different fashion, present in the reality of the greater, the model in Christian life for the incarnation is best had in the relationship of the individual Christian with the Christian community. The comparison is, of course, deficient in many respects; the incarnation keeps its uniqueness. Still, to the extent to which each of us, as an individual Christian, finds himself concretely encompassed by a loving Christian community, and to the extent to which that community is source of our Christian personhood and not threat to it, we are opened to the possibility of a similar, though infinitely more mysterious, relationship of duality in unity, total dependence in freedom, in the case of the humanness of Jesus which the divine Word has made his own.

This is, it seems to me, the full import of McIntyre's statement quoted above, "Christology happens only within a believing community, and the given upon which it rests is something which happens only to believers." There is no better example, perhaps, of the dependence of faith as doctrinal on faith as lived, of the Christological on the ecclesial, of knowlege on affective connaturality. The doctrinally creative power of charity, especially as exercised by the Christian community towards the individual, and on the other hand, the pressure towards heresy that is implicit where the individual Christian is either threatened or neglected by the community, likewise emerges.

To summarize what I have been saying: The life of Christian holiness, in its double aspect of 1) self-integration, and 2) mutual charity between the individual Christian and the Christian community, constitutes the most perfect instance within our human and Christian experience of the mystery of duality in unity. Its appropriation in lived experience and in theological reflection yields the closest approximation which we have to the transcendent mystery of duality in unity which is Christ. From the viewpoint of the title of this essay, and of the contemporary concern to let Jesus be fully a man, the thing to accent is the unhampered reality and value of the lesser partner to the union and, more positively, the bestowal of this reality and value by the very fact of union with the higher. As matter is ennobled, not degraded, by the fact that spirit makes it its own; as human spontaneity is preserved, not destroyed, in that self-integration which is Christian asceticism; as the Church, where she is true to herself, is creative mother and not threat to each of her children in his uniqueness; so does the Word's approach to a humanity born of Mary enrich it, *as human,* not snatch it from the human. In a word, our humanity, in its specifically Christian dimensions, becomes the principal avenue to understanding the humanity of Jesus Christ.

I conclude with three or four annotations on the above approach to the humanity of Jesus. The first remark is that we may reverse the direction of our understanding. Then it will be the humanity of Jesus which becomes model for our life of holiness.

As the utter freedom of his humanity comes home to us, there is less danger that we will, for example, conceive Christian asceticism as a cutting down on desire, or our relationship with the Church as a call to pull in our wings.

Secondly, the humanity of Jesus can be seen in its creative autonomy either in relation to the Word, as we have been doing, or in relation to the Father. It is in this aspect that the I-thou relationships of our human and Christian experience can serve more properly as analogues for understanding Jesus. Here Friedrich Gogarten's "mature sonship" beautifully expresses the towering paradox contained in the gospel Christ: the most creative and adult personality the world has ever seen, the man who has most decisively influenced human history, going about with the word "Father" constantly on his lips, and looking continually to that Other as source of his very creativity.

Thirdly, the line of reflection followed here suggests that the most serious challenge posed to Christianity by atheistic humanism, whether existentialist, Marxist or secularist, namely, that it enlarges God at the expense of man, is to be met at one and the same time ecclesially and Christologically. When Christian persons achieve a self-integration in holiness that does not inhibit the sheerly human in them but makes it flourish, and when the Christian community promotes instead of destroying the creative potential of its members, something of the mystery of Christ in his mature sonship shines forth.

Fourthly, a number of the questions generally discussed under the rubric of the humanity of Christ can be helped with the approach here taken. If one is really convinced of the principle of divine and human compatibility, he will feel less obliged, for example, to snatch Jesus from the limitations of human self-awareness, the need for real human decision even in the presence of moral good and evil, and the spontaneity of human passion and affection. The vocation of Christ to celibacy, about which the New Testament is completely silent, is not by that fact excluded

135

from Christological discussion, if one accepts that both Christian exprience and the totality of Christian doctrine have something to offer to our understanding of Christ.

One last remark. It cannot be too strongly emphasized that the foregoing is presented as *one* aspect of an integral Christology of the humanity of Jesus. I am not espousing some kind of gnostic short-cut which would dispense from the tedium of hacking a path through the thorny underbrush of textual criticism, evaluation of sources, relating stages of development in revelation and in tradition, conciliar history, etc. Obviously this integration is an enormous task, and the work of a community of scholars, not of individuals. The nub of the matter is how the various data and methodologies are to come together in a single methodology under some unifying principle. I am not so sure that Christology today possesses such an over-all methodology. We are presently in the process of recognizing and slowly assembling the parts.

IV.

Christology and Contemporary Philosophy

FREDERICK E. CROWE

IN THIS TITLE, the word contemporary probably defines a common frame of reference for contributors to the symposium. We are all concerned, one way or another, with Bonhoeffer's question: "What is Christianity, and indeed what is Christ, for us today?" So, surely, is everyone who believes in Christ and thinks at all about his faith. I can recall from my reading various articles that show this concern: on the laughter of Jesus, his subconscious, his sexuality and attitude toward women, his logotherapy, his questioning mind, his use of irony, his stature as a theologian, his reading in the Old Testament. The particular aspect of Christology that falls to me is indicated by the world "philosophy," and here more fundamental topics are in question; one might think of Bonhoeffer's own concern with the passing of the institutional in Christianity, or Teilhard de Chardin's vision of the place of Christ in an evolving universe, or Gogarten's view of Christ as taking on himself responsibility for our fateful entanglement with the word.

These are all legitimate topics of discussion, yet they are not quite the point that was suggested to me. This was "the challenge posed by contemporary philosophy to traditional Christological definitions and terminologies." The question was asked specifically about the formulation of Chalcedon on the two natures, divine and human, in the one person of Christ, and the extent to which such trends as linguistic analysis, phenomenology, process philosophy, etc., require its revision. Chalcedon is a sign of

137

contradiction, and I am not sorry to have had this particular aspect suggested to me. I think I should have had to come to it in any case, for it brings us up against the philosophical question that is really a challenge today, much more fundamental than the institutional and the evolutional and the existential themes.

Fundamental or not, the question of Chalcedon is squarely before us, as a few citations may show. There is the much-quoted statement of William Temple who, back in 1912, in the symposium, *Foundations,* said: "The formula of Chalcedon is, in fact, a confession of the bankruptcy of Greek Patristic theology." Of course, *Foundations* has been thought to mark a low point in Anglican theology, but Oscar Cullmann, who represents a high point in Protestant orthodoxy, says in *The Christology of the New Testament*: "all abstract speculation about the 'natures' of Christ is not only a useless undertaking, but actually an improper one." Well, Cullmann is a biblical and positive scholar and perhaps we cannot expect him to have much time for Chalcedon, but then you get the highly speculative Paul Tillich telling us in the second volume of his *Systematic Theology* that Chalcedon defined two natures "which lie beside each other like blocks and whose unity cannot be understood at all." Such judgments seem positively benign when you read Chalcedon referred to as "sheer verbal rubbish" (*Theology,* vol. 63, 1960, 290-293).

On the Catholic side one naturally finds a somewhat more conservative attitude, but even here there is recognition of Chalcedon as a plateau and not the summit. Thus, when the fifteen hundredth anniversary of the council came around in 1951, and the occasion was celebrated by three huge volumes, *Das Konzil von Chalkedon,* 2600 pages in all from a team of outstanding historians and theologians, Karl Rahner's contribution was called, "Chalcedon, End or Beginning?" From which the reader will surmise (rightly) that the answer is: a beginning. One is always glad nowadays to have Rahner on his side, and I associate myself with his forward-looking Christology; I think, in fact, that we can incorporate a great deal of the philosophies mentioned into our approach to Christology and considerably enrich it by means of their insights. They are not a challenge, therefore, in the sense that they require the overthrow of Chalcedon; they are a challenge to us to develop Chalcedon.

Nevertheless, Chalcedon is critically challenged, as the quotations from non-Catholic theologians show. It is challenged at a much more fundamental level. Further, I do not think it is possible to handle the issues involved without coming to something like absolutes of thought. Finally, I think the remedy for the defective philosophy is at hand in Bernard Lonergan's thought, but, since I simply cannot suppose that his views are understood, this paper will take on a didactic tone which cannot help but be disagreeable. There is my full apology all in a rush; I am sorry to be tendentious and fundamental and didactic, but after all I am governed by the necessities of the situation as I see them, and can write only what I believe to be true and important.

I need three headings to take up this question: the historical, the metaphysical, the foundational. The historical, in the modern use of the word, means not only the accurate determination of what happened or was said in the past but also the challenge it presents to us and the way we are constituted in relation to our past, positively or negatively. We have then to take as basis what exactly was decided at Chalcedon, study how that decision affects us today, and see what it means to "reinterpret" Chalcedon for our time. The historical leads to the metaphysical. It did so in actual fact as the Church moved from the patristic age to the medieval. It does so in principle insofar as the challenge of the past to us in our existential situation is partly intellectual. Explanation is as much an existential need as encounter and decision; there is an intellectual exigence to add metaphysics to Chalcedon. This seems odd, for many (not all) of those who reject Chalcedon do so on the grounds that it turned from the biblical to the metaphysical. But that is just one of the ironies of theology: Chalcedon was not especially metaphysical at all, but requires metaphysics of its successors. We are thus led inevitably to the foundational: are we, or are we not, to have a metaphysical Christology? This question must be decided on some better basis than mere like or dislike, or arbitrary decree, and so must come to basic issues of methodology and the prerequisites for dialogue between schools and approaches.

It is a complex matter to speak of the historical today in relation to Christ, without having an introductory chapter to explain your use of the word. Some will think immediately of the controversy on the Jesus of history and the Christ of faith; this pertains to my topic as an aspect, but only an aspect. Others will think of the historicality of Jesus himself, of his mind as conditioned by his time, of his decisions made in the responsibility his own situation thrust upon him. This, too, should be integrated into my topic as a component, but only as a component. What is in question here more generally is the historical character of all human thinking: that of the New Testament witnesses to Jesus, that of Jesus himself, that of all subsequent spokesmen for the faith of the Church. We are aware, in a way our ancestors were not, of the relativity of our concepts on all things under the sun and on the heavenly mysteries too, so it is a problem for us that we must adhere to one who lived a short life long ago and far away, and that we must hold to a doctrine uttered in the time-conditioned concepts of Palestine in the distant world of the Roman Empire.

There is, first of all, to start with a less formidable aspect, the multiplicity of our concepts about Christ. This appears in the New Testament itself with the successive efforts of different writers to present a theology or a concept of Christ. We are used to the idea that Paul, or the author of Hebrews, or John, has each a very distinctive Christology, but it comes as a surprise even to theologians to read a book like Sir Edwyn Hoskyns' *The Riddle of the New Testament* and discover what a remarkably thought-out view of Christ we have in Mark himself. The point appears much more simply in the many names given to Christ

—forty-two of them (some with sub-divisions) are scattered through the New Testament, according to the little book by Vincent Taylor, *The Names of Jesus*.

I presume this multiplicity presents no real problem to anyone. After all, the poets pile up image after image and concept after concept without exhausting their subject. ("O, what a rogue and peasant slave am I . . .", "This blessed plot, this earth, this realm . . .", etc.) Man himself, despite all the growth and differentiation of the human sciences, does not seem anywhere near the stage at which we can say: Now we know all there is to know about him. So the multiplicity of concepts about Jesus simply testifies to the inexhaustible wealth of his person and his nature and his role in history. Every advance in understanding what man is will constitute a new possibility for understanding the Christ, and that is the point of the studies on his laughter, his logotherapy, etc. Add to this his divine sonship and the mystery of his unity as the God-Man and it will be clear enough that the subject is quite simply and literally inexhaustible. The divine concept of what God is is simply one Word being uttered in an eternal Now, but the human concept of what God is will not exhaust the divinity in a succession of words uttered through eternity; much less then the succession of words uttered in human history.

There is, next, the apparent discontinuity of many of the names we give Jesus or the concepts we form about him: he is Alpha, Son of God, leader in faith, Amen, Cornerstone, and so on. But I do not think this will offer any real difficulty either, unless we think of doctrinal growth entirely on the analogy of a tree growing steadily in organic unity from one small seed of mighty potentiality. There *is* a growth like that, especially when you get theologians pursuing one line of thought with question following question in a kind of logical sequence. But you can also think of the growth of doctrine on the analogy of an orbiting ship's snapping pictures of the earth at odd moments; the pictures may not bear much relation to one another, but they are all snapshots

141

of the one reality and the more of them we have the more the total image takes on a unified pattern. Perhaps also we need a third analogy for the growth of doctrine, that of a tide washing farther and farther up the beach, receding at times to a considerable distance, but returning subsequently to a higher level than before.

Thirdly, there is the *real* question, that of the status of all these time-conditioned concepts in later times and other cultures. It seems to me there is a good deal of confusion here, and I would like to make my point firmly, without descending, if I can avoid it, to the language used by some of the critics of Chalcedon. First, truth has an absolute character that utterly excludes its contradictory; if it was true once that Jesus was asleep in the stern of the boat, it is forever true that at that time and place he was asleep in the stern of the boat, and similarly if he came as the Son of David, the Cornerstone, the Messiah, etc., it remains forever true that he came in those roles. One does not "reinterpret" these concepts or statements (except in the minor sense of language translation, as when one turns 'drachma' into 'dime'), one simply tries to discover as exactly as possible just what was in the mind of the original user. Secondly, whether the same statement can now be made of Jesus depends on its relation to his atemporal being and function; if it is true, however human the language, that he is eternal word of God, then he still is Word of God; if it is true, again in human language, that he is Redeemer of the whole human race, then this is a function that transcends any particular place and time, and is true as long as there are men to think about his relation to them.

There is another way of regarding the status of time-conditioned concepts, most simply defined in terms of "relevance." What is the impact today of calling Jesus by titles like Messiah, Son of David, I AM, the Father's YES, and so on? Here I find myself strongly with the radicals as against the fundamentalists. Recently I heard one of the latter on the radio telling me to believe on the Lord Jesus and I would be saved, and it struck me

142

with peculiar force how utterly alien this language was from modern man, how great the failure of the preacher to communicate with any of his audience who were not already won to Christ, and how pitiful the poverty of our imagination and creativity that we have failed so signally to do for our times what the New Testament writers or the early disciples did for theirs. "The Man for others" has become deservedly famous as something like a new name with a meaning for our time, but it stands out by its very loneliness. We have done a good deal of thinking on the finality of Christ in world-history, on the incarnation and process philosophy, on the existential attitude of Christ toward the world and his responsibilities in the world, but they have hardly given us new names; and they barely touch his transcendent relation to the Father and the Holy Spirit. There is room for even more radical approaches here than we have tried so far.

On the other hand, I find myself at odds with the radicals in their indiscriminate rejection of all the concepts of the past. Not everything human is just of its time, else it is pointless to speak of the human extending across the ages. There are concepts which are permanent even in theology, not because we have reached some exhaustive understanding of God and his mysteries, but because we have reached the limits of the human capacity to conceive; we have come to what is an ultimate for us. I think the concept, Word, in the Thomist sense of an inner word (which is not foreign to John's sense), is such a concept, and I think something similar can be said to apply to Chalcedon.

The particular concepts that have to be considered here are those of person and nature. The words so stick in the craw of many people today that one can hardly expect a hearing unless he jumps on the bandwagon of condemnation. The concept of person has a long history whose stages one can follow in Bernard Lonergan's *De Deo Trino* or in Karl Barth's *The Doctrine of the Word of God*. In Augustine it is a word whose meaning is a conundrum; in Boethius, Richard of St. Victor, and Thomas Aquinas there is the effort to find a logical definition; in the later scholastics, from Scotus to Tiphanus, there is the effort to analyze the constituent metaphysical elements; in the psychologists, beginning at a much later date, there is the effort to conceive personality in terms of internal experience; in our own day the trend is to the concrete life of persons, especially in relation to one another, with the use of art-forms of expression and the rejection of abstract formulations.

The point Lonergan makes is that there is a heuristic structure for the evolution of the concept of person, and that this structure is present already in Augustine, that prior stages of evolution do not exclude subsequent stages, that it is the heuristic structure that holds the whole process together and ensures that all are talking about the same thing. Furthermore I think we have to say that the fathers and the conciliar definitions use and sanction no more than such a heuristic concept. If that is the case, Chalcedon is not so much a time-conditioned attempt to be abandoned now for other equally time-conditioned attempts; rather it is the supposition and basis of all further attempts.

A first point is that the words sanctioned by the fathers received their theological meaning through the patristic use made of them. They did not stand in dictionaries already with a fixed meaning. This appears from the *Tomus ad Antiochenos* of Athanasius: the Arian quarrel was subsiding, he was trying to bring together the scattered Christian flock, but found some professing three *hypostaseis* (our present "person"), and some professing one *hypostasis* in God. He asked the former if they meant it in an Arian sense and was told no; he asked the latter if they meant it in a Sabellian sense, and again was told no. Thereupon he received both into communion with his church.

The point is that there was not yet a clear distinction between person and nature, that the words in use had no fixed meaning, that the governing factor was the "given" of scripture, that this "given" supplied a heuristic concept without being as yet expressed in a word, and that when the word was finally determined upon it had just the meaning with which that heuristic

144

concept endowed it. Thus also when Cyril talked at Ephesus of a union (in Christ) according to hypostasis, he was not first defining a "Greek" term and then applying it to Christ; what Ephesus determined, if one will take the trouble to study its history, was simply that he who was eternal Word was the one born of the Virgin Mary. The governing factor is simply the scriptural datum that *the one who* is eternal is *the same one who* is born temporally. And it was this that gave "hypostatic union" its meaning; the order was not the other way around.

The word, nature, enjoys a similar openness to development. It is, even more obviously than "person," conceived heuristically, meaning exactly what the interrogative "what" means. Lonergan's example here is fire; the nature of fire is conceived heuristically from descriptive accounts, which serve as a kind of pincers to hold the data for inquiry, and answers may range from an Aristotelian element to a type of oxidation, without upsetting the original heuristic concept. Now this is the kind of concept the fathers and councils had of Christ's natures. When Athanasius had to defend the Nicene definition of the Son's consubstantiality, he argued very simply that in scripture the same attributes are given the Son as the Father. This is an entirely heuristic concept.

What is the Son's nature: material? spiritual? light? intelligence? The concept allows for all: the significant word is "whatever": *whatever* the Father is, that the Son is too. When Chalcedon defined the two natures it used the same word, consubstantial with the Father in divinity, consubstantial with us in humanity. There is a delicate step forward in specifying the human nature as rational and material, but the main thrust of the definition is toward nature in that sense which Lonergan calls heuristic; the one scriptural quotation, "like us in everything but without sin," confirms this; the further phrase, "the properties of each nature are safeguarded" in the union, leads to the same conclusion. What are these properties? Chalcedon does not determine this in any detail; if later science discovers that man is a symbolic animal as well as rational, has a psyche which can get

145

out of order, plays language games, is historical and subject to indefinite progress, etc., etc., etc., well, Chalcedon is not affected and the theologian has no difficulty with all that.

So far as we have gone Christology is no more metaphysical than a politican who says, "My opponent who now advocates tax rebates is the very one who . . . ," or the President who sent the United States fleet into the Mediterranean danger spot with the remark, "We have to be men." The fully metaphysical aspect of Chistology emerges in the later scholastics when they try to determine the constituent factors of the God-Man. It is here that the full weight of the anti-metaphysical thrust should be directed; I have pointed to the irony in the fact that it is here, with a developed metaphysics, that the charge of hopeless bankruptcy at Chalcedon can be met.

The scholastic effort has to be seen as a struggle with a real problem that arose on the basis of Chalcedon and demanded an answer. It is given that we have not in Christ Someone who is God and someone else who is man. There is only One and, when the exigencies of thought forced the fathers to answer the question, One what? they settled on "person" as the best word to express their notion. Now this Someone was God and *became* Man, so he is a divine person and there is no human person. That sets the problem: what is the difference between being fully human and being a human person? Or: what constitutes personality? (Nowadays some prefer to speak rather of personhood, since "personality" has taken on a connotation of temperament and character and really pertains to the content of nature rather than that of person.) One scholastic answer, the one I assume here, is that the final constituent of personhood is the act of existence, so that the human and proportionate act of existence is lacking in Christ and is supplied by the divine act of existence.

Is it possible to see this as other than more verbal rubbish? I think so, but this is where I must become didactic. The problem is to give a meaning to the potency, form, and act of existence which are the components of a human person. The means to a

146

solution is the cognitional structure of experience, understanding, and reflection (leading to judgment) by which I know a human person or any object in my human world. If the reader will think of a very vivid dream in which he experiences violent terror, he will perhaps see how much understanding and reflection differ from experience. If he will think of some brilliant explanation he has at some time conceived of a problem that fascinated him, an explanation so brilliant that for a few days he walked on air—till he discovered that the explanation was defective, inadequate, and false, he may see how much reflection and judgment differ from idea. If he will correlate the cognitional now with the ontological he will see the relation of potency, form, and act and their unity in the composite being. He will see, I hope, that in terms of reality, they stand to one another (pardon the usage) as real, realer, and realest. He will see that it is the act of existence that gives the actuality to the whole, since the object of his dream seemed extremely "real" to imagination, and the object of his brilliant idea seemed extremely "real" to understanding, but reality was in fact lacking in both cases.

The difficult step is the next one. I do not see the act of existence, or feel it, or touch it, or perceive it, or "attain" it by any function of the faculty of experience. Furthermore, I do not understand the act of existence directly, or form a proper idea of it, or explain it in itself, or "attain" it by any function of the faculty of direct understanding. It is the object of judgment, which proceeds from a reflective grasp of the unconditioned in the way Newman describes in *An Essay in Aid of a Grammar of Assent,* and Lonergan in *Insight: A Study of Human Understanding.*

We are here in the sphere of the explicitly metaphysical. The act of existence is so metaphysical that Aristotle's *Metaphysics* did not succeed in isolating it from essence. It is so metaphysical that Paul Tillich did not really distinguish it from the human nature of Christ, and so could think only essentialistically of two natures "which lie beside each other like blocks." Nevertheless, it is not inhumanly metaphysical, for it is the object of everyone who uses the word "is" in an existential sense, and I need not point out that hardly any word is used more universally, or uttered with more conviction, even when the user utters it in a rejection of metaphysics. But, to get hold of this, one has to learn that judging is not seeing, and that most of my use of "see" in the preceding paragraphs was simply metaphorical.

If one "sees" that, I think he will be able to accept Chalcedon without perjuring his intellect and I think he can go on to enrich his Christology through the help of the modern philosophies. Our judgment of the act of existence gives us an analogy for the unity of the God-Man which does not in any way make it appear like two blocks side by side, unless the reader thinks of his own essence and existence as two blocks side by side. At the same time it allows for the complete humanity of Christ, and the full acceptance of any results achieved by the ever expanding field of human sciences, with the one exception stipulated by scripture and Chalcedon—but perhaps we may concede that sin is not really essential to the human. If I may finish my didactic section with a picture, I suggest the image of a heaven filled with pure light, which gives reality to the color of the earthly world without depriving it of its proper character and certainly not lying beside it like block beside block. In some such way the divine being joins human nature in Christ to become the one God-Man.

I have not much space left in which to discuss the positive contribution the modern philosophies might make to an up-to-date Christology. But a man with a gun at his head is not apt to think very enthusiastically of the positive features of the encounter. Insofar as phenomenology, *als ob* philosophy, logical positivism, and, despite its name, even existentialism, do not or cannot take full account of the act of existence in its distinct reality, they simply remove the basis for a Christology that is faithful to the word of God and Catholic dogma; it is useless then to talk of positive contribution. On the other hand, once their signal oversight is remedied, we can enrich our Christology with their insights. I will try to indicate that now in a few extremely brief paragraphs.

Thus, I would hope for nothing but good from the positive contribution of linguistic analysis. Anyone who has spent a few years with the dialoguing generation will give a warm welcome to any movement that forces people to pay attention to the exact meaning of their language. But I should not be critical simply of the amateurs; James Barr has some extremely pointed criticisms of the linguistics of exegetes in the Kittel dictionary, and Paul Van Buren of similar deficiencies among theologians. On the other hand, the contribution here can only be minor, partly because the best work both in positive and systematic theology has taken great pains with its language, and partly because, when you have done your homework in language, you are only ready to begin theology.

Process philosophy, on the other hand, could make a major contribution, in my opinion. Not only because we have to take more account of the scriptural data on process in Jesus himself (Luke 2:52; Hebrews 5:8), but because a full Christology includes the relation of Christ to history, and we are in a much better position to give a theology of history than the disciples were in their speeches in Acts or Eusebius in his *Praeparatio evangelica.* There is a far more difficult question on becoming in God, but we cannot avoid it in Christology, if we are to take seriously the Johannine doctrine that the Word *became* flesh. It does seem that our older scholasticism left this question somewhat unexplored and was more rigid here than the necessities of faith and reason required. Not only the process philosophers but serious theologians are striving today to assign a more adequate meaning to that word, "become." Perhaps we can move toward understanding contingent "process" in God by means of an extrapolation modeled on the Thomist extrapolation towards the "procession" of the eternal Word (*Contra gentiles,* IV, c. 11). The series might look like this: we begin with our own potential knowledge (by anticipation) of all that is, and note that it *be-*

comes actual and determinate in us by specific increments; from this we move to the process in the human Christ and the blessed, where you have actual knowledge of the Totality, but items *become* specified by a kind of descent from the Totality to particularity; and finally we move on to God who *is* the Totality and *becomes* the particularity, Man, without ceasing to be the All, in an analogous descent (Paul's *kenosis*).

Phenomenology is not so easily applied to Christology. What could its distinctive contribution be? We can omit idealist forms at once, but even the bracketing of existence leaves it powerless before the real problems of Christology. There is a strong emphasis on the phenomena of consciousness, and a good technique for distinguishing and isolating its contents, but we have little access to the consciousness of Christ. We deal immediately with inkmarks on paper, and I do not know whether a phenomenology of vicarious experience offers much that we do not get from careful historical work fortified by imagination and hypothesis. I am inclined to think that the profitable field for exercise will turn out to be the phenomena of church life, doctrine, practice, worship, spirituality, as observable today, rather than Christology proper.

Existentialism, though deriving from phenomenology as a method, has more significance for Christology by reason of its content: situation in the world, attitude to death, achievement of what one can become, responsibility for one's choices—all this could greatly enrich our Christology and our Christian life. It has been a real question for me how much Heidegger's life as a Jesuit novice, with its long exercises on death and decision, had to do with his philosophical thought. As to Christ himself, the effect of such a study of his life would be to put him into human history the way other great men are there, as one with whom we can identify. In a similar way personalism would enlarge our understanding of Christ, providing especially a better basis for our doctrine of his relations with others, though I would say Christology would also contribute to personalism, forcing a greater accuracy in conceiving personhood, requiring recognition of the role of nature in inter-personal relations, and relating the metaphysical to intersubjective experience. In fact, one might expect such a two-way commerce between Christology and philosophy in all the regions of the latter.

This short article has to make room for final considerations of another order than the impersonal. The central issue throughout has been the meaning of the word "is." The issue of the historical, and the relevance today of the ancient belief that Jesus is the Christ, the Son of God, are settled ultimately by the meaning of "is." The place of metaphysics and the continuing significance of Chalcedon are measured by the role one assigns to "is." And finally, the meaning of "is" settles the questions now debated on objectivity and non-objectivity: to say in faith that Christ is God takes Christology out of the chaos of religious sentiment and the vagueness of encounter and the blindness of mere subjective decision and sets it in the cold light of objectivity, just as to say that God is the Subject who is never an object is in fact to make God an object and set him (may he pardon us) in the cold light of objectivity.

That debate on non-objectifying thinking and speaking in contemporary theology seems to me just the latest manifestation of failure to get hold of the word, "is." It is difficult to get the lines to form clearly; I do not wish to exaggerate; at the Drew University consultation on this theme in 1964 a surprising number of theologians held out for objectification. But I think the non-objectifying mood is prevalent; it is an attitude, a murmur, it is in the air; it is the unvoiced supposition of many a philosophy; and I state frankly that I have been fighting it throughout this article.

Chalcedon is indeed challenged by modern philosophy, but not by the regional insights of this, that, or the other movement, rather by their attitude to the foundations of all philosophy, as well as of theology, science, and the conversations of daily life. The question here is that of truth, being, objectivity, reality; to spend time on linguistics and process and so on, seems to me a little like fiddling while Rome burns. But when we go to foundations we are not involved in anything so simple as learning a new idea; nothing less is involved than a fairly complete intellectual conversion, for which we need, besides intelligence, a certain youthful mentality, a certain openness of heart, and maybe a good shot of divine grace. There is no use guessing whether I or anyone lacks these requisites; we have to try to dialogue anyway; I insist only that dialogue come ultimately to the foundations themselves of all thought and dialogue.

V.

The Ethical Teaching of Jesus

CHARLES E. CURRAN

CONTEMPORARY THEOLOGY has shifted its gaze from heaven to earth, from God to man, from the after life to the present life. Human existence and its meaning are the primary problems of contemporary theology. The world today is ageric—modern man is not a contemplator but a doer. Dogma and speculation for its own sake have very little appeal to man today. Within the Catholic Church some are questioning the primacy attributed to liturgy over life itself. Is liturgy not the celebration of life rather than the font and source of all life? Life is the most important reality.

The Christian Church and the individual Christians are reading the signs of the times. Christians need to speak to the actual life of man today. What does the ethical teaching of Jesus mean for contemporary human existence? However, the Church must carefully avoid just talking. Words without deeds are like the Pauline sounding brass or tinkling cymbal. The credibility gap merely widens when the pious mouthings of the Church are contradicted by its own life and actions.

The Christian trying to realize the meaning of human life naturally turns to the ethic of Jesus. The ethical teaching of Jesus is not a detailed blueprint for human activity, but the follower of Jesus at least begins his quest by examining the ethical teaching of the scriptures. Many speculative problems arise from a consideration of biblical ethics and modern existence. Theology

153

today is discussing secularity, the relationship between the immanent and the transcendent, the connection between human progress and the coming of the kingdom, the meaning of history. An older theology struggled with the problems of nature and grace or law and gospel. A thorough consideration of all these issues lies beyond the scope of the present article. The essay will merely attempt to indicate the relevancy of the ethic of Jesus for the contemporary Christian.

What is the ethical teaching of Jesus? In general, Jesus calls his followers to live a life in union with God and neighbor. Many theologians summarize the moral teaching of Jesus under the category of love. The three synoptic accounts mention the twofold commandment of love of God and neighbor as the core of the ethical teaching of Jesus (Mk. 12:28-34; Mt. 22:34-40; Lk. 10:25-37).

Why is the twofold love commandment called a new commandment? Love of God and neighbor was central in the teaching of the Old Testament and in many other religions. One distinctive characteristic of the love ethic of Jesus is the insistence on an indissoluble interior bond between the love of God and the love of neighbor. The follower of Jesus is recognized by his love for others. The judgment scene of Mt. 25 indicates that man's relationship to God is known and manifested in his relationship with his fellow man. The follower of Jesus cannot claim to love God and yet neglect his neighbor who is hungry, thirsty, naked, alone, or in prison. John says very poignantly that man cannot love the God he does not see if he does not love the neighbor whom he does see (1 Jn. 4:20). The ethic of Jesus does not eschew life in this world; rather, the authentic love of God is found in a loving concern for others. The follower of Jesus can find no excuse (not even worship at the altar) which takes precedence over his loving concern and forgiveness for his neighbor.

A second characteristic of the love ethic of Jesus centers on the universality attached to the concept of neighbor. To love friends

154

is easy. To love when one is loved in return requires no self-giving. But Christian love for others is modeled on the love of Jesus for us. Jesus loved us while we were yet sinners. Jesus' love for us did not depend on what we could give him in return. The love of Jesus is completely disinterested and gratuitous in the sense that his love in no way depends on the loving qualities or the response of men. Jesus' love is creative, not responsive; giving, not possessing. Who are the privileged recipients of the love of Jesus? The strong, the influential, the wealthy, the intelligent, the respected? No, the privileged recipients of Jesus' love are the poor, the children, and even sinners. The non-value of the recipients of the good news of salvation is a startling fact.

The Christian is called to love just as Jesus has loved. The greatest example of Christian love is love for enemies. The enemy can give the lover nothing in return. In fact, the enemy returns hatred for love. The enemy might react with vengeance and annoyance, but love of enemies remains the great sign of Christian love. Our love for others does not depend on what they can do for us. Since the love of Jesus does not depend on the loving qualities of others, the object of his love is universal. The parable of the good Samaritan illustrates the universality of neighbor in the love ethic of Jesus. The neighbor is the person who is in need. The priest and the levite walk by the man in the road; but the Samaritan, a foreigner and enemy, has compassion on the man in need. Love is not just liking but a loving concern for the neighbor in need.

Perhaps the ethical teaching of Jesus as the complete giving of self to God and neighbor cannot be perfectly expressed in any human formula or concept. There are theological difficulties in reducing the ethic of Jesus even to the twofold commandment of love of God and neighbor. The love of the Christian for his God and his love for his neighbor are not the same kind of love. Love of God is the adoring gratitude of one who has received all from the giver of life. Love of neighbor is a creative giving and a redemptive forgiving which does not depend on the

155

lovable qualities of the other. The two loves are different. The scriptures seldom speak of man's love for God as *agape* precisely because of the difference between God's love for man and man's love for God.

Even man's relationship to his neighbor cannot be adequately explained in terms of *agape*—the loving concern which is a total giving independent of the lovable qualities of the other. The human relationship of love does at times require that I love the other precisely because of his loving qualities. A human person does want to be loved in himself and for what he is. Bishop Pike has criticized Professor Fletcher for reducing the entire Christian ethic to *agape*. There are times when *eros* as a responsive and possessive love or friendship as a mutual love are absolutely essential for human well-being. The theologian should be cautious in thinking that he can reduce the ethical teaching of Jesus to any neat human formulae. H. Richard Niebuhr claims that no human virtue as such can adequately explain the ethical teaching of Jesus.

However, all can agree that the ethical teaching of Jesus calls for the giving of self to God and neighbor. The neighbor in need, according to many biblical passages, has the first claim on the love of the Christian. However, we must examine this ethical teaching in more detail. The most prolonged statement of the ethical teaching of Jesus is found in the composite arranged in Matthew around the literary form of the Sermon on the Mount (Mt. 5-7). Luke brings together much of the ethical teaching of Jesus in his shorter Sermon on the Plain (Lk. 6:20-49). Matthew begins the Sermon on the Mount with the beatitudes. Although Luke employs the beatitudes in a sapiential perspective and the more primitive form of the beatitudes was probably a messianic proclamation, Matthew employs the beatitudes in a catechizing and moralizing way to outline the characteristics which mark the life of the follower of Jesus. Matthew's spiritualization of the beatitudes (the poor in spirit and the clean of heart) and the peculiar emphasis on justice or righteousness indicate that Mat-

156

thew is trying to describe the moral life of the follower of Jesus. The Christian is called to be the light of the world and the salt of the earth through love, meekness, mercy, forgiveness, peace-making, and the pursuit of righteousness.

Matthew then continues to describe the ethical teaching of Jesus as the completion and fullness of the law. Matthew first contrasts (perhaps by way of completion and not antithesis according to W. D. Davies) the ethical teaching of Jesus with that of the scribes, the theologians of the time. The six antitheses or completions of the ethical teaching of Jesus concern anger, chastity, divorce, oaths, forgiveness and love of enemies. The section ends with a call to be perfect just as our heavenly Father is perfect. The parallel verse in Luke is a call to be merciful or compassionate as our heavenly Father is merciful (Lk. 6:36). Matthew begins chapter six by comparing the attitude of the Pharisees and the followers of Jesus on the matters of almsgiving, prayer, and fasting. The follower of Jesus is concerned with a true change of heart and not just a rigid external observance. In the final section of the Sermon on the Mount, Matthew outlines other characteristics of the followers of Jesus. Jesus asks for a complete and loving trust in himself which leads to the abandonment of all other persons and things. Thus the literary device of the Sermon on the Mount capsulizes the ethical teaching of Jesus as found throughout the New Testament.

A meditative reflection on the moral teaching of Jesus raises embarrassing questions. Do the Church and the followers of Jesus really put into practice the ethical teaching of their Lord? Can the Church truly say to Jesus: "When you were hungry, thirsty, naked, lonely, abandoned, and in prison, I was there to comfort you"? Does the average person living today see reflected in the life of the Church the ethical teaching of Jesus? Is the primary concern of the Church the neighbor in need or is the Church more interested in preserving and augmenting its image, status, wealth, and power? Is the Church truly credible when it does raise its voice on particular issues, since so often there is only

157

loud silence on other problems involving the neighbor in need? Has the Church left all to follow Jesus or is it trying to serve two masters? When the hierarchical Church does speak on a particular issue, how often are the words accompanied by appropriate actions, even to the giving away of earthly power and possessions? Does the Church really take seriously the ethical teaching of Jesus?

However, one cannot merely point an accusing finger at the Church. How about myself as a Christian? Am I really willing to give all that I possess for my neighbor in need? Am I really willing to forgive my enemies the same way that Christ did? How difficult it remains to speak well of those who have hurt me in the past. Am I always willing to turn the other cheek or to walk an extra mile? How often do I really go out of my way to help others?

There exists an even more embarrassing question: can anyone be expected to live the ethical teaching of Jesus? At first glance, all are compelled to admit the beauty and sublimity of the ethical teaching of Jesus. However, the moral demands of Jesus are radical and seemingly impossible. The disciple of Jesus leaves all things to follow his master. Luke, who is the evangelist of total renunciation, even goes so far as to call for hatred of father and mother, brother and sister (Lk. 14:26-33). Can anyone truly live the ethical teaching of Jesus?

The ethic of Jesus seems totally unreal when applied to the particular problems that so often arise in our lives. How can a Christian not worry about what he is going to eat or drink? What minister of God's Word would ever say to an improvident father that he should not worry about food, clothing, and shelter for his family? Can a wife forgive her husband and welcome him with open arms if he constantly beats her and the children? Can I as a Christian stand by and turn the other cheek when other innocent people (for example, young children) are being attacked? How practical is it not to resist the evildoer? Who can possibly give to everyone who asks? Is the gospel injunction of

158

turning the other cheek an apt solution to the complicated problems of American involvement in Vietnam? In any war?

Even the Church does not follow the ethical demands of Jesus. Just after speaking about divorce, Matthew reminds the followers of Jesus never to take any oaths but to restrict their speech to yes and no (Mt. 5: 33-37). However, the Roman Catholic Church has insisted on a number of oaths that must be taken by priests and teachers. Even on such a practical matter as judicial processes and matrimonial courts, Church procedure is practically never willing to accept the word of the Christian.

A true follower of Jesus cannot dismiss his whole ethical teaching as irrelevant and meaningless for daily human existence. Some explain the difficulty connected with the moral teaching of Jesus as arising from the fondness for imagery and exaggeration, which is associated with the Oriental mentality. The beam in one's eye, the camel and the eye of the needle, forgiveness seventy times seven times, all these expressions embody overstatement and exaggeration. Undoubtedly Jesus reflected the thought patterns of his own culture, but can the entire moral teaching of Jesus be satisfactorily explained in terms of Oriental exaggeration? Within a Lutheran tradition some want to interpret the Sermon on the Mount as *Moyses Moysissimus*—the law of Moses in the nth degree. The important function of law is to bring man to acknowledge his own weakness and sinfulness. The Mosaic Law brought man to Christ not by continuous development, but through discontinuity. The Law made man aware that he could find salvation not in the works of the Law but only through faith in Christ Jesus. The radical and impossible demands of the Sermon on the Mount only intensify the function of law which brings man to realize his sinfulness and need of redemption through faith in Christ. Although such a solution does serve as a partial explanation of the problem, the *Moyses Moysissimus* solution does not really take seriously the ethical teaching of Jesus.

A few have tried to take literally the ethical teaching of Jesus

159

as universal norms for moral conduct which are always and everywhere binding. Such biblical fundamentalism quickly clashes with the problems of everyday human existence. Common sense and experience remind us that man cannot accept the ethical teachings of Jesus as laws of conduct which are always obliging in similar circumstances.

The Catholic theological tradition has generally ignored the problem created by the radical ethical demands of Jesus. At least on a popular level, Catholic teaching maintained that only a few people were called to perfection. Such people followed the evangelical counsels and generally entered the religious life. The vast majority of men living in the world were content with just observing the commandments which are binding on all men. Catholic theology thus ignored the problem created by the radical moral teaching of Jesus. However, the consequences of ignoring the problem have been evident in Catholic life and practice. Only with Vatican II does popular Catholic teaching stress the universal vocation of all Christians to perfection. Catholic theology has not developed a theology and spirituality for life in the world because people outside the religious life were content with just obeying the commandments.

Many serious attempts to come to grips with the radical ethical teaching of Jesus hinge on the question of eschatology. Interestingly, contemporary theologians are also calling for a renewed eschatology. The eschatological views see the ethic of Jesus in connection with his mission in proclaiming the reign of God. The ethic of Jesus is above all a religious ethic, intimately connected with the reign that Jesus proclaimed. The reign of God calls for a complete and radical response from the hearer.

Albert Schweitzer well represents the school that labeled the moral teaching of Jesus an "interim ethic." In reacting against liberal Protestantism, Schweitzer stressed the eschatological dimension of Jesus' mission. Jesus expected the kingdom of God to come even before his disciples returned from their first missionary journey. When the kingdom did not come, Jesus went up to

160

Jerusalem to precipitate the coming of the kingdom by his death. The strenuous ethic proposed by Jesus was for the very short interim that would precede the final coming of the kingdom. The ethical teaching of Jesus cannot be lived and sustained over a long period of time. Jesus' ethic is intimately connected with his own mistaken eschatology. Today, most theologians have rejected the opinion proposed by Schweitzer. The reign of God is not all future; to some extent the kingdom of God in Christ is already present and working in the world. Even many who maintain that Jesus believed in a very quick coming of the final stage of the reign of God do not think that Jesus would have preached a different ethic even if he had realized that the final stage of the kingdom would not arrive for a long period of time.

Perhaps the ethic of Jesus was meant only to describe life in the final stage of the reign of God and has no practical meaning for life here and now. Jesus did not propose a moral teaching for life in this world but was merely describing the life in the final coming of the reign of God. Again there is some truth in such an assertion, but the follower of Jesus cannot conclude that the ethical teaching of the master is completely irrelevant for Christians living in the world of today. Even the conflict and troubling situations described by Jesus seem much more applicable to the situation of our own daily lives than to the description of some future state of blessedness.

The ethic of Jesus is closely aligned with his mission in proclaiming the reign of God. The final stage of the reign of God is coming. The reign is already begun but is now hastening toward its conclusion. The eschatological dimension at least adds a sense of urgency to some of the ethical teachings of Jesus (for example, anger, lust). But there is also a content to the ethic of Jesus which is influenced by the presence and impending fulfillment of the reign of God. The ethical teaching of Jesus is a constant reminder of the absolute claim which the presence of the reign of God makes on the follower of Jesus. Jesus does not propose universal norms of conduct which are obliging for all Christians

161

under all circumstances. Rather, in a very graphic way Jesus pictures man before the call of the reign of God's love. The reign of God places an all-engaging claim upon the hearer. Nothing else matters or counts when compared to the reign of God proclaimed and inaugurated by Jesus. Many of the ethical sayings of Jesus confront the individual with the inexorable claim of the presence of God's call. Jesus' graphic descriptions prescind from all other circumstances which might enter the picture. The neighbor in need and the follower of Jesus are placed face to face in a dramatic fashion.

The complexity of human problems is cast aside. Jesus prescinds from all other circumstances and conditions while showing the claim of the reign of God and the neighbor in need upon the individual follower. No mention is made of the binding obligations which a man might have to his wife or family. Jesus prescinds from all such realities and simply shows in a very stark and dramatic way the radical claim of the reign of God and the needs of the neighbor upon his followers. The Christian, like Jesus himself, should be willing to sacrifice all for others. One can understand better the sayings about turning the other cheek, walking the extra mile, giving to everyone who asks, imitating the lilies of the field, hating father and mother, plucking out an eye or cutting off a hand which would separate man from God, as illustrative of the radical demands of the presence of the reign of God.

The gift of the reign of God puts an unconditional claim on the believer. But what does such a simplistic view of reality mean for the follower of Jesus who lives amid the complexity of modern human existence? Very often the Christian is confronted by many people in need. The Christian has manifold responsibilities that are always on the horizon. Can a Christian so give himself and his time to the neighbor in need that he forgets his familial obligations? What value is the simplistic evangelical description of the dramatic confrontation between an individual and the call of the kingdom or the neighbor in need?

162

The radical, seemingly impossible ethical teaching of Jesus is more than rhetoric. Jesus indicates the goal and direction that should characterize the life and actions of his followers. "Give to everyone who asks" is an impossible ethical imperative, but such a demand indicates the constant thrust that characterizes the life of the Christian. I cannot claim everything I have as my own and dispose of it in any way I want. The Christian realizes that his talents, treasure, and abilities are in the service of the kingdom and the neighbor in need. There are times when the follower of Jesus might not be able to turn the other cheek; but the model of patience and forebearance, coupled with mercy and not vengeance, always remains meaningful. Occasionally the Christian might deem violence necessary to protect innocent human life (for example, a young child being attacked by a demented person), but the thrust of the radical teaching of Jesus can never be forgotten.

Eschatological considerations introduce an inevitable tension into Christian ethics. The tension results from the fact that the reign of God in Christ is now present and is going forward toward its fullness. We are living in the time in between the two comings of Jesus. The reign of God is present but not yet fully present. The incipient presence of the eschaton calls for a continual growth and development. The followers of Jesus can never rest content with the present. The eschatological future is to some extent now present and urging the Christian forward. The true follower of the New Law can never say: "All these I have kept from my youth." The ethical teaching of Jesus calls for a continual effort to overcome the obstacles and shortcomings of the present moment.

Unfortunately, the recent Catholic tradition has forgotten the eschatological tension both in the life of the individual and in the life of the Church. Theology did not insist upon the radical teachings of Jesus. In popular teaching the Christian ethical demands were reduced to a comparatively few, negative, universal norms which were to be observed by all. Such norms not only

163

gave a negative tone to the Christian life, but comparatively easy norms of conduct robbed the Christian life of its inherent dynamism. The Christian could be content with having observed a comparatively few norms of morality. The Christian found a false sense of security in such norms and occasionally succumbed to a pharisaical attitude. On a wider scale the Church itself suffered from the same defect. The charge of triumphalism rang true in the conciliar halls of Vatican II. The Church forgot its pilgrim status and lost the dynamic thrust of continual growth and conversion. The radical ethical teaching of Jesus prevents either his Church or his followers from ever remaining content and smug in the present stage of life.

Specifically in the area of moral theology, Catholic teaching has tried to avoid the tension created by the ethics of Jesus. As a result Catholic theology very frequently has lost the eschatological dimension of growth; or, less frequently, has required of all a goal that was not always attainable. The loss of the dynamic thrust in moral theology can be seen in the teaching on the right to life. Catholic theologians have not been in the forefront of those who were arguing for the abolition of capital punishment, the suspension of nuclear testing, the cessation of war. Why not? Catholic teaching over the years developed a very intricate system or theory for dealing with problems of life and death. Direct killing of the innocent is never permitted; but the state has the right to kill malefactors, and individuals may kill others indirectly or in self-defense. However, such a norm, considered only in itself, lacks the dynamic thrust in favor of human life which should always characterize the Christian life. The principles governing the questions of life and death solve complex problems too easily. The follower of Jesus can never be content when forced to take a life. Every taking of life is a falling short of the radical ethic of Jesus. Perhaps at times it is necessary to take human life; but a Christian can take life with only the greatest remorse and reluctance.

Likewise in the question of war, theologians tend to dismiss too easily the deaths of thousands of people because they are only "indirect" killings. There may be times when the follower of Jesus must act according to the principles of indirect killing, but the Christian can never lose sight of the thrust imposed by the radical ethic of Jesus. Personally I cannot be a total pacifist in the sense that at times resorting to violence might be necessary to defend innocent people. However, the follower of Jesus always strives in the direction of pacificism. When killing is deemed necessary it can only be as a reluctant accommodation to the needs of the present time.

In many other areas Catholic theology has too easily accommodated itself to the present moment and forgotten the radical ethical demands of Jesus. Problems of slavery and race immediately come to mind. The Church and the theologians too easily acquiesced in predominant social patterns and structures. The Church cannot be altogether proud of its historical record on behalf of the freedom and dignity of man. Theologians and Church leaders have also been absent from leadership in the fight for the equality of women. The institutional Church seems to have perpetuated a system of colonization rather than to have fought for the rights of people to govern themselves. In the ninth century Pope Nicholas I condemned physical constraint and torture; but a few centuries later the Church used torture and violence to further its own dubious goals. Papal teaching on justice and the rights of the working man is a comparatively bright chapter in the history of the Church. But history also reminds us that Karl Marx recognized the problem almost half a century before Leo XIII wrote his encyclicals.

The followers of Jesus and his Church can never forget the radical ethical teaching of the Master. However, the imperfections and sinfulness that characterize the present times will mean that the Christian often falls far short of the goal described by Jesus. Accommodation to the present reality is a necessity at times. But the absolute claim of the reign of God and the needs of our neighbor never allow the Christian to be content when it

165

is necessary to fall short of the radical moral teaching of Jesus. The Christian always possesses an uneasy conscience. Compromise and adaptation to present needs can only be accepted reluctantly. Catholic theology has too often forgotten the uneasy conscience of the Christian in confronting the imperfect and sinful situations of the present time. Jesus calls his followers to be the light of the world and the salt of the earth.

On the other side of the paradox, there are times when the universal norms in Catholic theology do not sufficiently take into consideration the reluctant but necessary possibility of not fully accomplishing the moral demand of Jesus. Perhaps the universal norm absolutizes what is a radical demand of Jesus which is not always achievable. The biblical teaching on divorce may be an example. (Naturally one cannot settle the teaching of the Catholic Church on divorce merely from biblical evidence, but the solution proposed according to the biblical understanding may very well be applicable to the present understanding of divorce in the Church). In the Sermon on the Mount in Matthew the two verses on divorce follow the radical maxim of plucking out an eye or cutting off a hand if the eye or the hand lead one astray. The divorce passage is followed by the saying of Jesus that his true followers will never take any oaths but will be content to make their speech a plain "yes" or "no." In Mt. 19 the matter of divorce is approached in the context of the two opposing opinions existing among the scholars of the Old Law. Jesus definitely upholds the indissolubility of marriage. Jesus explains the permission given by Moses in the Old Testament on the grounds of the hardness of the heart of the people. However, there is in Mt. 19:9 the puzzling exception clause (except for unchastity *porneia*) which also appears in Mt. 5:32.

Within the New Testament times there are accommodations in the teaching of absolute indissolubility. The famous Pauline privilege represents a falling short of the ideal proposed by Jesus. Paul, according to some exegetes, allowed converts to the faith to marry a new wife if their heathen wife wanted a separation

166

(1 Cor. 7:12-16). Exegetes have developed many different theories for the famous incisions in the gospel of Matthew. Although scripture scholars disagree on the exact meaning of such exceptions, many would agree that the exceptions were probably added to the primitive statements by the early Church. The exceptions may well represent some type of accommodation within the early Church to the radical ethical demands of Jesus. The accommodations made in New Testament times, whatever they may have been, are not the only possible accommodations that the Church and Christians might have to make in the course of time.

The radical ethic of Jesus, although seemingly impossible, is relevant precisely because the presence of the reign of God tending toward its eschatological fulfillment places an absolute claim upon the follower of Jesus. Even when the Christian must fall short of the radical demand of Jesus, he cannot rest content with the accommodation to the needs and imperfections of present reality. The dangers in any ethic of pure accommodation are manifold. The collaboration of citizens with the war aims and activities of their governments is perhaps the most painful and obvious example for the modern Christian. The conscience of the Christian can never rest content with any type of accommodation, but always seeks new ways to pursue the direction and goal pointed out in the radical ethics of Jesus. The ethic of Jesus for the contemporary Christian involves a creative tension between the present and the final stage of the reign of God.

Unfortunately, man finds such tension difficult to live with. Some eliminate the tension by forgetting about the future and the continual call to growth and development. Others overthrow the tension by naively forgetting the present reality. Until very recently Catholic theology and life dissolved the tension and the frustration by forgetting about the radical ethics of Jesus and the consequent call for continual growth and even revolution. Absolute norms capable of being observed to the letter provided man with a false sense of security. Catholics acted as if they had all the answers to the problems confronting mankind. The

167

certitude and the security of the Church were a rock against the shifting sands of human existence. Various types of security were built into the system in addition to the watered down ethical demands which gave a reassuring sense of security to those who obeyed them. Indulgences, First Fridays, and First Saturdays were all means of providing assurance of eternal salvation. The Church had all the answers to the problems that confronted man and his society. The Church itself did not know doubt, confusion, growth, pain, and tension.

Catholic life and theology in the post Vatican II era no longer claim to have the security and certitude that characterized Catholic life and teaching just a few short years ago. However, there is still a tendency to avoid the doubts, growing pains, and frustrations of a pilgrim people and a pilgrim Church. For Catholic life today the older securities and certitudes are gone forever, but many still look, somewhat naïvely, for a false sense of security. In opening up the Church to the world, in opening up ourselves to others, we reveal our own uncertainties, frustrations and weaknesses. In the midst of such frustration men easily seek a false sense of security. Post-conciliar life in the Church has witnessed a number of new Messiahs appear on the horizon with great expectations, but the hopes of their followers are quickly dashed against the realities of human existence in the times in between. Many pinned their hopes on the liturgy in English or lately on an entirely new liturgy, but experience shows that the liturgy will never become the New Messiah. Many other Messiahs have appeared—ranging from Martin Buber to Harvey Cox to the scriptural renewal. But the eschaton has not yet come. Perhaps the pessimism of Sartre serves as an excellent reminder to the naive personalism and optimism of many today.

Some Catholics have abandoned a triumphalism in the Church only to embrace a triumphalism of the world or the secular city. I finally believe that the mission of the Christian and the Church is in service of the world, but the present state of the world is not entirely salvific. There is too much suffering and inequality in

168

our own country, let alone in a world blighted by injustice, ignorance, and hunger, for the Christian to be content with the present situation. Professor Charles West of Princeton Theological Seminary, in describing the meeting on Church and Society sponsored by the World Council of Churches in Geneva in the summer of 1966, remarked about the opposition to the theological advocates of the secular city. West claims that the majority of theologians from the underdeveloped countries were "theological guerrillas" who saw revolution as the only way of shaking off the shackles of contemporary political and social structures. The "theological technocrats" of the secular city were amazed at the vehemence of the revolutionaries.

To live with the eschatological tension is difficult. The Christian, too, experiences doubt, frustration, opposition, and resistance to any growth. One who realizes the difficulties in breaking away from his own selfishness and sinfulness also understands the slowness of growth in the structures of human existence. To become resigned to the present is just as inadequate a solution as to expect miraculous progress without opposition or frustration. For the Christian the virtue of hope allows him to live the eschatological tension. Hope constantly beckons in the direction of the final stage of the kingdom of God. The follower of Jesus can never rest content with the present situation of his own change of heart or the present situation of humanity. But hope also strengthens the follower of Jesus against the frustrations and opposition that accompany any growth. Hope makes the Paschal Mystery of Christ a reality. Only by dying does the Christian rise in the newness of life.

Despair looms all too easily on the horizon for one who expects the eschaton to come too easily or too quickly. The greatness of God's gift to man is the fact that man has his role to play in bringing about the new heaven and the new earth. The radical ethic of Jesus could very easily bring one to despair because of the impossibility that it entails. However, the ethic of Jesus is both gift and demand. Man's inability to live according to the

169

strenuous moral teaching of Jesus is a constant reminder of his need for God's mercy and forgiveness. At the same time the radical ethical demand serves as a constant reminder to the Christian to open himself ever more to the call of God and neighbor. The Christian creatively tries to make himself and his world. All the old securities and certitudes are gone. There are no false props that the Christian can use. Christian maturity demands that the follower of Jesus stand on his own feet and carve out his human existence despite all the frustrations and doubts of life. The Christian as a pilgrim traveling to the new heaven and the new earth never has the luxury and the security of one who has already arrived at his final destination. In the insecurity of the journey only his hope in the Word and Work of God gives him the courage to continue. Hope is the virtue that allows the Christian to live the tension of the reign of God present but not yet fully here.

There are tendencies in the evangelical ethic to abandon entirely the life of man in this world. However, the contemporary Christian realizes that the needs of his neighbor can and must be met at the present time. The Christian's hope in the final coming of the reign of God does not furnish him with any blueprint for human development and growth. Only a naïve biblicism would expect to find in the scriptures the solutions to the problems confronting man and society today. The ethical teaching of Jesus urges his followers to creatively find solutions to come to the aid of the neighbor who is in need.

Like the individual Christian, the Church too must take seriously the moral teaching of Jesus and the virtue of hope. The primary concern of the Church should be the neighbor in need. The Church constantly needs to re-think the ways in which it tries to accomplish its primary purposes. The tendency to seek security in the means that were helpful in the past is all too tempting. There is also the temptation to seek security in other things and not in the Word of God in Christ. For a long time the Church tried to find its security in the protection of the State.

Now the temptation seems to be for the Church to find its security in brick and mortar institutions. Structures and institutions will always be necessary, but they only serve to help the Church be faithful to the mission and teaching of Jesus which puts primary emphasis on the neighbor in need. The Church should not seek false security in status, wealth or power. The pilgrim Church finds its only security in the promise of its founder.

The relevancy of the gospel ethic of Jesus is the challenge and vocation given to the followers of Jesus and his Church.

VI.

A Non-Violent Christology

JAMES W. DOUGLASS

IF CATHOLIC CHRISTIANITY is measured by the essence of its claim, by a faith in the universal truth of Jesus Christ, scripturally given and dogmatically protected, rather than by the conduct of its formal membership, then the presence of Christ becomes in the last analysis independent of the corruption of a sinful Church. What this means in theological terms is the precedence of grace over nature in the unveiling of God's presence in man, thus eclipsing any natural claims to moral pre-eminence—including the religious pride and moral postures of self-proclaimed believers—by the dual mystery of God's frequent absence in belief and of his often striking presence in unbelief. What a genuinely "universal Catholicism" means in regard to the presence of Christ in the world is that such a presence must be defined in a living way, as Christ himself defined it passively in terms of those in suffering need and as his own life and death unfolded his presence actively in suffering love.

In seeking out the presence of Christ in his world, Christians must therefore become less and less interested in themselves as Christians and focus instead on the living reality of Christ, whether in belief or unbelief, as the invitation of suffering need and as the graceful response of suffering love. What is then seen to be common to Christ's passive and active presence in the world is man in the state of suffering, as he first cries out in suffering for the aid of his brother and then as in the person of the brother he lays down his goods and his life in suffering response to that cry. If it is recognized that suffering is the one earthly reality with which God identifies himself universally in the person of Jesus Christ, who becomes present to suffering through the love of the Holy Spirit, it will be seen that the Catholic faith—by re-emphasizing the active presence of Christ as suffering love over those dogmatic formulations which, however true, have been frozen rather than fulfilled—can be true to its self-definition as a witness to the living and universal Christ.

It may be suggested therefore that a living and scripturally founded doctrine of the incarnation will center on suffering love as the redemptive reality and active presence of Christ in the world. From this standpoint, much of the Catholicism we know today (in America, for example, on the issues of race and peace) can be understood and evaluated best as an incarnational heresy, which is to say, as a choice made for a theoretical faith, imbedded in a milieu consciousness, to the exclusion of the living Christic reality of suffering love. The truth of Jesus, while remaining dogmatically protected, has not become flesh in a living, suffering belief. Modern Christianity has been incarnate instead only in the wrong flesh, that of self and of the extended culture-self.

The significance of Mohandas Gandhi, for a Christianity which has capitulated to its various milieux and thus become an incarnational heresy, is that Gandhi concentrated his entire life and being on the Christic reality of suffering love. Gandhi recognized peace and revolution as integral. He experimented with the Christic power of peace, suffering love, to realize the social revolution demanded by conscience. By not allying himself with Western Christianity, Gandhi kept himself independent of the incarnational heresy characteristic of it and worshipped none of the gods of established disorder. He was therefore free to reopen the way for a return to the Gospel of Peace and to the revolutionary power of the cross which stands at its summit.

In view of the milieu-Christianity of the West, the relationship of the Hindu Gandhi to the person of Christ may be described as the most living belief in the incarnation given in our time, even

173

while recognizing that Gandhi did not confess Jesus as the only Son of God. For Gandhi had a profound sense of the suffering, loving Christ. Though he never claimed to be a Christian, Gandhi often testified to the importance of Jesus' suffering as a factor in his undying faith in non-violence.

Gandhi rejected Christianity for the sake of Jesus. He understood and revered Christ as catholic and could not reconcile the universal meaning he saw in him with the imperialist faith he met in Christianity. In rejecting the milieu-Christianity of the West, he rejected as well the Church and doctrines he associated with it. Gandhi did not accept Jesus as the only Son of God because that doctrine as presented to him by friends anxious to claim him for Christianity always struck him as too exclusive. If God could have sons, all men were his sons. For Gandhi as for Bonhoeffer (in a striking parallel of both words and spirit), "Jesus preached not a new religion, but a new life. He called men to repentance."

To define the catholic Christ of Gandhi more precisely, one can say that Gandhi committed himself to Christ morally in the Sermon on the Mount and existentially in the cross. Concerning the Sermon, which he felt "was delivered not merely to the peaceful disciples but to a groaning world," Gandhi wrote: "The teaching of the Sermon on the Mount echoed something I had learnt in childhood and something which seemed to be part of my being and which I felt was being acted up to in the daily life around me. . . . This teaching was non-retaliation, or non-resistance to evil."

The cross too, was a reality meant for all men: "The Cross, undoubtedly, makes a universal appeal the moment you give it a universal meaning in place of the narrow one that is often heard at ordinary meetings." Gandhi followed Christ in identifying genuine faith and discipleship with the taking up of one's personal cross. In a talk given to a group of Christians on Christmas Day, he said: "We dare not think of birth without death on the cross. Living Christ means a living Cross, without it life is a living death."

As for the Christianity which Gandhi rejected, there the Christological problem of our time may be posed with reference to that milieu-consciousness, whether it be found in German, American or any other national Catholicism, which has so often meant capitulation for the Christian conscience. Our Christological problem would then rightly take the form of the same two questions Jesus asked the disciples in the passage that is the center of the earliest gospel (Mark 8, 27-29), with the difference that in our case we can hardly hear Jesus' decisive second question. The first, preliminary question, "Who do *men* say that I am?" is virtually the only one modern Christians have recognized. But that is a sociological question, one of current opinion, to which the proper answer is simply the kind of descriptive response given by the disciples in Mark: "Some say . . . Others say . . ." Yet the contemporary Christian answer to this question has been either the basis for dismissal or a substitute for faith.

On the one hand, Christians have heard this first question as "Who do *secular* men say that I am?", and have dismissed their answers as the expressions of a belligerent unbelief. On the other hand, they have heard the question as "Who do *Christian* men say that I am?" and have accepted those equally milieu-given answers as the form of their own faith instead of recognizing them as the reflections of a popular religiosity. In neither case has the response to Jesus' first question served the purpose he intended, namely, to serve as the background for an altogether personal confession of faith paralleling that of Peter. As for Jesus' second and decisive question of faith, "But who do *you* say that I am?" which abruptly cuts off each disciple from the support of his secular-Christian milieu and confronts him with the fearful task of personal decision, the Christian of today normally does not even hear it. The question of a deeply personal, and therefore self-critical response to Christ does not arise in a

175

milieu-Christianity. For it is there that Christ is defined for all by consensus, which is to say, by cultural dogma.

In the absence of any real theological recognition of the incessant demand of Christ, "But who do you—modern disciples —say that I am?" cultural dogma has easily prevailed. The cultural faith of men in the church-going Jesus who comforts the comfortable and afflicts the afflicted has removed the Church from Christ's urgent demand for a living faith in himself. Christology is today the most neglected area of theology in the Catholic Church because the Church has not yet distinguished herself radically enough from her milieu to be able to hear the critical question of her master, "But who do you say that I am?" The Church is still too absorbed in resisting the answers of secular man and in defending the answers of "Catholic culture" to hear the question asked of her real self by the person to whom she is wedded. Nor can the problem be solved on a deeper institutional level by retreating from the milieu into a properly dogmatic understanding of Christ. While a milieu can never provide the substance of faith, it will always exist as its context. The truth of the Council of Chalcedon is unable to answer Christ's question to the modern disciple. When Chalcedon's formulation is taken as finally definitive for the Church today it will be found in fact, as Karl Rahner has shown, that a contemporary consciousness will have overlain fifth-century concepts so as to revise them into the figure of a mythological Christ.

If there is to be a living ontic Christology today, then there must also be an existential one—to grant new life and clarity to terms which have to be translated by theologians before the meaning of the Creed is evident. An extended re-definition of "ontological person" and "nature" in an effort to re-create for us their original meaning and vividness will simply not do for a living belief in Jesus Christ today. The glory contained in the ontic meaning of the man-God is dependent on a prior existential perception of his humanity. One can assume that such a perception was present in the ontic categories themselves at a time

176

when they carried more weight than they do now. But today, in a very different idiom, there are too many unrecognized heresies already deadening the community of faith for us to avoid trying to do anew what was always necessary from the beginning: to know Jesus fully as man in order then to confess him fully as God. We must seek to know Jesus fully as man if we are to free ourselves both from the cultural Jesus who reveals only the gods of our time and from the mythological Jesus, the god charading in human form, who hides beneath our professions of the Chalcedonian formula. And to know Jesus as man is to know him in terms of that concept by which he knew himself; it is to know him as *ebed Yahweh,* the Suffering Servant of God.

The Suffering Servant of Yahweh is, first of all, a profoundly Jewish concept, rooted in the Servant poems of Isaiah and exemplified in the living history of Judaism. The primary meaning of the *ebed Yahweh* as given in Isaiah is that the Servant of God through his innocent suffering and death takes the place of the many who should suffer instead of him. The truth revealed in the *ebed Yahweh* is that salvation comes through suffering.

The beginning of Jesus' consciousness that he had to realize the task of the Suffering Servant can be traced to the moment of his baptism by John in the Jordan. The words of the voice from heaven, "Thou are my beloved Son, with thee I am well pleased," are a quotation from the opening line of the *ebed Yahweh* poems. In Isaiah these words are addressed by Yahweh to his Servant. For Jesus to have heard them spoken to him at his baptism must have compelled a recognition that he had to take on the full role of the *ebed Yahweh,* introduced in Isaiah as favored of God but destined in the unfolding drama of the poems "to pour out his soul to death."

The development of Jesus' conscious identification with the *ebed Yahweh* can be followed through the gospel in his more and more frequent references to his suffering and death as central to the work he must accomplish. This rising sense of the *ebed's* impending task is supported by Jesus' claim that Isaiah 53 will be fulfilled in himself. The one other concept which figures prominently in Jesus' own formulation of his work, that of the Son of Man, is united with the theme of the Suffering Servant: "For the Son of Man also came not to be served but to serve, and to give his life as a ransom for many." Although Jesus refers to himself in the gospel as the Son of Man because this title, with its eschatological overtones, is more comprehensive, he nevertheless merges it with the meaning of the *ebed Yahweh* so that the vocation of the *ebed* becomes the main content of the Son of Man's earthly work.

The decisive question Jesus asked of his disciples, "But who do you say that I am?" was not answered by Peter in terms of the *ebed Yahweh*. Rather, Peter's response was "You are the Christ." What is significant about this profession of faith is that Jesus wasn't satisfied with it. Not only did he go on to link his own messianic vocation to great suffering, "to teach them that the Son of Man must suffer many things, and be rejected . . . and be killed," but he also sharply rebuked Peter's suggestion that such suffering was somehow avoidable: "Get behind me, Satan! For you are not on the side of God, but of men." Thus, suffering, rejection and a sacrificial death are essential to define the Christ. To profess a true faith in Jesus Christ is to profess a faith in Jesus the Suffering Servant.

At this point the words of Gandhi, "Living Christ means a living Cross, without it life is a living death," find their foundation in Jesus' statement of what it means to follow him. For a faith in Christ is not possible without the symbol and demanding reality which sums up a Christocentric life: "If any man would come after me, let him deny himself and take up his cross and follow me." Though Gandhi did not claim to be a Christian, the example of Jesus' suffering was at the root of his faith in nonviolence. For him the suffering of Jesus so defined the law of Love that love and suffering were seen as one in a single flame of life. And it is thus, in terms of suffering servanthood, that Jesus defined his own vocation on earth and the vocation of any man who would travel his way.

Faith without crucifixion is meaningless. "Christianity," therefore means nothing to Christ: "Not everyone who says to me, 'Lord, Lord,' shall enter the kingdom of heaven, but he who does the will of my Father who is in heaven." If it is thought that the implications of this statement are too strong to apply it to the Church, then there are also Jesus' words in the presence of his mother: "Whoever does the will of God is my brother, and sister, and mother." If we admit that Jesus loved his mother as much as he loves the Church, we can be safe in assuming that he would not hesitate to identify only those who through their suffering love do the will of God today as "my bishops, my clergy and my laity."

Because the Suffering Servant is the key to Jesus' own understanding of his mission on earth, and thus the key to our understanding of his humanity, we shall be able to affirm the full truth of Jesus' humanity only by passing over to the standpoint of suffering servanthood. And, as we have seen, it is only by passing through Jesus' humanity that we can feel the overwhelming mystery of his divinity. The essence of his humanity, suffering servanthood, is a reality which can hardly be understood except through an existential commitment to it as such. There can be no theoretical appropriation of the meaning of suffering as it is expressed in the *ebed Yahweh* and in Jesus. Philosophers have not thought such thoughts, nor can they be expected to as philosophers, for reason will refuse to admit the necessity of embracing suffering in love until a committed life has lost itself in that salvific mystery.

To follow to its conclusion Mark's Christological passage, we can understand Jesus' explanation of cross-bearing, "whoever loses his life for my sake and the gospel's will save it," as the description of an existential passing over to the standpoint of Jesus' humanity and through the suffering love of Jesus' hu-

179

manity, to the overwhelming mystery of incarnation. This mystery is complete when the Son of Man "comes in the glory of the Father," but it is again a mystery whose realization is dependent on a passing over to the standpoint of suffering servanthood: "For whoever is ashamed of me and of my words in this adulterous and sinful generation, of him will the Son of Man also be ashamed, when he comes in the glory of his Father with the holy angels." The only way to affirm, and be caught up in, the glory of Jesus in the Father is to affirm with one's own life the cross of Jesus' humanity. In this loving cross of the believing community, resurrection is not on the way: it is here.

But in view of all the self-proclaimed believers who deny that living cross in practice, it is apparent that "this adulterous and sinful generation" is a permanent phenomenon; it may be that its primary locus today is within Christianity. When the gospel has become a fixture of culture, and thus has been crowned with irrelevance, the discipline required to pass over to the standpoint of Jesus crucified must receive its inspiration from beyond that culture. For no milieu-Christianity professes a living faith in the cross. To pass over to the standpoint of the Suffering Servant, one must learn to see with new eyes, one must be struck by the lightning shock of the cross.

This kind of shock was provided during the great nonviolent campaign for Indian independence in 1930-31. At one stage row upon row of unarmed and praying Hindus marched into the blows of steel lathis wielded by British-directed police. Gandhi's volunteers by the thousands walked into certain injury and possible death. Gandhi and his followers deliberately offered their bodies and their lives to the British, thus resisting them in spirit and in truth. As Indian casualties rose, British self-justification fell. India's eventual assumption of power came through blood and crucifixion, not because the British were particularly kindhearted. It may be true that a different imperialist power, whether Communist as in Hungary or capitalist as in Vietnam, would have raised the cost in suffering even higher in an effort to hold off India's independence. But to those who witnessed scenes such as those at the Dharasana salt works in 1930, where hundreds of Gandhi's followers were beaten mercilessly, the British seemed brutal enough to make the confrontation between armed might and the power of suffering love a genuine one. In any event, Gandhi's faith in non-violent resistance was realistic enough not to rest on the presumably civilized sensibilities of the opponent or the hope of an early victory. Gandhi rooted his non-violent faith in voluntary suffering without limit.

The logic of non-violence is the logic of crucifixion and leads the man of non-violence into the heart of the suffering Christ. The purpose of non-violence is to move the oppressors to perceive those whom they are oppressing as human beings. Men commit acts of violence and injustice against other men only to the extent that they do not regard them as fully human. Non-violent resistance seeks to persuade the aggressor to recognize in his victim the humanity they have in common; when that is fully recognized violence is impossible. Through the power of voluntary suffering, the victim becomes no longer a victim but instead an active opponent in loving resistance to the man who has refused to recognize him as man. The greater the repression, the greater the inhumanity, the greater the power of suffering love necessary to begin restoring the bonds of community. Suffering as such is powerless. Love transforms it into the kind of resistance capable of moving an opponent to acknowledge his victim's humanity.

We can understand, then, why Gandhi looked to Christ as the supreme example of non-violence: on the cross suffering love received its fullest expression, even in the eyes of one who could not affirm Christ as uniquely divine. Gandhi knew that the man who died on Golgotha understood his entire life and mission as pointing toward that voluntary death, yet regarded it not as futility but as complete fulfillment. Jesus of Nazareth had no other purpose in life than the cross of suffering love, which is to say, he had no other purpose in life than life itself.

But for the believer, the inner dynamic of redemption can also be understood in terms of non-violence. If it is the purpose of non-violence to move men by suffering love to a recognition of their common humanity, it is the purpose of the cross to move us in the same way to a recognition of all men in Christ. The cross moves us, first of all, to an acknowledgment of Jesus' own suffering humanity. In order to profess a faith in Christ, as Peter and the disciples learned, we must profess him first in the scandal of suffering and rejection which summarizes his humanity. But to identify oneself in faith with the Christ of the cross is to acknowledge that here is the ultimate self-disclosure of God in man, in the action of suffering love unto death and in the words of Christ embracing all men, victims and executioners alike: "Father, forgive them for they know not what they do." With these words and with the cross embodying them, Jesus revealed so profound a union between himself and mankind that the crucifixion cannot be seen in isolation from a single injustice in history, nor can it be separated from the personal confrontation of victim and executioner in any single injustice. By the crucifixion violence and injustice have everywhere become *crucial*, cross-centered.

In inflicting violence on one another, men know not what they do, for they know not the sacredness of their brothers' and their own humanity, which at its innermost core is one with the humanity of Christ. The violence of men at any place or time in history is the violence of Golgotha. And the victim is everywhere and always the same: the man of the cross. To recognize the humanity of the Christ of the cross is to recognize all men in him, who in his suffering is one with all those by whom he has been murdered. To pass over to the suffering servanthood of the man Jesus is to see, through his forgiveness, his redeeming presence in all men, oppressed and oppressors alike, and to see therefore the possibility of his redeeming mediation of any human conflict through suffering love. To profess a living faith in the Christ of the cross is to affirm the redemptive reality present in every cross

of suffering love enacted in history. Christ becomes present everywhere in suffering servanthood and crucifixion. In and through
this presence he redeems mankind from division and leads it into
community.

In thus interpreting the cross from the standpoint of belief, we
may again confirm that interpretation best by returning to the
witness of Gandhi. When India finally gained its independence
from England in 1947, Gandhi could take no part in the victory
celebrations. The partition of India and the creation of Pakistan
had been accepted, against Gandhi's plea for unity, as the necessary condition for independence. The ensuing, intensified Hindu-
Muslim conflict threatened to inflame both countries. Against the
rise of mass violence, independence was an empty victory. Therefore, the seventy-eight-year-old Gandhi went to Calcutta, into a
Muslim house in an area where the stones were slippery with
fresh blood and the air acrid with the smoke of burning homes,
and there he undertook a fast unto death. His fast would end
only if and when sanity returned to Calcutta.

To most Indians, as to the other people of the world, Gandhi's
decision to fast seemed irrelevant to the violent city about him.
Yet Calcutta's response to Gandhi's self-imposed suffering grew
as his suffering deepened and threatened to take his life. Even
for the majority who could not understand Gandhi's methods or
philosophy, it struck them that if anyone had to suffer for the
continued killing of the city, it should not be Gandhi. Many
wanted to stop his suffering. They gathered weapons from streets
and homes and brought them to Gandhi offering them in return
for his promise to break the fast. But Gandhi persisted, continuing his suffering until the city itself began to fast and suffer with
him. Hindu and Muslim alike shared his pain and through that
sharing the power of feeling was restored to a community which
had become numbed to its inhumanity by constant violence.

As Dr. Amiya Chakravarty has written of the fast: "Suffering
was happening in a social and moral vacuum, with no response
from peoples whose minds had lost all human sensitiveness. It

could only be reciprocated and then redeemed by the process of suffering. Then, out of sharing and involvement would arise a new situation; it would not be merely change but transformation."

When the fast was finally broken, Calcutta rejoiced and the warring communities joined in great feasts, while Gandhi sipped his glass of orange juice.

The transformation which Gandhi sought and was given through the cross is the transformation spoken of by the angel at the open tomb: "He is not here; for he has risen." Or more pointedly in Luke, "Why do you seek the living among the dead?" The cross raises the dead to the living because the cross itself is living, as Gandhi described and followed it. For Gandhi dared not think of birth without death on the cross. He also said, "God did not bear the cross only 1900 years ago, but He bears it today, and He dies and is resurrected from day to day." To the suffering servant, resurrection is as present a reality as crucifixion, although present only in and through the cross. Only in yielding up one's spirit, "Father, into thy hands I commit my spirit," is there granted the power to roll back the rock so that the dead can become the living. Only in suffering love unto death is a Calcutta reclaimed from the valley of the dead. Only through the servant's gift of life in the darkness of death can the violent be returned to life, for it was after Jesus' death that the centurion and those who assisted him in that death confessed, "Truly this was the Son of God."

Does not a full commitment to Jesus' humanity of suffering servanthood necessarily involve an existential commitment to the overcoming truth of his divinity as well? To answer yes with particular reference to Gandhi's witness is not to claim Gandhi for Christianity, but to claim to see the full meaning of Christ through Gandhi, in a living cross and resurrection which would be true to Gandhi's own understanding of what it means to live and to die. The cross is revolutionary not simply because it raises men to another life but because it transforms them into the fullness of that life on this earth. The revolution of peace is realized in Calcutta, not heaven, because only the wounded flesh and spilled blood of Calcutta can provide the matter of a new heaven and a new earth. The spirit of a new earth must also be in Calcutta, as it was in the Christic figure suffering into love the violence of the city, and in the community thus re-created.

Because he envisioned the face of God as Truth, Gandhi experimented with truth in a lifelong struggle to see God face to face. In the course of that struggle, which became in part the struggle of India and finally the British Empire and the world, Gandhi encountered God as suffering love. In realizing through his experiments that the God of Truth is found through the God of suffering love, Gandhi passed into the redeeming truth of the incarnation.

VII.

The "Presence" of Jesus

BERNARD J. COOKE

"If CHRIST be not risen, the gospel we preach to you is vain and
your faith is vain." These words of St. Paul are as relevant today
as when he first addressed them to the Christians of Corinth in
the first century of the Church. For more than a century now the
scholarly criticisms directed against the claims made by Christianity have focused on the issue of Christ's resurrection.

It is interesting to notice the way in which Catholic theological
reaction to attacks on the resurrection of Christ reflects our gradual recovery of a more integral notion of the Church. In the
apologetics that characterized most Catholic thought in the nineteenth century and the first half of the twentieth, the resurrection
of Christ was viewed as the key "proof" of his divinity and of
the Church's claims. With the decline of this kind of apologetics
the resurrection of Christ is seen, not so much as a link in a
logical argument but rather as the very source of the Church's
existential reality.

If the Church is truly the body of Christ, if the Church is to
function as the sacrament of Christ, Christ himself must still be.
Unless Jesus still lives as the risen Lord, the Church has no claim
to uniqueness among the religions of mankind. Christianity would
be reduced to faith in a message left it by a great founder—but
actually not even this would be the case, for the gospel of
Christianity is the good news of the resurrection.

Without the resurrection of Jesus, none of the descriptions of

186

the Church given by Vatican II in its decree "Lumen gentium" would be true. They all presuppose that the Church is part of the continuing mystery of Christ himself. They presuppose, moreover, that the risen Christ is somehow present to this community of believers which is the Church. This raises the basic question: what do we mean by the "presence" of Christ?

Admitting our inability to achieve a fully adequate understanding of Christ as he now is, the risen Lord, we must still work toward as accurate an understanding as is possible. At the very least, we must strive to rid ourselves of misunderstandings. History indicates that such misunderstandings have, during many centuries, blocked a more correct insight into the nature of the Church and of its sacramental actions. To be more specific: the resurrection of Jesus does not mean that he "came back to life"; rather, it means that he passed from the kind of human life we know into a much fuller manner of being human. Nor does it mean that the risen Christ is "up in heaven," as if he is at a spatial distance from us; Christ is exalted in the mystery of risen life, but this is a matter of intrinsic human fulfillment rather than of geographical location.

Denying such obvious misunderstandings of Christ's risen state may seem trite. Yet such notions have been widely accepted; and they have been deeply imbedded in Christian imagery regarding Christ. As long as they remain in any form they tend to block our grasp of the fact that the resurrection is a mystery of Christ's *presence* to us.

Presence to men throughout the centuries that follow upon his earthly career is much more than a modality of Christ's resurrection. This presence is the central finality of Christ's risen human existing. Perhaps things might have been otherwise; but the New Testament literature assures us that Jesus is now the risen Lord *for our sake*. Without men to be present to, Christ could not be in risen life as he now is. Jesus chose passage into new life, in order to give himself more fully to his human brothers and sisters; this choice to give himself to us humans

187

continues to dominate his consciousness as the risen Lord—the symbolism of his eucharistic self-giving makes this clear.

In a sense, it could not be otherwise. Risen life is the full expression of human existing; and Jesus passed into this fullness of manhood with his resurrection. But presence to other humans is so intrinsic to our human fulfillment that it is difficult to see how Christ could be in this state of human perfection now if this state did not involve presence to men.

At first blush this seems to create grave difficulties, difficulties that arise from our own faith experience. It is quite clear that while we accept the reality of the risen Christ in faith, we have no direct experience of his presence in our midst. We neither see, hear, nor touch him. We possess none of the ordinary indications of interrelationship that mark our human presence to one another. As far as our ordinary means of perception are concerned we can scarcely avoid the conclusion that he is "away from us."

Without attempting to minimize the very real questions that are raised in this matter—for these touch close to the heart of the problem of Christian faith—we might indicate that part of the problem comes from our tendency to associate the reality of presence too closely with spatial location. In our ordinary experience of presence to one another, some proximity is always involved. Even when we become present to one another at a distance, as by letter or telephone, there is still some type of spatial link that spans the intervening distance.

As we examine more deeply the reality of presence, we see that in itself it need not involve such spatial connotations. Presence between persons is essentially a matter of communication between one and the other, by which a person becomes conscious of another, by which a person insofar as he is known becomes "interior" to another person. True personal presence is basically a question of one person's being aware of another, of persons entering into conscious communion with one another.

Within this reality of personal communication there are almost limitless levels of identification and communion. I may say "Good morning" to a stranger on the street and the extent of our relationship to one another is quite minimal. A conversation carried on with a business associate would be in most cases an instance of deeper awareness of one another. And if I were involved in an intimate conversation with a very dear friend, perhaps consoling him or sharing some hope or dream, our presence to one another would be quite uniquely different. In this last case, I would be revealing myself as a person to this friend, truly giving myself in my deepest consciousness of myself. At least during the conversation I would be existing for this other person; and in a true friendship this being for the other person would endure as a constitutive factor in my own personal self-identity. To be for this friend would be a part of what it means for me to be me.

It would seem, then, that the critical element in presence is to *be for another person.* While for us humans in our life in space and time this "being for another" does involve spatial nearness, this nearness in space seems accidental to the basic reality of presence. Conceivably, if one were free of the limitation of spatial-temporal location, presence would still be possible if one existed for another. This seems to be the case of Christ's presence to us. Though his present risen existence is not commensurate with our space-time continuum, he is constantly present to us because of the fact that he exists humanly *for us.* In this sense it is most correct to say that Christ is "the man for all men."

Quite obviously we can discuss all this only on the presupposition of faith. If, however, we do accept the basic revelation of the gospel, the datum of revelation is clear: The Son of God in becoming man has sought and found a most remarkable identification with us humans; the incarnation is the realization par excellence of the most basic law of love and friendship, to find identity with the beloved. This means that the entire human career of Jesus, through the years of his earthly life and into his continuing risen life, is a self-giving to men, a being for men.

189

Because the finality of the incarnation is directed to the entire human race, the mystery of Christ's presence somehow touches all men. Vatican II has recalled this fact to us, but it does little more than point to the fact, and our theological understanding of this matter is most inchoative. We can see, though, that this basic and universal reality of Christ's risen presence to men will have far-reaching implications for our ecclesiology and our missiology.

Bracketing momentarily our ignorance in this regard, we might strive to investigate more thoroughly the reality of Christ's presence as it touches the community of Christian faith which is the Church. Here we seem to encounter considerable complexity. While there is only one Christ who is present to Christians, the modes or bases of his presence are multiple.

First, there is Christ's presence to the Christian community because of his *sharing with these believers his own redemptive mission and activity*. This is the mystery of Christ's priesthood, which he continues to exercise through the historical witness and action of Christians. There is only one mission, only one priesthood, only one redemptive action—Christ's. Those who belong to the Church do not have a mission or a priesthood or an apostolate that is derived from Christ's but distinct, or that is consequent to his in human history. "As my Father has sent me, so also I send you." And just as the Father who sent him continuously worked in and through Jesus, so the risen Christ continues his saving work through his followers.

This presence is directed essentially to the community of faith, and each individual Christian shares in it by virtue of his insertion into this communty by baptism. While it is correct to say that Christ is thus present to each Christian, that each Christian bears the reality of Christ into his daily life, we must beware of an individualistic understanding that would see Christ as somehow contained "in" each Christian. Instead, it is the people of God, the community of believers, that is the object of this priestly presence of Christ. Indeed, this presence will become more in-

190

tense, it will operate more effectively for the salvation of all men, in proportion as the Church is consciously and generously open to accepting its priestly mission.

Since Christ shares with his followers in the Church his redemptive mission, he also shares with them his human destiny in his unending union with his Father; this is inseparable from his task of bringing men to this Father. In the practical order the risen Christ carries on the functional realization of his destiny by acting through the Church, which is his body and his sacrament. Those who belong to the Church share in this way in Christ's destiny, and their own destiny is inextricably linked with his.

In addition to this priestly mode of presence to the Church there is a second way in which Christ is present to Christians: he *shares with them his own personal identity.* Of course, it is true that in one sense no person can give to another his own identity, for this is unique and distinctive. Yet it is also true that in a genuine friendship each person strives to give himself to the other, a true friend is an *alter ego.* So Christ who is bound to us in love shares with us his own divine identity.

When in a deep friendship we strive to share our identity, we do so by communicating to another the insights, the motivations, the experiences, by which we identify ourselves. To the extent to which a friend can appropriate to himself these bases of our own self-identity he can identify with us. For Christ the most profound root of his personal identity is his relationship to the Father. Christ is the Son, who gives us a share in his own sonship by giving us his Father as our own Father. We can begin to appreciate the extent of Christ's identification with us, of his being *for us,* when we learn to accept the fact that we "are not only called, but actually are, sons of God."

Christ, the risen Lord, is present to Christians by sharing with them his priestly mission and his own identity as Son. At this point in our discussion, however, it may well seem that we are dealing with obscure truth that bears little or no relationship to our experience; indeed, the whole matter may seem not only mysterious but almost magical. We touch closer to our Christian experience when we discuss the third mode of Christ's presence to Christians: he is present to them *in their faith.*

Here again we can profitably reason from our ordinary human experience of friendship. When I accept a person as my friend I increasingly come to know that person, I increasingly allow him to occupy my consciousness, I increasingly give myself over as a knower (that is, as a person) to my friend. As the friendship deepens, my friend truly begins to "dwell within me," he abides with me even when we are geographically separated from one another.

John's gospel tells us that this law of friendship applies to our relationship to Christ. "If any man loves me, my Father will love him, and we will come to him and take up our abode with him." And St. Paul prays for the early Christians "that Christ may dwell by love in your hearts." This is, as it were, our human side of making Christ's presence to us possible. As we have been saying, presence is constituted by being *for another;* but one can only be for another effectively if that other person accepts this offer of friendship.

Christ's presence to us requires, then, our openness to him in faith, a faith that is not a purely rational acceptance of abstract religious truths but rather a total personal acceptance of him, the risen Christ. To believe in Christ is not only to accept the fact that he is and is risen, it is to accept him as being *for us men.* It is to allow him to be effectively present to us.

Christian faith is meant to be a consciousness of the reality and of the presence of the risen Christ. It is an awareness of him, who is our brother and friend, an awareness that is different from any other, because it does not have a grounding in ordinary sensible experience, but none the less real. The centuries of Christian history indicate that this awareness is not an illusion, that it has dominated the consciousness of countless men and women who have been among the great people who have graced our earth.

When such awareness of Christ's living reality and close friendship is found in the community of faith and in the people who comprise it, their faith consciousness is truly a *locus* for the presence of the risen Christ in our world. Other men and women who deal with these Christians are thus in the presence of Christ, whether they are conscious of it or not. If they come to know these Christians more deeply, discover in conversation and friendship the faith these Christians possess, they may themselves come to a growing realization of the reality of Christ and so be led to faith. For Christians to bear in their consciousness the presence of their risen Lord and to reflect this in their human attitudes and activity is to a great extent what we mean by the over-used term "Christian witness."

More than that, Christ's presence to Christians—by their sharing his mission and sonship, consciously accepted in faith—is meant to be a force for transforming the lives of the men whom Christians meet and with whom they live and work. If Christians truly live in the awareness of the relationship they bear to Christ, this will inevitably change their attitude towards people. They will reverence others, be deeply concerned for their genuine human welfare, emphathize with them in their problems and sorrows, devote themselves to bettering their lives. In this way, Christ himself through the impact he has on Christians in faith will be working to redeem the lives of all men. At least in part, this seems to be what the Second Vatican Council was talking about when it described the Church as the sacrament of Christ.

All we have been saying so far seems to lay a heavy burden on Christian faith. Faith is unquestionably the key to the presence of the risen Christ to our human life, and therefore the key to the transforming and redeeming power of Christ in our midst. Yet for many men, Christians as well as non-Christians, this seems to be a shaky foundation on which to build one's life. Christian faith is indeed a risk, in many ways the ultimate risk. And while our present generation is by no means the first to have seen this risk, it is hard to find another historical period in which the very possibility of God's intimate dealing with men has been more widely and critically challenged. Many a reader of this article may think it quite presumptuous to be discussing the presence of the risen Christ at a time when our contemporaries are talking about "the death of God."

It may just be, however, that coming to grips with the question of faith in the risen Christ will be the only adequate way of dealing with the "death of God." We are able to know the divine only in so far as it manifests itself to us; and our Christian faith tells us that only in Jesus can we find the proper and ultimate revelation of God. To a Christian the denial of conscious contact with the reality of the risen Christ means the denial of any human understanding of who God is.

Yet, how do we know that our Christian faith is not an illusion? How do we know that Christ really exists as the risen Lord, and that he is actively present to us in our lives? Very simply, because he tells us so. Admittedly, this sounds like an outrageously naïve answer. In attempting to justify it, we must study a fourth mode of Christ's presence to us, his *presence through communication* with us.

We need not dwell on the fact that communication with one another is absolutely basic and essential for us human beings if we wish to be present to one another. By word, gesture, an action of kindness and concern, we make clear to another person that we are for them. Without such communication, the community of friendship could never be established. And any growth of the friendship is dependent upon constant and deepening communication. So also, because we Christians are humans, the presence of Christ to us in faith must be rooted in some form of personal dialogue between Christ and ourselves.

Certainly one element in the case is the earthly career of Jesus, those years when he communicated in perceptible human form

194

with his disciples and some others of his contemporaries. At least
in essence his teaching has come down to us through the witness
of the early Christians. So, we do have the possibility of responding in our thought and life to the message of Jesus. If our response to Christ were, however, nothing more than this
"dialogue" with the Jesus of history, we could not be involved in
the kind of communication that is necessary for a friendship. The
impact of the historical Jesus could be present to us; but this is
quite different from the presence to us of the risen Christ now.

What we must do, difficult though it be, is reflect upon what
we mean by saying that *Christ speaks to us—in one another, in
scripture, and in sacrament.* Though these three are distinguishable one from another, they are experientially intertwined. Of
the three, the one that seems to be psychologically most basic is
Christ's speaking to us in one another.

We have already treated of this somewhat in talking about the
witness that believing Christians give by their faith. We can now
stress the point that this witness finds its most important function
within the Christian community itself. Any one of us who
searches for the criterion of his faith will discover that he is
dependent upon the faith of fellow Christians. For most of us a
sense of reality with regard to the risen Christ came from our par-
ents, was reinforced by teachers, and—if we were fortunate—
found continuing support during our adult life in the Christian
faith of our friends. Observable faith in the lives of these people
whom we respect and love has been an unreflective but critically
important basis for our own judgment of faith. This is why each
one of us comes to Christian faith in a community of faith.

Present as he is to these Christians in faith, Christ speaks to me
the reality of his risen human existing, speaks the reality of his
being for me also. In this process of communicating to me
through the faith of my fellow Christians Christ makes himself
present to my consciousness. This is not merely a matter of the
first beginnings of my faith; throughout the years of growth and
development that should mark my life as a Christian, Christ's

presence to my Christian brethren should continue to speak to me. Each Christian (and in some sense each human) is a "word" of Christ to me, a word of challenge to which I must respond.

It is not just the faith of individual Christians that is meant to be word of Christ addressed to me in faith; the communal faith of the whole Church bears the presence of Christ to me. To "dialogue" with Christ and so deepen and sharpen my awareness of his present activity in my life I must learn to listen to the developing faith of the Church as a whole. In this regard, an experience such as the one we have had in Vatican II is an immeasurable advantage.

This process of Christians' testifying in faith to one another and clarifying for one another the mystery of Christ's presence in their midst has been a reality from the earliest days of the Church's life. The very first generation of Christians enjoyed, however, a special benefit: their own faith was grounded, not on the witness of others, but on their own immediate experience of Jesus' public life and Passover into risen life. Because of the privileged validity of their witness, the infant Church gathered the record of the teaching of the apostles into that collection of inspired writings we call the New Testament. Each succeeding generation of Christians has spoken its faith, not just by using appropriate human language but also by speaking the word of scripture. In this way Christ continues to speak through his apostles during all the centuries of the Church's life.

Scripture is truly word of God, not just word about God. Scripture is truly sacramental. When it is proclaimed in a Christian community, it expresses not only the living faith of Christians today and the continuing faith of the historical Church; it expresses the mind of Christ as he is present in faith to this community. In responding to the word of the bible a Christian is in dialogue both with the community of faith and with Christ himself.

Much the same kind of communicating between Christians and the risen Christ is established in the celebration of the sacra-

196

ments. As a matter of fact, scripture and sacrament are inseparable elements in the one process of God's speaking to men. Sacraments, though, are enacted word; everything about them, not just the spoken word, is meant to convey meaning to the community of believers who share these actions. The very name they bear, "sacraments," indicates that the basic purpose of these actions is to communicate understanding in faith to Christians.

The actions we humans perform speak for us; we have the adage that "actions speak louder than words." Sacraments speak for Christ because he is the one who acts in the sacraments. But he acts in sacraments through the agency of his Church which is his body. It is the very action, then, that we Christians carry out in sacraments which is the action of Christ, for we are acting as his body; what we are doing, he is doing in and through us. In order to hear what it is that Christ is saying to us in these actions, we must listen to what it is that we ourselves are doing. Only if sacraments are this kind of response to Christ's communication with us will they become occasions for deepening Christ's presence to us in faith.

Through this triple "word"—the faith of fellow Christians, scripture, and sacrament—the risen Christ continues to communicate to us in faith. The presence effected by this communication is not a "new" reality, as if Christ becomes present to us in such situations and then is again absent. Instead, this presence in word is an intensification of the enduring presence that comes by his sharing with us his priestly mission and sonship. Friendship is an enduring reality which is brought into sharper reality and focus by conversation between friends; this is essentially what is involved in Christ's presence to us in the Church.

Perhaps the best way of illustrating the interaction of the various modes of Christ's presence is to describe the presence of Christ in the action of the Eucharist. As a group of Christians assemble for the Mass, Christ is already present in their midst because he is sharing with them his own priesthood. It is by virtue of this shared priesthood that these Christians then proceed to the

197

priestly act of sacrificial worship. As the word of scripture is proclaimed to them they are meant to be brought into closer union with the mind of Christ who is speaking to them; and so their personal relationship to him is deepened, his personal presence to them made more profound. Christ is present in and to the word he speaks, in order to be more present to those who receive this word.

When we men wish to communicate most importantly with one another, mere words are insufficient; we search for other signs or symbols that may impart the meaning we wish to speak. So, too, Christ in the eucharistic action: in order to convey to the assembled Christians the incredible reality of his love for them, Christ uses the sign values of both food and the human body, combining them in the mystery we try to designate by the term "transubstantiation." Christ is immediately present to the "species," that is, the aspects of bread and wine that can carry significance, so that they be a word which makes it possible for him to be deeply present to the faith of the assembled Christian community. Christ's presence to the eucharistic species cannot be understood in isolation; it has reality and meaning only as a part of the process of communication by which he is present in faith to Christians.

Finally, the eucharistic dialogue between Christ and the Christians who are participating in the action comes to unitive expression in the reception of the body of Christ; for communion is the goal of communication and the fulfillment of presence. And while this eucharistic intensification of Christ's presence is meant to be a high point in our Christian experience of faith, it is by no means the exclusive occasion of Christ's presence. Christ continues to be present to those who had shared in the Eucharist when they have dispersed to their daily tasks.

We might note that the reality of Christ's presence to us is not a peripheral topic in our contemporary theological discourse. It could not be, for it stands at the heart of the processes we call "revelation" and "redemption."

Revelation, as we understand it in the context of Old and New Testament, has always been a matter of God's presence to human consciousness in faith. The prophetic experience, that is so much of the source of Old Testament faith understanding, is essentially an insight into the earthshaking presence of Yahweh to his people Israel. Christ's own human understanding, in which all Christianity is rooted, is the conscious result of that unparalleled presence of God to man which is the incarnation. And throughout the centuries of Christian history, Christ has continued to reveal himself and his Father in the process of self-giving presence that we have tried to describe.

It is this continuing self-revelation on the part of the divine persons that has made it possible for Christians to be and grow as a community of believers. It is this continuing self-revelation that still makes it possible for us today to enter into personal friendship with Christ through faith.

If the mystery of Christ's presence to us is inseparable from the process of revelation, it is equally inseparable from the action of redemption that the risen Lord carries on still in our world. Redemption is most basically a matter of changing people, redirecting them in their conscious and affective life so that they achieve the destiny that is properly theirs. Such a reordering of men's attitudes and decisions cannot be achieved by imposition or laws or religious institutions. Only the impact of persons, particularly of the divine persons, can challenge humans to deepened realization of their personhood.

This is exactly why Christ remains active in our lives, present to us through the mystery of the Church. Under the impact of his being for us, we may respond to this challenge of friendship, receive him openly in faith, and develop into the kind of persons he desires us to be—in brief, into sons of his Father. While redemption has many facets, human transformation by the presence of the risen Christ stands at its very center. A soteriology that does not incorporate this basic reality of Christ's presence will necessarily be abstract or legalistic or both.

199

We are Christians because of the presence of the risen Lord in our lives. It is the influence of his presence that has Christianized us to the extent that we can claim that that desired effect has occurred. Only this presence can make our faith other than a tragic mockery and our religious practices other than refined superstition. In proportion as one understands this mystery of Christ's presence, he understands what Christianity really is. In proportion to his acceptance of this presence he becomes truly Christian.

VIII.

Jesus and the Church

J. M. CAMERON

IT IS VERY COMMON to judge this or that action of men, this or that ecclesiastical practice, this or that institution in Church or State, by an appeal to "the mind of Christ." What ground we may have for this appeal is not clear. There is a plain temptation to identify our preferences and likings, our moral prejudices, all that supports our situation in the world and assists our ambitions, with the mind of Christ. We are also tempted, though this may at bottom be the same temptation, to understand talk about the person of Christ as having a transcendent reference only, to belong to the order of the supernatural understood as an order that is clearly separable from the world of work and warfare, of Negro ghettos and commuter suburbs, of "telegrams and anger." Both temptations, interwoven as they may often be, appear at every social and intellectual level.

There is not so much difference as one might suppose between the trivializing piety represented by the epicene statues of the Sacred Heart and the equally trivializing location, by some existentialist theologians, of the reality of Christ in the consciousness of that believer who is not even, properly speaking, a believer, for he takes the historical actuality of the death and resurrection of Jesus as ultimately dispensable. One can see that to yield to such temptations is to play tricks with oneself; but it is not easy to see how we are to state what it is to use Jesus, the one who is spoken of in the New Testament writings both as the man who suffered through his obedience to the will of his Father and as

Kyrios, the exalted Lord, as a standard, a criterion and a pattern
for men in the twentieth century.

For Catholics and Orthodox, and other Christians whose lives
are religiously speaking inconceivable outside the context of
ecclesiastical institutions, there is a further problem. It is through
the sacred writings, the sacraments, the common fellowship of
such institutions, that we know about the Lord and that Jesus *is*
the Lord (and therefore, necessarily, standard, criterion and pattern) and it is impossible that we should know about Jesus in
any other way. It is true, men can know about Jesus as they know
about Socrates or Confucius or Mary Baker Eddy; but this would
not be to know that Jesus is the Lord, and therefore standard,
criterion and pattern, but to know that some men use the term
"Lord" as applying to him. No man can call Jesus Lord, so
the New Testament writers assert, except by or in the Holy
Spirit; and the gift of the Spirit is a gift to a community of men
and a gift that makes of men a genuine community. And yet this
community, just because it is fully human, is conditioned by history and marked by all the frailties and crimes that belong to
human institutions, and is thus itself subject to the judgment of
its Lord, that Lord whom we nevertheless encounter only in and
through this community of men.

But if the institutional is the mode in which we encounter the
Lord, wouldn't it always be presumptuous—this is a problem
raised in Dostoevsky's story about the Grand Inquisitor and is the
ground of the Inquisitor's sophism—to say of this or that deliverance or practice of the ecclesiastical community that it is
contrary to the mind of Christ? More, wouldn't it be self-con-
tradictory to do so if the mind of Christ is to be known only in
and through the experience of the community?

My question, then, has two aspects. One is concerned with
what it is to commend Jesus as the pattern of the authentically
human in our own day. The other is concerned with what is
darkly problematical about the presence of perversity and evil
in that very community for which Jesus is the Lord and within

which we learn that Jesus is the Lord and encounter him as the Lord.

Strong personalities create movements of one kind or another. There are Dickens societies . . . Sometimes the cultus of a saint, of St. Philip Neri, for example, or St. Vincent de Paul, is in part provoked by the special flavor of his personality. Samuel Johnson has many devoted admirers who will exchange characteristic anecdotes about him with gusto. Modern totalitarian movements are stamped with the demonic personalities of their leaders. Within such movements there are manifestations of which we can say that they are authentic, faithful expressions of the personality in question. A given anecdote can be said to be Johnsonian, another not. A particular story about a saint will ring true or ring false. Now, such judgments are possible only because we can give an independent account of the personality of the man concerned; and we thus have a criterion of judgment that is superior to the details of the concrete tradition generated by the personality. Can we say that the relation of Jesus to the tradition and the community that historically takes its origin from him is of this kind?

If there is one thing that a century's work in New Testament studies seems to have put beyond question, it is that an account of "the historical Jesus" which, as it were, gets behind the account of him given in the apostolic preaching cannot be given. The relation of Jesus to the Church is thus not of the kind we have been considering. The old idea that we can contrast the simple teacher of the synoptic gospels with the supposedly hellenized figure of the Pauline or Johannine theology is plainly false. The Jesus of Mark is as much the strange, commanding, Messianic man who generates the great Christological controversies of the fourth century as the Jesus of Paul or of John or of the writer to the Hebrews.

From this it has been argued that "the Christ of faith" is a datum and that the historical Jesus is a figure about which we can say remarkably little, except that a man of that name existed and that there is some now irrecoverable connection between him and the figure given to us in the apostolic preaching. There is nothing necessary about such a conclusion. It is a perfectly possible hypothesis that the apostolic testimony is that of witnesses who are striving to express in various modes the impact of the man Jesus with whom some of them had lived and conversed, who had been present at his crucifixion, seen him after his death, and had given their lives to the proclamation "that Christ died for our sins in accordance with the scriptures, that he was buried, that he was raised on the third day . . . and that he appeared to Cephas, then to the twelve" (1 Cor. 15:3-5).

Indeed, we might hold that this hypothesis is more consistent with what we can recover historically than any other. It is, at any rate, the hypothesis upon which Christians stake their existence; and I shall take it as not only the expression of the most primitive Christian faith but also as a genuinely historical assertion; the Christ of faith is what the first witnesses made of the Jesus of history, expresses their convictions, which we as believers make our own, about the person and role of Jesus.

Given this position, we are still strongly inclined to suppose that the essence of the Christian proclamation is that salvation comes through a conscious relation between the individual believer and the person of Jesus; and with this goes the view that reflection upon this conscious relation enables us to judge this or that practice, action or what not as in accordance, or not, with the mind of Christ. How I stand reflectively in relation to Christ is then fundamental, the testimony of others, the judgments of the Church, having value only in so far as they conform to what I know at, so to speak, first hand. This view, for which there is some support in common forms of Christian devotion, both Catholic and Protestant—Orthodoxy, so far as one can tell, does not have such forms—is a misconception of what the apostolic proclamation is and implies.

The New Testament tells us what God has accomplished for men through the life, death and resurrection of Jesus. Our salvation is something essentially and necessarily prior to our knowledge of it. To stand in a conscious relation to the fact of our redemption is to believe, to accept it, or to disbelieve and therefore to reject it. The visible community of the Church is for the most part, excluding very young children and idiots, who may nevertheless be true and lively members of the Church, composed of those who have heard, perhaps fragmentarily and with much of purely human origin mixed with it, the good news of what God has accomplished in relation to the entire human family and who thus stand in a conscious relation to the apostolic proclamation; and this consciousness can become deeper and more explicit through attention to the Word of God for men, that is, Jesus Christ, of whom the *entire* scriptures speak, the Word listened to primarily in community (where the believers are gathered together) and in sacramental worship.

Every detail of the Church's life witnesses to God's initiative: in listening for and to the Word, in baptism, in the Supper of the Lord, in the rebuilding of the links with God (that is, *in via,* with his holy community, the Church) that are broken by sin, in the making of Christian families. In all these the initiative is that of God. He comes first to us, that we may come to him.

Now, it is quite strictly a grace, that is, something absolutely not to be expected or in any way merited, that a man should be able to stand in a conscious relation to his own redemption; and what holds true of the individual believer holds true of the community of believers. It follows then that we as individuals and as members of the believing community stand in this relation to the redemption on behalf of all the others, that is, of the vast majority of the human race who are quite unable, for temporal or spatial or other reasons, to stand in a conscious relation to their redemption. The believing community exists not only to present Christ to the world but to *be* the presence of Christ to the world; and the presence of Christ as humiliated, rejected, crucified, as well as glorified and at the right hand of the Father. The presenting of Christ is not the presenting of a set of affecting

205

pictures, or the presenting of a remarkable personality; but the proclamation—and the simultaneous realization—in and through the Church's historical existence of the astonishing news of what God has accomplished in Jesus Christ. Speaking to the Gentiles, Paul puts it thus: "Just as you were once disobedient to God but now have received mercy because of their disobedience [that is, that of Israel], so they have now been disobedient in order that *by the mercy shown to you* they also may receive mercy. *For God has consigned all men to disobedience, that he may have mercy upon all*" (Rom. 11:30-32).

What the Church does, what she is summoned to do, is then both to represent and to be Christ in the midst of a world already redeemed, though this redemption does not yet appear plainly, not even in the historical existence of the Church, for the Church is the *sign* of God's reign, not, as it were, its naked form. There would seem, then, at first sight, to be no such problem as that which we raised earlier, namely, how we are to know the mind of Christ in such a way that we can look at ecclesiastical practices and structures and judge them by the intentions of the Lord of the Church. If the Church in its historical existence *is* the presence of Christ to the world, at least sacramentally, that is, as a sign, then it looks as though we can only appeal from the Church to the Church; and this seems impossible. But it is also plain and beyond argument that whole features of ecclesiastical life, both now and in the past, merit the most obvious condemnation in the light of what we may learn about the mind of Christ from the New Testament witness.

This is not only a hard problem; it is also a momentous one, for how we solve it will determine how we are to understand the meaning of the present crisis through which the Church is passing. It is possible to intone, for example, *ecclesia semper reformanda,* as though this were a commonplace familiar to all and not something intimately connected with heartbreak and suffering in every generation. We can take the present crisis as above all one concerned with ecclesiastical machinery and liturgical forms, whereas it is concerned with what the Church is in its depths, the encounter of God with man, in sin and in grace.

Karl Rahner has noted a "mysterious monophysite undercurrent" in our ordinary Christology, above all perhaps in our devotional life outside the liturgy. This is one of the ways in which we fail to take historicity seriously. If we take the mission of Jesus with complete seriousness as a genuinely historical phenomenon, then he is not for us a transcendent figure who took on the appearance of a man for a space of time, but a man who belongs to his time, not to ours, not even to the time of the preaching of the gospel, to the hellenistic world; for he preached only to Israel, he stood only within this tradition, that of the Law and the Prophets. That he stands in a relation to every man throughout human history is brought about by what happens within this one historical situation. It is within *this* situation that he "emptied himself, taking the form of a servant, being born in the likeness of men . . . humbled himself and became obedient unto death, even death on a cross" (Phil. 2:7,8).

To expect timeless truths to be distilled from a contemplation of this situation is to fail to take seriously the historical character of God's speaking to men in the human existence of Jesus. If he comes to us in *our* situation, to Peter or Paul or to the Christians of later ages, it is in virtue of what was then accomplished, forever. The balance here is hard to state rightly. It was "under Pontius Pilate" that he suffered for us. His speech, the forms of his thought, the very method by which he was put to death, all these belong to a particular time long past; and yet we give to what then happened a universal significance, not in the sense that the universal fractures the historical moment that hides it and is then expressible in terms that apply to all times and places—this does not happen: there is a *semper explicanda* as well as a *semper reformanda*—but rather in the sense that he is present to and within *all* historical situations in virtue of what happened within the one historical situation. This belongs to the logic of revelation and redemption; not that we have *a priori* insight into how revelation and redemption *have* to be apart from what is historically given.

It is then within our own historical situation that we may hope to encounter Christ as pattern and standard. But of course historical situations are not monadic, shut off from each other in brute separation and particularity. Our own situation is what it is in part in virtue of God's being present to it in the sign, the sacrament, that is the Church, just as God was present to the disciples in the sacrament of the man Jesus; but the Church has a historical origin as well as its present historical actuality, that is, what we are now is open to as well as shaped by the crucial situation out of which the Church came. Thus, every detail in the gospels, every sentence in the letters of the apostolic writers, is precious to us. More, these things are normative, not as the axioms of a timeless system, but as witnesses to what was once done for us. And since what was done was done within a particular historical tradition, that of Judaism, Judaism too is precious to us; indeed, for faith it becomes our own history, is ceaselessly repeated in the liturgy. In the unforgettable phrase that appears in the Canon of the Roman Mass, after the *anamnesis,* Abraham is spoken of as our ancestor, our forefather. We are engrafted branches on the holy root of Israel (Rom. 10:13-24).

The task of discovering what the mind of Christ is for us today is thus neither a task of historical research nor a task in which we are free to discard what belongs to our historical past. This can be illustrated from one of the earliest crises in the history of the Church, a crisis for the overcoming of which there was no decisive saying or practice of the Lord. I have in mind the dispute over circumcision, the controversy that rent the early Church. What was in question was whether belief in the apostolic preaching involved, in the case of Gentiles, conversion to Judaism. Equipped with hindsight, we are inclined to be astonished that over this issue Paul was compelled to resist Peter "to the face" (Gal. 2:11). But the question was not and is not absolutely clear. It is, in one sense, quite true that to become a Christian believer is to be converted to Judaism. Jesus is the expected Messiah; we receive the gift of the Spirit "who has spoken by the prophets"; to be incorporated in Christ is to be made one with the very flesh of Israel, the flesh of kings and prophets who had longed to see Christ's day and in the end were not disappointed; Abraham is our ancestor, our forefather.

That it is nevertheless in accordance with the mind of Christ that conversion to Judaism should no longer entail conformity to the ritual and ceremonial law is not something founded upon a clear dominical pronouncement but something that had to be worked out, in debate, in the circumstance of the preaching of the good news in the hellenistic world, to the Jews first, and then to the Gentiles. That in Christ distinctions of ethnic origin, of sex, of social status, are overcome is an entailment of the preaching but one which is gradually and sometimes fitfully perceived; it is an entailment that in our own day, as we have sadly to note, is still imperfectly grasped and sometimes rejected. Indeed, we may want to say that perhaps the victory over the Judaizing tendencies in the early Church was too complete, so that one side of the complex truth is suppressed. How else are we to explain the sacrilegious phenomenon of Christian anti-Semitism?

That there should be a debate between the Church and the world has always been recognized. That there should be a debate within the Church, and that this is the normal way in which we come to know the implications of the Christian proclamation, this has become clearer as a result of the Council, though it is a truth that is written large in the history of the Church. But we cling to the idea that there are *two* debates and that the debate between the Church and the world is between those who have a clear, systematic, well ordered *gnosis* integrated with a clear, systematic, and well ordered complex of ecclesiastical institutions, and those who stand essentially outside the Church. As I have already argued, this is a basically mistaken view. The entire human world lies within the scope of the redemption; and the distinction between the believing community and those who are

209

outside it is between those who have received the grace of a reflective consciousness of that redemption which has been given to, if not yet fully appropriated by, all, and those who are in a state of ignorance. This is the ground of that reverence for and proper curiosity about the world that was so distinctive a mark of John XXIII's attitude to the problems of our time; and the ground of his belief that there is much for the Church to learn from the world.

Human society is most radically affected by the process of redemption. To dig a great trench between the Church and the world is to attempt to separate what God has joined together in the redemption. "For [God our Father] has made known to us in all wisdom and insight the mystery of his will, according to his purpose which he set forth in Christ as a plan for the fullness of time, to unite all things in him, things in heaven and things on earth . . . he has put all things under his feet and has made him the head over all things for the church, which is his body, the fulness of him who fills all in all" (Eph. 1:9,10 and 22,23).

There is of course a deep division: between what is of grace and what is of sin, between obedience to God and idolatry, between the liberating truth and the enslaving lie. But this is a division within all human communities, ecclesiastical communities included, and within each individual man, believer or not. To show this division and to show us how, through grace, it may be overcome is the function of those many who are called to be witnesses, as prophets or teachers or martyrs. Not all who are thus called respond; but in every generation there are those who respond, most often in humility and obscurity, as in the case of the man who was perhaps the greatest witness to the truth in modern times, the Austrian peasant Jägerstätter (see Gordon Zahn, *In Solitary Witness*, 1964). It should also be noted that the civil rights movement, a movement only possible in a world radically affected by the process of redemption, has produced those who have witnessed to the truth through their deaths. James Chaney, Andrew Goodman, Michael Schwerner, James

210

Reeb are names that will not be forgotten. Those who suffer for the sake of justice are at the very heart of the gospel's concern.

Bonhoeffer has an interesting argument on this point. He notes that in our Lord's time it is the tax-gatherers and the prostitutes who are nearer to the kingdom of God than the respectable and law-abiding (Mt. 21:31); but that there are situations in our own day—he has Germany under the Nazis in mind—in which it is the just, in a quite worldly sense, who are close to Christ, not far from the kingdom. What this shows is that "Christ belongs both to the wicked and the good. He belongs to them both only as sinners . . . as men who in their wickedness and in their goodness have fallen away from the origin" (*Ethics*).

Are there any points, within the Church and within the world of our own day, where we can see a fruitful dialectical opposition that can be compared with the controversy over circumcision, or that controversy over Catholic teaching on civil and religious liberty that was settled definitely only at the Council? Each man will compile his own list. Both in the compiling of the list and in the resolution of the issues listed, we may be confident that we have the opportunity to encounter Jesus Christ in our own situation. He will come to us as Lord that through him and in the Spirit we may ask for the will of the Father to be made effectual, here, as in the heavenly places.

Let us suppose, then, that we have compiled our list, and that it includes such issues as contraception, the implications of the Christian calling for social and economic life, the duty of the Christian to the State under the conditions of modern warfare, the possibility of the ordination of women, and so on. Plainly, there is no guarantee that these issues will be resolved rightly or that they will even be posed rightly; there is not even a guarantee that we shall be aware in our own day that a given human phenomenon or possibility *is* an issue for the Christian conscience. Sensitiveness in matters of civil and religious liberty was very late in coming and the definitive changes of Vatican II were resisted to the end in the Council and are still resisted in practice

211

here and there. For centuries Christians failed to see, what would today be universally allowed, that chattel slavery is contrary to the mind of Christ. Such tasks, then, have to be approached with great humility and with a feeling for the ironies of history. Progressives and conservatives alike have at this point to take heed lest they fall victims to those forms of bad faith characteristic of their respective outlooks.

Is it in any way possible to state the conditions under which issues can be perceived as issues for the Christian conscience and can be resolved in such a way that a later generation may say that how they were resolved was in accordance with the mind of Christ? I think something can be said about this; and once again I think we can profit by looking at the great dispute over circumcision. The first witnesses and preachers are all of them Jews, children of the promise. Whatever traces of hellenistic thought forms there may be in the teaching of some of them, notably Paul and John, this is not combined with Judaism in a spirit of syncretism but is wholly subordinate to the categories of the revelation to Israel. The *ecclesia* is the new Israel or a continuation of the old Israel (1 Pet.). Further, Judaism is in this period a proselytizing religion and conversions to Judaism among the Gentiles are commonplace. "Devout men from every nation under heaven" (Acts, 2:5) enter the family of Israel, are circumcised and strive to keep the law.

In such a situation it must at first have seemed inevitable that conversion to the New Israel would entail, as well as what was crucially new in the Christian proclamation, circumcision and the acceptance of the law. There were dominical sayings that could be taken in this sense. It is clear even from the compressed and schematic account in the Acts of the Apostles, from echoes of the dispute in the synoptic gospels and from the references in Paul's letters, that it was only after a long and bitter conflict that the infant Church became clear that the implication of the preaching was that Christians could not be bound by the legal

212

and ceremonial requirements of Judaism, that there was no necessary connexion between the *ecclesia* and the synagogue.

Two things must be said about the conditions under which the discussion was possible and the issue in the end resolved. First, the institutional structure of the primitive Church is loose and polycentric; and to say this is not to deny the leading role of Peter and the decisive role of the witness of the apostles. Secondly, there is immense respect for charismatic authority, both as it shows itself in those who exercise institutional authority as well —Paul is the most extreme and obvious case, since his apostolic authority can be understood as springing from a unique charisma —and as it shows itself in men who stand outside the rudimentary institutional structure. Apollos (Acts, 18:24-28), who may be the author of the Letter to the Hebrews, is an example of this.

Now, it would be foolish to set out as a possible program for the Church today a return to the loose institutional structure of the primitive Church. All the same, we may see in the present epoch of reform the possibility of a measure of polycentrism and of a growth in respect for charismatic authority. Few would now deny that the centralization of the government of the Church in the West, and the repressive methods of the Holy Office, have produced among clergy and laity alike a passivity before institutional authority and a suspicion of charismatic leadersip that have together kept the Church from a serious confrontation with a variety of issues, some of which I have already listed. It would be a mistake to suppose that centralization and inquisitional discipline are alone responsible for this. The Orthodox churches have an even more melancholy record of passivity and withdrawal before the great secular issues that are also issues for the Christian conscience; and while we are all indebted to Protestantism for the prophetic witness of a Barth or a Bonhoeffer, we rightly shrink from the mere worldliness or the amiable heterodoxy into which contemporary Protestantism too easily dissolves. The great hope of the ecumenical movement is

213

that it should, by bringing within the Church the rich traditions of eastern Christianity and the Biblical concerns of the Protestant churches at their best, give to our life a more diversified structure, a more arresting texture. It is under such conditions, now as in the apostolic age, that the great issues can be posed and resolved.

It seems, then, that what at first we took to be absurd, that we should encounter Jesus Christ in the tensions and conflicts of the Church's institutional life and that issues may be posed and resolved by appealing from the Church to the Church, are possibilities after all. Only if we slip into a monophysite or docetic view of the Church—and these are the characteristic deformations of the Catholic religious attitude, in ecclesiology as in Christology, just as Arianism and adoptionism represent characteristic Protestant deformations—shall we be tempted to deny this. It is in our own historical situation, with all that belongs to it of darkness as well as of illumination, that we may hope to encounter Jesus Christ and to have his mind; but it is Jesus Christ we hope to encounter, and he is the Lord of this as of every other human situation; and to seek him is to find that we are not and cannot be separated from him. To be anxious and tormented, at least in a radical way, over the destiny of the humanity that has been redeemed and over the future of the Church, the sign of redemption, is implicitly to doubt that Jesus is the Lord.

IX.

Good-By Chalcedon, Hello What?
A Response

WILLIAM HAMILTON

OUR PRESENT theological ferment still has to do with the doctrine of God, and will continue so for some time to come. But in the midst of all our talk about God-talk, we've begun to recognize that our Christology (will we dare talk about Jesus-talk?) will have to manifest the same kind of risk that has become necessary and appropriate in our talk about God. Protestants have scarcely begun this new venture, so this symposium is both an important straw in the wind and a brick for our new building. All of us have reason to be grateful to the editors and the authors involved.

Chalcedon, it seems, is not to be in the center of the stage. It is barely inside the stage door. In these articles, it appears centrally only in Frederick Crowe's engaging attempt to persuade us that the intentions of the fifth-century fathers can be uncovered by a re-interpretation based on Lonergan's ontology. Surely even this shows us once again that any attempt to revive the *anhypostasia* ends up with a theologically impermissible reduction of the full humanity of Jesus, as when Father Crowe writes that "the human and proportionate act of existence is lacking in Christ and is supplied by the divine act of existence." The use of contemporary thought-forms to elucidate the fathers is likely to tell us more about the user than the used, and Protestants will be reminded of Bultmann's essay defending the World Council of Churches' doctrinal formula of Jesus as God and Savior, which purchases assent

215

to the formula by the rather dubious tour de force of making Cyril into a latent Bultmannian.

If we don't have Chalcedon, what do we have, and what should we have? Before coming to this, it may be useful for me to set down, quite imprecisely, some of the basic Christological styles that Protestantism has manifested over the last thirty years. This approach will do several things. It will permit me to be most useful to the continuing dialogue by being as Protestant and as opinionated as I can be; it will provide an alien structure to use for purposes of comparison; and it will show, I think, that part of the post-Chalcedonian mood in contemporary Catholic thought is consciously or unconsciously engaged in the task of recapitulating recent Protestant theological history. This latter point does not seem to me to be wholly healthy, for we do not serve one another best when we try to be most like the other.

In any case, recent Protestant Christology in America can be traced through five stages.

1. At the beginning of the neo-orthodox revival in America, in the mid-thirties, the church was strongly influenced by the Christology of Reinhold Niebuhr: the crucified Christ of suffering love, the one who confronts us with a radical (though empty) demand and with a radical (and not so empty) word of healing. No direct ethics or politics appeared possible from this Christ, so our politics and ethics became prudential and secular. The gulf between the church and the world, between *agape* and justice, received no theoretical bridge. In this collection of essays, Charles Curran seems to be working along very Niebuhrian lines. Christology, he tells us, is not to be located in the church, but in the world (we will return to this theme), and as with Niebuhr, we really do not have a Christology at all, but a lucid portrait of the ethics of Jesus and a call to obedience. Curran's admirable essay takes a Protestant reader back to "The Relevance of an Impossible Ethical Ideal," one of the finest and most influential of Niebuhr's writings. It is very close to that, and nearly as good, and that is meant as high praise indeed.

2. Niebuhr's Christology of suffering love was neither Christ-

ology nor ethics, and in the late Forties, as the continental theology came to be studied and absorbed, a new style came to the fore, and it was represented by Donald Baillie's admirable *God Was in Christ*. This was a deliberately irenic work that tried to be faithful to the dogmatic tradition as well as to be an historical-critical uncovering of the Jesus of history. The key to Baillie's project was his analysis of the "paradox of grace" as a piece of human experience which could cast some light on "very God, very man" of Chalcedon. Thomas Clarke, in this collection of essays, recalls Baillie's approach. He defends the legitimacy of using human experience as material for Christology (the actual human experience he stresses is remarkably like Baillie's paradox of grace) and he tries consciously to mediate between a too ecclesiastical and too worldly approach. Raymond Brown's essay on the resurrection also tries to locate a mid-point between an uncritical liberalism attending too much to the needs of modern man and an equally uncritical fundamentalism of tradition. Father Clarke's defense of a general incarnational theology as the background of the incarnation of the Son, further relates him to the worlds of Baillie and William Temple.

3. The Christology of Baillie was better as Christology than as ethics or politics. If it helped us find our way into the Church's past, it did not move us into the world of the present. The next Christological style might be described as that which emerged from the Americanization of Barth. The American Barth, it should be noted, was quite different from the Scottish one; *Church Dogmatics* IV/1 went to America, IV/2 went to Edinburgh. This meant that the human God, the suffering God (it is surely the Lutheran-Barthian world that is reflected in Bonhoeffer's "only a suffering God can help") enabled American thinkers to keep in touch both with the doctrine of the two natures and with the earlier image of the suffering Christ of Niebuhr. The Americanization of Barth proved, however, to be more fruitful for the church than for the world, and it was the American theologian as the grateful student of Barth that entered fully, for the first time, into the Catholic-Protestant dia-

217

logue. Barth became the ideologue of that dialogue in its initial
stages, as he had become, earlier, the theologian of the W.C.C.

4. The Bultmann-Barth controversy in Europe, as received in
America, developed our fourth Christological style. We received
Bultmann well after Barth's influence had taken hold, and indeed, Bultmann was received by a different community—by the
New Testament scholar, rather than by the theologians and the
preachers. Thus the impact of Bultmann in the Fifties wasn't
really a theological event at all in the narrow sense. It didn't help
us engage the problem of the two natures; it didn't really directly
help us in our Christological ethics at all (how can you find an
ethical structure for a spoken word or an eschatological act?),
but it turned us back to the old problem, which we once thought
Baillie had settled, of faith and history, but in new terms and
with new questions. Up to now, the Christologies had attempted
either to help us move back to the church's tradition or out into
the church's task into the world, or both. Bultmann and the post-
Bultmannians seemed interested in neither, for their concern was
to move us into scripture. Christology became transformed into
hermeneutics.

Avery Dulles presents, in this collection of essays, an admirable and lucid survey of the Bultmannian and post-Bultmannian
style. He notes its excesses, stays in the center, and seems to conclude as do the Anglicans (Turner, Mackinnon) and the German Lutherans (Stauffer, Althaus, Jeremias) that there is in the
New Testament a solider core of historical material than the
Bultmannians believe. But, when we read Father Dulles more
carefully, we notice that he is really talking about a kind of history that is different from mere factuality or chronicle. If we cannot preserve the basic historical character of the New Testament
kerygma, he seems to say, by using the concepts of history of the
practicing historians, we had better find another concept of history
that will enable us to preserve what must be preserved. So what
he really means by history is encounter, a sense of one's own
historicity, and he comes out about where H. Richard Niebuhr,

Richard R. Niebuhr, and the early James Robinson came out. "Once history is viewed," Father Dulles writes, "as an interpersonal event which may call for nothing short of a real conversion in opening of self to what previously lay beyond the range of expectation, the gospels assume greater historical significance." It is surely too desperate and fearful to devise, in order to rescue the New Testament from modernity, an almost private definition of history, one but dimly related to the work of practicing historians. In spite of such efforts, *Geschichte* has proved unable to vanquish *Historie*.

Since I am looking at the essays contained in this special issue through unashamedly Protestant eyes, it should be noted here how the current Catholic explorations of a "theology of presence" look from the outside. "Christian presence" appears to be very big just now. We are watching it emerge in the struggle against scholasticism in the doctrine of God, and in Bernard Cooke's essay we watch, with great interest, as it is put to work in Christology. It comes out, it would seem, very ecclesiastical, very pious—indeed, and about the place Protestants used to come out when they used their version of the same basic idea, "encounter." If your "presence" is indeed our "encounter," we can only say "good luck," and wait for the collapse.

5. Except for Gerhard Ebeling and some of the most recent work of James Robinson, the post-Bultmannian "new quest" gave us our bibles but not our world. The final Christological style I wish to mention attends to this undone task. This might be called incarnation as secularization. Here, the incarnation is interpreted as God becoming the wholly worldly man in Jesus. Thus, the man in Christ is to become, as a disciple of this Jesus, the worldly man, the man for others. It is not clear that this style has any overpowering advantages over the others, but it is here, I suspect, that much of the new work in Christology will be carried on. Will it be able to meet the three-fold test I have been asking of the other styles: the ability to drive us back to our historical tradition, the ability to drive us into scripture, the power

to move us into the world of our time? It would appear that it would certainly be able to do the third (though the ethical action of this style has been more impressive than the theory); that it might be possible to do the second (the work of James Robinson, Robert Funk, and Herbert Braun can be called to mind); and that it may have to give up any claim to do the first task at all (in much the same way that the case against scholasticism is being developed by Eugene Fontinell, Leslie Dewart, and Michael Novak). If we did admit to the inability of this "secular" Christtological style to return us happily to 325 or 451, it would not be because the Trinitarian and Christological formulas are "Greek" or "couched in substance metaphysics," but because they fail the church today in its primary task of proclaiming Christ to the world.

Perhaps the most striking question that underlies all of these essays, sometimes openly, sometimes lying concealed, is this: "How, to what extent, and to what end, can Christology be liberated from ecclesiology?" In many ways, I think this is the most important question for all of us to attend to today, and I am grateful that this symposium has brought it so interestingly to the fore. Part of the answer, of course, is that it cannot and must not be so liberated. Protestantism will never revert to its perennial temptation (which it learned, recall, not only from liberalism and from Luther but from Augustine—"God and the soul") to construe Christology as the rendering of the relation of the solitary believer to Christ. The important issue is not individualism versus community, but rather: "Just where in the world is that community prepared to be conformed to Christ?" Father Cooke and Mr. Cameron seem certain that this community is rather specifically identified with the visible church, and the latter writes the only sentence in this collection that genuinely horrified me: "To be anxious and tormented, at least in a radical way, over the destiny of the humanity that has been redeemed and over the future of the Church, the sign of redemption, is implicitly to doubt that Jesus is the Lord."

Where is the community prepared to be conformed to Christ? It may be the church; it may be in the church; it may not. It will certainly be in the world, whatever else. Thus, if I am constrained to confess that the worst sentence in this collection comes from a layman, it pleases me to be able to confess that the best sentence comes from a layman as well. It is this, from James Douglass' superb essay: "On seeking out the presence of Christ in his world, Christians must become therefore less and less interested in themselves as Christians and focus instead on the living reality of Christ, whether in belief or unbelief, as the invitation of suffering need and as the graceful response of suffering love."

This seems to me the direction most worth taking today. Protestant ethics is vacuous, and desperately needs some Christological reflection. We watch the dying gasps of our Catholicizing koinonia-ethics ventures, the striking shallowness of the situation-ethics and new morality debates, and Paul Ramsey's wonderfully non-conformist attack on the liberal establishment and John Bennett, giving comfort (through no fault of his own?) to Bill Buckley and David Lawrence. The rest of us run about in frustration, wondering what statements to sign and what laws to break. Douglass' invitation is a dangerous one, and there will always be those around to tell us we have reverted to the liberal heresy or to mindless activism. There are great dangers here, many mistakes likely, and a lot of work. But if we acknowledge we are bound to do our Christology in this way, and that we are seeking that community in which it can so be done, it is worth the risks.

I am writing these notes on October 28, three days before the celebration of the 450th anniversary of the nailing of the ninety-five theses to the door of the castle church at Wittenberg. In my morning paper is the story of Father Philip Berrigan and the Protestant minister James Mengel breaking into the office of the draft board in Baltimore and pouring blood on the records. If we can read this as clue to a common Christology, we have begun the long road back to our obedience and discipleship.

PART THREE

Spirit

I.

The Spirit in the New Testament

J. MASSINGBERD FORD

THE THEOLOGY of the Holy Spirit in the New Testament presents several problems, three of which are as follows. Firstly, in the synoptic gospels there are comparatively few references to the Holy Spirit, and Jesus' own teaching is confined to seven sayings, some of which New Testament scholars regard as interpolations by the early Church. Secondly, the Spirit is sometimes used "impersonally" and sometimes "personally." Thirdly, there are two extremely enigmatic sayings concerning the Holy Spirit: St. John says that the Spirit "was not yet" because Jesus was not yet glorified (Jn. 7:39); the disciples at Ephesus declare that they "have never even heard that there is a Holy Spirit" (Acts 19:2).

Why do the synoptic gospels speak so little about the Holy Spirit? The answer may lie in the problem of Christology itself, especially as regards the Divine Sonship of Jesus.

In recent times our picture of Judaism in the first centuries A.D. and B.C. has been changed considerably. Instead of a certain uniformity of belief and practice scholars have found an increasing diversity. It is within this setting that we must set the formulation of both New Testament Christology and Pneumatology. With few exceptions (such as the Elephantine community of Jews in Egypt, for example), the Jewish people contemporary with Jesus held resolutely to a monotheistic belief, but beyond this there were lively discussions concerning the transcendency and immanence of God. Some schools of thought sought to avoid any suspicion of anthropomorphism or tangible mystical experiences. They were, if you will, the rationalists of the day, who sought to make the biblical text more acceptable to "modern man" by "demythologizing" and allegorization. On the opposite side stood those who admitted certain and varying degrees of anthropomorphism and accepted wholeheartedly the intervention of Providence in human affairs: some of these thinkers believed they experienced the sensible presence of God in various modes. Some accepted many writings, especially of a mystical nature, which later were precluded from the canon; they were inclined to read certain biblical texts almost literally. One pertinent example is the dispute between the schools concerning Exodus 15:3: "The Lord is a man of War, the Lord is his name." All could say that God is not a man but some could aver "that God reveals Himself as man for the sanctification of Israel." In the same strain it was reported that God appeared as an old man in the Temple when Simeon the High Priest was offering sacrifice.

It was those who believed so fervently in the immanence of God in this world, and expected him to take an interest in the smallest detail of human life, who went to such lengths in their beliefs. Essentially it was a belief in the presence and activity of Yahweh under various guises and in different forms.

Therefore, when we turn to the question of Christology and Pneumatology we must first ask about the Jewish beliefs in the presence of Yahweh. The theology of the Spirit is only one section of this. The presence of Yahweh in biblical and extra-biblical works is expressed under some of the following titles:

The Word: There are two main Semitic words for this, *Dibbur* and *Memra. Dibbur* usually denotes the spoken word, while *Memra* seems to have been a more concrete hypostasis of the Deity and to have something of a personality. So, for example, the *Memra* of God walks in the garden of Eden, closes the door of the ark; conducts himself as a support for Abraham and Moses, and, in a text known to Roman Catholics from the Christmas Mass, smites the first-born in Egypt:

226

For while gentle silence enveloped all things,
and night in its swift course was now half gone,
thy all-powerful word leaped from heaven, from the royal throne,
into the midst of the land that was doomed,
a stern warrior carrying the sharp sword of thy authentic command,
and stood and filled all things with death,
and touched heaven while standing on the earth (Wis. 18:15–17).*

Although many Jewish readers might accept this type of text as mere metaphor, others concurred with the possibility of such an apparition of the deity. The paraphrases of the Hebrew lessons recited in the synagogue taught the congregation that the *Memra* had delivered them from Egypt, accompanied them on their travel to the promised land and been "God with them" throughout life, but they also looked forward to a second redemption wrought by the Word. Thus, when the people listened to Deuteronomy they would hear "When the Word of the Lord shall reveal himself to redeem his people, he will say to all the nations: Behold, now that I am he who am, and was, and will be, . . . I, in my Word, kill and make alive . . ."

That is they learnt that the *Memra* would have a central role in salvation history.

Wisdom: Closely associated with the *Memra* with its "personal" aspects was the concept of Wisdom conceived as "created" before the world, the "firstborn" who had a part in creation and delighted to be with the children of men (Proverbs 8:22). It is not sufficient to see Wisdom merely from the primocanonical books; for example, one can see from Wisdom of Solomon that the personification of Wisdom is very close in function and character to the *Memra.* In Wisdom 10:1—12:27 the historical illustrations of the power of Wisdom bear close affinity to those of the Word in the *targum* (that is, the Aramaic free translation of the Hebrew Bible).

* All biblical quotations are taken from the Revised Standard Version.

227

The Shekinah and the Glory: Akin to the manifestations of Yahweh expressed by Spirit, *Memra* and Wisdom are the concepts of *Shekinah* and Glory. Whereas these, to all intents and purposes, were the invisible or intangible activity of Yahweh, the *Shekinah* and the Glory were often the visible, well-nigh palpable aspect of Yehweh in the world; both were usually a sign of his favor. *Shekinah* is not a biblical word but is frequent in the *targumim* and very frequently is interchangeable with "Holy Spirit." It derives from a Semitic root meaning to dwell and can mean the royal residence or sovereignty but it is also used of the immanence of God among his people. The *Shekinah* often appears as a light or bright cloud, and her activities are sometimes interchangeable with that of the *Memra.*

"Glory" is difficult to dissociate from *Shekinah*: It is God's splendor, honor and power. In the *targum* one often reads "the glory of the Shekinah of Yahweh"; it is used consistently for the divine and heavenly mode of being and is presented as the object of perception. It is the *Shekinah* and the Glory which lead the Israelites in the desert in the cloud and fiery pillar, are revealed on Mount Sinai to Moses, descend on the Tent of Meeting (Exodus 33:7-11) and fill the Temple (1 Kings 8:10-13). Many believed that the *Shekinah* accompanied her people into exile, suffered and wept with them and that they would bask in her Glory in the world to come; that is, they would be before the throne of Glory.

The concepts of the throne of Yahweh and His Glory are brought to a climax in Isaiah 6 and in Ezekiel and Daniel:

Ezekiel *1:26-28*	Ezekiel *8:2-4*	Daniel *7:9-10, 13-14*
And above the firmament over their heads there was the likeness of a throne, in appearance like sapphire; and seated above the likeness of	Then I beheld, and, lo, a form that had the appearance of a man; below what appeared to be his loins it was fire, and above his loins it was like	As I looked, thrones were placed and one that was ancient of days took his seat; his raiment was white as snow, and the hair of his head like pure

a throne was a likeness as it were of a human form. And upward from what had the appearance of his loins I saw as it were gleaming bronze, like the appearance of fire enclosed round about; and downward from what had the appearance of his loins I saw as it were the appearance of fire, and there was brightness round about him. Like the appearance of the bow that is in the cloud on the day of rain, so was the appearance of the brightness round about.

the appearance of brightness, like gleaming bronze. He put forth the form of a hand, and took me by a lock of my head; and the Spirit lifted me up between earth and heaven, and brought me in visions of God to Jerusalem, to the entrance of the gateway of the inner court that faces north, where was the seat of the image of jealously, which provokes to jealousy. And behold, the glory of the God of Israel was there, like the vision that I saw in the plain.

wool; his throne was fiery flames, its wheels were burning fire. A stream of fire issued and came forth from before him; a thousand thousands served him, and ten thousand times ten thousand stood before him; the court sat in judgment, and the books were opened. . . .

I saw in the night visions, and behold, with the clouds of heaven there came one like a son of man, and he came to the Ancient of Days and was presented before him. And to him was given dominion and glory and kingdom, that all peoples, nations, and languages should serve him; his dominion is an everlasting dominion, which shall not pass away, and his kingdom one that shall not be destroyed.

These texts show once again the idea of God appearing as if in human form. A persuasive, yet somewhat neglected, argument has been presented by Père André Feuillet (in *Revenue Biblique* —60, 1953, 170-202, and 321-346). He recalls the influence of Ezekiel on the book of Daniel in general and suggests also that Ezekiel has influenced the idea of the Son of Man. Both Ezekiel and Isaiah see the glory of Yahweh, that is, *"des manifestations de la transcendence divine dans la nature et dans l'histoire."* For Ezekiel the glory of God, is, as it were, materialized. Not only can the seer localize the divine glory, he describes it ". . . *'C' est comme une figure d' homme'."* The upper part of the body is like gleaming bronze, the rest like brightness and the rainbow (cf. Ezek. 8:2). The phrase "like a figure of a man" is used to describe angels, but if one relates the background of Ezekiel to the mysterious figure of the Son of Man in Daniel it appears to be *"une sorte de manifestation visible de Dieu invisible."* Feuillet concludes that, taking into consideration this and other data, one may suggest that the Son of Man in Daniel belongs to the category of the divine and is like *"une sorte d' incarnation de la gloire divine, au même titre que la silhouette humaine contemplée par Ezechiél* (1:26)." To him is given glory and dominion.

This, therefore, is the acme of the presence, activity and visibility of the "Spirit" or presence of Yahweh. It is this type of Jewish Pneumatology which may have prepared the way for the incarnation of Christ. It is in this context, too, in which we may understand Baruch 3:35-37 concerning wisdom:

> This is our God;
> no other can be compared to him!
> He found the whole way to knowledge,
> and gave her to Jacob his servant
> and to Israel whom he loved.
> *Afterward she [Wisdom] appeared upon earth*
> *and lived among men.*

Most scholars could accept this as Christian, yet the quotation is no more difficult to accept than the statements about "seeing" the *Shekinah*, or Glory of God, or "seeing" God as an old man in the Temple. The least that one may assert is that the Jews as a whole did not overemphasize the transcendence of God but some, indeed, stressed the immanence, and these may well have been more ready to accept the incarnate God. We must not for-

230

get that very many Jews did accept Jesus. Sometimes one is apt to think that all rejected him and only the Gentiles accepted him!

Let us turn now to the New Testament to see whether some of the passages may suggest that 1) Jesus was considered the Incarnate Word, *Shekinah,* Glory, Presence, Wisdom or Spirit of God and 2) whether Jesus fulfilled in a new way the signs and wonders manifested by these aspects of the "spirit" of Yahweh for the Chosen People.

The infancy narratives of Matthew and Luke show this fairly clearly. In Matthew the "Genesis" of Jesus is as follows: Mary conceives from (the) Holy Spirit (literally, in the Semitic language, of the Spirit of the Holiness); how else could a Jewish writer express "Emmanuel" (God with us,) the immanence of God with His people? In Luke this is even clearer. As René Laurentin and others have shown so aptly, for Mary's conception of Jesus, St. Luke uses the verb for the Spirit overshadowing the desert tabernacle and, once again, there is a hint back to Genesis. Moreover, the influence of Daniel is felt, especially Daniel 9:17: "Now therefore, O our God, hear the prayer of thy servant, and his supplications, and cause they face to shine upon thy sanctuary that is desolate, for the Lord's sake."

The purpose of the Old Testament allusions is obvious. The presence of Yahweh to his people, the Daughter of Sion, is fulfilled when Jesus dwells within the womb of Mary, who has become the personification of the people of God in a concrete way. The parallel between Mary and Jesus and the *Shekinah* and ark is continued in Luke 1:39-44, 56 because just as David moved the ark, which symbolized the presence of Yahweh, allowed it to remain at Obededom for three months and danced before it at Jerusalem, so Mary stays with Elizabeth for three months, John leaps before her, and finally she goes to Jerusalem.

However, the clearest "*Shekinah* infancy narrative" is St. John's Prologue. It is a hymn celebrating the Word (*Memra*) and/or *Shekinah* become flesh. Here the concepts of "Word," "Dwelling" and "Glory" are closely associated, as C. F. Burney

231

saw some years ago. The word "dwell" suggests the Jewish doctrine of the *Shekinah* "or visible *dwelling* of Yahweh among His people, typified by the pillar of cloud standing above the Tent of Meeting, as subsequently in Solomon's Temple." (C. F. Burney, *The Aramaic Origin of the Fourth Gospel.* Oxford 1922, p. 35) The phrase "we behold his Glory" is "a clear reference to a second term in the *Targums* to describe God's Self-manifestation to mankind, the Glory of the Lord. The *Targums* employ *Yehara* (Fear), like *Shekinah,* in paraphrasing passages which, as they stand in the Hebrew might be taken to describe the appearance of God in bodily form" (p. 36) Burney refers to the hypostatization of the Word in Ps. 107:20, Ps. 33:6. He concludes, "This is evidence that, so far from his owing his logos-doctrine to an Alexandrine source, he is soaked through and through with Palestinian Jewish thought which is represented by the *Targums.* Nor would the teaching of the Prologue need time for its development. Any disciple of our Lord who had heard the Targumic rendering of the O.T. in the synagogue, and who was capable of recognizing a superhuman power shining through the Master's Personality in His mighty acts, of detecting the Divine voice in His teaching, and at length of apprehending that in His Presence on earth God had come to dwell among men, could hardly fail to draw the inference that here was the grand fulfillment of O.T. conceptions so familiar to him through the Aramaic paraphrase" (p. 39).

Thus in all the evangelists' infancy narratives, Jesus is shown to be the incarnation of the Spirit or presence of Yahweh but not the Father himself. The mystical or anthropomorphic ideas became historic.

Now we should take a glance at a few examples of the correlation between the characteristics and functions of these manifestations of Yahweh and the symbolic actions and historical events which occurred in Jesus' life. We shall confine ourselves to parallels with the phenomenon known as the *Gilluy Shekinah.* This means a special revelation of *Shekinah* usually in a concrete mode and often on a definite occasion. The word *"Shekinah"* need not necessarily occur in the text but the revelation is of God himself.

The Baptism of Jesus: A *Gilluy Shekinah* was supposed to have occurred at the crossing of the Red Sea. One citation reads: [He revealed Himself in . . . two opposite ways] "so as not to give the excuse to the Nations of the World to say that there are two Powers . . . He was in Egypt, He was at the (Red) Sea; He was in the past, He will be in the future . . . ; He is in this world, He will be in the World to Come." (Max Kadushin, *The Rabbinic Mind,* Blaisdell, 1965, p. 230.)

However, Professor W. D. Davies, in *The Setting of the Sermon on the Mount* (Cambridge, 1964), has demonstrated a more illustrative background. He cites several ancient Jewish texts which show the tradition that Yahweh Himself was revealed crossing the Red Sea:

". . . when the Holy One . . . revealed Himself at the sea, no one had to ask: 'Which one is the king?' But as soon as they saw Him they recognized Him, and they all opened their mouths and said: 'This is my God and I will glorify Him." In short, God himself was seen at work *at* the crossing of the sea.' Professor Davies also calls attention to the fact that in the *Mekilta* (Commentary) on Exodus 14:13:

"The Holy Spirit . . . then rested upon them [the Israelites] presumably to give them confidence in the presence and power of God. At the same moment, Israel is compared to a dove . . . also, although the express phrase 'the heavens were opened' is not used, this is what is implied to have happened, because squadrons of the heavenly hosts appear to the Israelites' sight, that is, they are granted a vision in which God reveals his power to save."

Against this background we may suggest that the people saw in the baptism of Jesus a parallel to the revelation of Yahweh at the Red Sea. This also appears to have been the background to Jesus' walking on the sea, (Matthew 14:28 ff. and parallels).

Compare "Thus says the Lord, who makes a way in the sea, a path in the mighty waters . . ." (Isaiah 63:16-20). We might say, therefore, that a *gilluy Shekinah* occurred at the river Jordan.

The Manna and the Multiplications of Loaves: The relationship between the "Spirit of Yahweh" and heavenly food and the light it sheds upon Jesus' actions is seen most clearly in John 6. The first part of this discourse reflects the banquet proffered by wisdom in Proverbs 8 and 9 and is, therefore, a wisdom motif possibly illustrating that "Man does not live by bread alone" (cf. Jesus' temptation); but the second part turns to the manna which was provided in the wilderness. In some circles there was a Jewish tradition that the manna was the *ziv* (radiance) of the *Shekinah* which was endowed with physical properties; this was the nourishment of Israelites in the desert, of Moses on Sinai, of the angels and of the first in the world to come. In John 6, therefore, the person of Jesus probably is associated with the concepts of Wisdom and *Shekinah* and he says that he will be the sustenance of those who eat his body and blood. In baptism Jesus repeats the event of the Red Sea, in John 6 the event of the manna in the desert.

The Transfiguration: This is a climax in the earthly life of Jesus as regards the *Shekinah* motif and in one way it is a corollary to the Lucan birth narratives. Jesus is transfigured in terms not unlike the visions of Ezekiel, Daniel and the Apocalypse and a *bath qol* (a voice from heaven which often occurs when a decision has been reached) identifies him as the Son of God. However, the account which harmonizes most completely with the Jewish concept of the *gilluy Shekinah* is found in 2 Peter 1:16-19:

"For we did not follow cleverly devised myths when we made known to you the power and coming of our Lord Jesus Christ, but we were eyewitnesses of his majesty. [Note that "majesty" is predicated of Christ.] For when he received honor and glory from God the Father and the voice was borne to him by the

234

Majestic Glory, 'This is my beloved Son, with whom I am well pleased,' we heard this voice borne from heaven, for we were with him on the holy mountain. And we have the prophetic word made more sure. You will do well to pay attention to this as to a lamp shining in a dark place, until the day dawns and the morning star rises in your hearts."

Here we have the very term "Majestic Glory" which denotes the presence of the *Shekinah,* but Jesus is clearly seen as "Son." Further, we are taken back, not so much to the Feast of Tabernacles but to Mount Sinai (the Jewish Feast of Pentecost) where the giving of the law and the bestowal of prophecy are given.

Thus far, we have attempted to see the New Testament writers' feeling toward an expression of their concept of Jesus of Nazareth. For them, through the human nature of Jesus, shone the glory of the *Shekinah* which had returned in the fullness of its power to the earth. The point reached eventually is perhaps a binitarian view of the deity. The later sections of the New Testament and the early patristic works were to develop more precisely and definitively the trinitarian concept which is hinted in the New Testament. But perhaps the absence of many references to the Holy Spirit in the synoptic gospels and the oscillation between the character and functions of the Spirit and those of Christ in the Pauline epistles may be explained by the fact that at first Jesus was almost identified with the "Spirit" of Yahweh. This may also account for the impersonal references to the Spirit.

The declaration of Jesus as the Son of God by a *bath qol,* by his living relationship with the Father and by his own designation as "Son of Man" * (which I believe to be an euphemism for the Son of God), persuaded Jesus' disciples toward a binitarian view of the deity. After Jesus' resurrection and ascension he sent his Spirit upon his disciples. It would appear that first of all they

---

* The Greek for the title "Son of Man," literally translated is "The Son of the Man," where it is used without reference to Jesus, the Greek translation would read "the son of man."

thought of this Spirit as the Spirit of Jesus analogous to the Spirit of Yahweh, that is, a manifestation of him, a facet of his risen person but as not a distinct person.

What eventually could have persuaded them that there were three persons in the deity? To answer this we must try first to obtain an understanding of Pentecost. Pentecost appears to have occurred on the Jewish Feast of Weeks, which commemorated the Covenant on Mount Sinai and the Giving of the *Torah;* it was also the birthday of the Jewish nation. Apparently there were current Jewish beliefs that the *Shekinah* had her original home among men but that She had gradually withdrawn into the upper heavens owing to the increasing sin of mankind. Yet, through the merits of seven righteous men, She gradually returned until by the time of Moses She was prepared to rest upon every individual on Mount Sinai and every individual would have the power to prophesy. This tradition is illustrated by the following text from *Numbers Rabbah* XIII, 2:

". . . When Adam sinned, the Shechinah withdrew to the first . . . heaven, when Cain sinned to the second . . . the generations of Enoch to the third (*et cetera*) . . . Then six righteous men arose, and they brought the Shechinah back to the earth. For Abraham brought it back to the sixth heaven, Isaac to the fifth . . . Moses finally brought it back from the upper world to the lower world [that is, the earth]. For indeed the wicked cause the Shechinah to ascend from the earth, while the righteous cause it to dwell on the earth. When exactly did the Shechinah come down upon the earth? On the day when the Sanctuary was set up, as it is said, 'Then the cloud covered the tent of meeting, and the glory of the Lord filled the Sanctuary'." (Compare this passage to John 3:13.) *

---

* This is one tradition. Another tradition is remarked by H. Parzen, in "The Ruah Hakodesh in Tannaitic Literature," *Jewish Quarterly Review,* n.s. 20 (1929-30) 51-76. The following quotation is from p. 54: "Generally speaking, there were two momentous ages which may be regarded as landmarks in the prevalence of the Ruah Hakodesh (Holy Spirit) in Israel's midst. Up to the time of the 'Ascension' of Elijah, the Rabbis be-

However, the Israelites committed the sin of the Golden Calf and the Shekinah was obliged to withdraw. Therefore She was destined to rest only upon chosen individuals. Yet many Jews looked to the restoration of the Holy Spirit in the Messianic Age, and they quoted Joel 2:28-32 to that effect:

And it shall come to pass afterward, that I will pour out my spirit upon all flesh; and your sons and your daughters shall prophesy, your old men shall dream dreams, your young men shall see visions: And also upon the servants and upon the handmaids in those days will I pour out my spirit. And I will shew wonders in the heavens and in the earth, blood, and fire, and pillars of smoke. The sun shall be turned into darkness, and the moon into blood, before the great and the terrible day of the Lord come. And it shall come to pass, that whosoever shall call on the name of the Lord shall be delivered: for in mount Zion and in Jerusalem shall be deliverance, as the Lord hath said, and in the remnant whom the Lord shall call.

Then they believed the Holy Spirit would rest upon all, Jew and Gentile, slave and free, man and woman. The early Christians believed that this happened at Pentecost after the ascension of Jesus: this was the promise of the Father (Luke 24:49), for when Jesus had atoned for sin all obstacles to the restoration of the Holy Spirit to the whole community had been removed. St. Luke portrays Pentecost as analogous to the conception of Jesus. The power from on high descended not only upon Mary but upon the whole assembly which she had prefigured. They conceived in a spiritual sense the Spirit of the resurrected Jesus; perhaps they thought they received the second person of the deity rather than the third.

Yet Pentecost also shows affinity to the baptism of Jesus. The gifts received by the Church and the signs and wonders which the

---

lieved, the Ruah Hakodesh was experienced by Israel most frequently. With his 'secretion' a diminution set in which reached its climax with the death of the last three prophets, Haggai, Zechariah and Malachi. With their demise the Ruah Hakodesh also passed away, (note 8 Tosefta, Sotah 12, 5 and 13, 2)." This tradition is interesting in view of the Elijah typology of St. Luke.

spirit of Jesus performed through them enabled them to go out on a public ministry like Jesus after his baptism. The whole Church as a body reproduced the ministry of Jesus. This is shown in theory in St. Paul's teaching in 1 Corinthians 12:4-11:

Now there are diversities of gifts, but the same Spirit. And there are differences of administrations, but the same Lord. And there are differences of administrations, but the same God which worketh all in all. But the manifestation of the Spirit is given to every man to profit withal. For to one is given by the Spirit the word of wisdom; to another the word of knowledge by the same Spirit; To another faith by the same Spirit; to another the gifts of healing by the same Spirit; To another the working of miracles; to another prophecy; to another discerning of spirits; to another divers kinds of tongues; to another the interpretation of tongues: But all these worketh that one and the selfsame Spirit, dividing to every man severally as he will.

It is shown in practice in the Acts of Apostles. One notes that, except for the gift of "tongues" and "interpretation," all the ministries described in 1 Corinthians 12 were formerly performed by Jesus. He spoke with wisdom (Matthew 13:54) and brought knowledge; he healed; he performed miracles; he possessed the gifts of prophecy (Mark 14 *passim*) and he was able to discern the spirit of man (John 2:25) and to cast out evil spirits. In the same way, the Spirit of Wisdom, Understanding, Knowledge and Counsel are remarked in the disciples (Acts 4:13; 16:10; 20:22-27 16:6-10) because Isaiah 11:2-5 (the servant's endowment with the Spirit) has been fulfilled in them, too. They performed miracles similar to those of Jesus and preached and were rejected in the same way: they were sustained by the Spirit of Might. Above all they produced in the community a unanimous spirit of joy, peace and love, the fruits of the Spirit (compare Galatians 5:22-26).

In traditional Judaism, it was the Holy Spirit who enabled men and women to possess these gifts and they were endowed with these not merely for their own sanctification but for the building up of the community. In his informative article Dr. Parzen speaks about the character and functions of the Holy Spirit in Judaism. He summarizes the subjective effects of the Holy Spirit as follows: "To sum up briefly what the Ruah Hakodesh (the Holy Spirit) from the standpoint of effect means . . . It connotes prophecy and wisdom, poetic inspiration, spiritual purity and spiritual exaltation" (p. 75). These were fully realized by Jesus and yet we never hear of his being called as a prophet or inspired by the Holy Spirit: in reality the Holy Spirit does not need to rest upon him because he is the Son of God by nature. But the Church as a whole is endowed by grace with the gifts of the Spirit, which were given only to chosen individuals in the Old Testament. This means that the Holy Spirit is no longer given by measure (John 3:34) or to a Chosen Race but to all who believe on the Lord Jesus. Further, the Church at her Eucharistic worship represented the same gifts or ministries as illustrated by Parzen. St. Paul describes them in 1 Corinthians 14:26-33:

How is it then, brethren? when ye come together, every one of you hath a psalm, hath a doctrine, hath a tongue, hath a revelation, hath an interpretation. Let all things be done unto edifying. If any man speak in an unknown tongue, let it be at the most by three, and that by course and let one interpret. But if there be no interpreter, let him keep silence in the church; and let him speak to himself, and to God. Let the prophets speak two or three, and let the other judge. If anything be revealed to another that sitteth by, let the first hold his peace. For ye may all prophesy one by one, that all may learn, and all may be comforted. And the spirits of the prophets are subject to the prophets. For God is not the author of confusion, but of peace, as in all churches of the saints.

At this worship they share in the resurrected body and blood of Jesus.

So the Christian community finds itself producing the life of Jesus by the power of the Spirit. It is then, perhaps, in the actual experience of this, that they begin to realize that the Holy Spirit is a distinct person from Jesus and has come as another Paraclete (both Jesus and the Holy Spirit appear to have been called "Paraclete") when Jesus ascended (John 16:7). Hence it may be that the word "given" was added to the Johannine text "the Spirit was not yet" and this also may explain why the disciples at Ephesus apparently had heard of "Jesus" but not of the Holy Spirit. They must have heard of Jesus from John the Baptist.

This essay has suggested that the Pauline epistles (perhaps on the whole our earliest witness to Christian thought) vacillated between Christ himself and the Spirit; St. Paul also alternates between an impersonal and a personal use of the Spirit. The synoptic gospels in some passages see Christ as the incarnation of the *Shekinah*; in other passages there seems to be a distinction. His designation "The Son of The Man" fulfilled the prophecies of Ezekiel and Daniel concerning the "incarnation" of the Glory of Yahweh. St. John gives more information about the Holy Spirit as distinct from Jesus, but, in what are, perhaps, earlier strata of the gospel material Jesus is seen as the incarnate *Shekinah*. The Acts of Apostles see the Spirit of the resurrected Jesus descend upon the infant Church but then give some hints that the Spirit is distinct from the Spirit of the risen Jesus. In early patristic works there is the same ambiguity between Jesus as Logos and Wisdom and the Spirit as such; it is only later that separate treatises are devoted to the Holy Spirit.

We need not be disturbed by the slow evolution of Pneumatology, but perhaps the contemporary Western Church should express some regret in having been slower than the Eastern Church to recognize the dynamic activity of the Holy Spirit. The encyclical of Leo XIII and Pope John XXIII's "New Pentecost" threw the activity of the Holy Spirit into high relief, and the present neo-Pentecostalism and other Spirit-filled movements may (or may not) show us more of his Power. The extraordinary charismata and the almost miraculous unity of understanding, love, peace and joy in the eucumenical movement today suggest that these signs, like those in the Acts of Apostles, are efficacious, prophetic symbols that in the Holy Spirit Christians may see soon the realization of Jesus' prayer ". . . that they may all be one; even as thou, Father, art in me, and I in thee, that they also may be in us, so that the world may believe that thou hast sent me" (John 17:21).

II.

The Spirit in Catholic Thought

EDWARD D. O'CONNOR

IN THE NEW TESTAMENT, the Holy Spirit appears as the dynamic principle of the Christian life. He led Jesus about in his life on earth and, after the resurrection, was imparted to all the disciples in order to cleanse, renew, vivify, strengthen, illumine, teach and guide them. In modern times, however, for many Christians he has become simply the third person of the Blessed Trinity—a colorless, odorless, tasteless entity with no evident practical *raison d'être.*

This has not come about simply through a gradual accumulation of oblivion down through the centuries. The truth is that the Holy Spirit went into a sort of eclipse very soon after the apostolic era, and has been emerging from it gradually, and with occasional setbacks, ever since. Our own day is at once the depository of the sediments of neglect that date particularly from the eighteenth century, and the witness to a rediscovery of the Spirit that fulfills a movement that began in the third century.

To trace this history,* we must distinguish between two spheres: the manifestation of the Spirit in the Church, and the knowledge

* There does not yet exist an adequate history of the theology of the Holy Spirit. The present essay is meant as nothing more than a sketch of the contours of such a history, and an indication of areas that require fuller exploration. No doubt, many of the judgments made here will eventually need to be qualified; they are offered with that understanding.

Already, in this "second edition" of the paper that appeared in Commonweal, I have modified the paragraphs devoted to St. Augustine, in order to place the emphasis more justly on the positive side of his pneumatology, and have slightly rephrased the statement about Adam Moehler.

242

of the Spirit by the Church. The initial eclipse occurred in both these spheres; but from then on their histories are quite different. The manifestation referred to here consists of the extraordinary charisms such as prophecy, healing, speaking in tongues, discernment of spirits, etc. In the primitive Christian community, as it can be glimpsed through the Acts of the Apostles and the Epistles of St. Paul, they occurred with a frequency that astounds modern readers. In the course of the second century, however, they diminished: the gift of tongues seems to have disappeared altogether; prophecy and the power of healing and miracles became the prerogative of rare and exceptional individuals. Charismatic activity never completely disappeared from the Church; every age has had its miracle workers, prophets and inspired preachers. Nevertheless, a definite change seems to have taken place from a regime in which the operation of charisms was normal in each local church, to one in which their appearance is a rare phenomenon that provokes astonishment and even a kind of scandal.

This change does not seem to have evoked any comment from the earliest Christian writers, who were its contemporaries; hence we can be sure that it came about gradually, and that there never had been a time in which all Christians were charismatic in this sense. For the same reason, it is impossible to trace the history of the transition. However, it must have been substantially complete before the end of the second century, when the Montanists laid claim to a new spirit of prophecy, reviving that which had died out in the Church at large.

This relative disappearance of the charisms must be one of the most momentous changes that ever took place in the history of the Church. Traditionally, it has been explained on the grounds that charisms were necessary for the expansion of the Church in primitive times, but are no longer. However, there are critics who charge that the development of hierarchical offices in the sub-apostolic Church choked out the original charismatic leadership, or more simply that the primitive fervor was gradually lost, causing the Spirit to withdraw. In truth, however, each of these explanations is glib and inadequate; all of them need to be reconsidered in the light of a deeper understanding of the role of the charismatic in the Church.

One principle, enunciated by 1 Corinthians 13, and confirmed and clarified by the collective spiritual experience of the Church, is that the chief and essential action of the Spirit in the Church does not lie in the manifest charisms, but in the invisible work of sanctification. The charisms are given in the freedom of the Spirit when and in what measure they are useful. Their presence is not a sure sign of sanctity, and their relative disappearance does not imply a withdrawal of the Paraclete from the Church. In fact, the continual emergence of saints in all eras is a surer sign of his unfailing fecundity than those manifestations of which St. Paul could say, "If I should speak with the tongues of men and of angels, and have not charity, I have become a tinkling brass and a sounding cymbal."

When we turn from the sphere of manifestation to that of knowledge, our history grows more complex. Here, too, there occurred a partial eclipse in the second century.

The early generations of Christians were not able to appreciate the full riches of the apostolic teaching. On the subject of the Holy Spirit, as on many other topics, there is an evident impoverishment when we pass from the New Testament to the apostolic Fathers or the apologists. It is as though the human mind had been quite unable to assimilate all at once the rich nourishment left it by Christ. The Church could take in, as it were, only a few basic ideas at the start; it had to live off them, be formed by them and grounded in them, before it would be able, as there was occasion, to turn to some other point that had meanwhile lain more or less dormant, and begin to draw out its potential.

There is a special reason why the Holy Spirit in particular suffered from neglect. Of all the divine persons, he is the most difficult to conceive. The Son, of course, is the easiest, because of

244

his human flesh. The Father occupies, as it were, the place always attributed to the one God before the revelation of the Trinity; in addition, he has appropriated the name of Father, so rich in meaning associations. But the Spirit resides in an obscure unimaginability which doves and tongues of fire do little to relieve.

It is true that the Spirit has the great advantage of being the one sent by Christ to stay permanently with us, and act in us. Accordingly, the earliest idea of the Spirit, that which scripture itself gives us, conceives him in function not of his nature, but of his activity. However, this is all the more reason why, when his works ceased to be so manifest, his person became harder to keep in view.

In any case, it seems that the second-century apologists, Justin, Athenagoras, Irenaeus, Theophilus and even Clement of Alexandria, all had an inadequate notion of the Holy Spirit. Some scholars go so far as to claim that these writers regarded the Spirit as nothing more than the spiritual presence and action of Christ, although others defend their orthodoxy. But the very fact that such a controversy is possible indicates how vague and indefinite their notion was.

The great question which preoccupied the Church Fathers was how to conceive of the Son of God in a monotheistic religion. The Trinitarian and Christological debates of the third, fourth and fifth centuries were all aspects of this one problem. The question of the Spirit was dealt with mainly as a corollary. This mentality is evident in the "Apostles" Creed (ca. 200) which, after a long clause about the Son, adds only "I believe in the Holy Spirit . . ." for the third person. In fact, the Church was to require many centuries, not only to settle the place of the Son in its doctrine, but also to assimilate him fully into its piety. This task was not completed (if it ever can be completed) until the establishment of devotion to the Sacred Heart beginning in the seventeenth and eighteenth centuries.

The question of the Holy Spirit was, however, forced upon the

245

attention of theologians during the fourth century, by the appearance of the *"pneumatomachoi"* who expressly denied his divinity. This was easy enough to do, since the nature of the Spirit is not dealt with directly in scripture. Hence, paradoxically, it was the nature and person of the Spirit that first became the object of theological discussion and dogmatic definition, if we prescind from the minor, although not insignificant discussions raised by Marcion (d. ca. 160). The activity of the Spirit, about which scripture has much more to say, received relatively less attention from the theologians.

The great point which had to be made was that the Holy Spirit is not just the power of God active in the world, but is a distinct person, equal to and coeternal with, the Father and the Son, even though he proceeds from the Father and is not a Son. Arguing from the activity attributed to the Spirit in scripture, the great doctors of the fourth century, Athanasius, Basil and Gregory Naziansen, established this doctrine for all future ages. The fruit of their labors is expressed in the "Nicene Creed," which still reflects the dependence of the pneumatological question on the christological: ". . . and in the Holy Spirit, the Lord and giver of life, who proceeds from the Father, who together with the Father and the Son is adored and glorified, who spoke through the prophets."

Whereas the nature of the Spirit and his place in the Trinity thus came to be settled relatively early,* his activity in the sanctification of souls took much longer. In fact, it has not yet received the comprehensive formulation it requires. But down through the ages, different cultures and different epochs have each added their contribution to a pneumatology which is only today beginning to discover its full stature.

---

* In the ninth century, a fierce debate arose when the Greek Church objected to the Latin addition *Filioque* to the Nicene Creed. This addition expresses the doctrine received throughout the Latin Church that the Spirit proceeds not only from the Father, but also from the Son. Discussion of this point, which still goes wearily on, has provoked an endess literature all out of proportion to the importance of the matter.

The same Greek Fathers who established the divine personality of the Spirit also gathered together the biblical doctrine on his work of restoring and sanctifying fallen human nature. With growing firmness and boldness, they taught that human nature is in a true sense divinized by the presence of the divine spirit. This doctrine attained its greatest richness in Cyril of Alexandria (d. 444), and bore fruit in the mysticism of an unknown writer who published circa 550 under the name of Dionysius the Areopagite. In stressing the personal presence of the uncreated sanctifier, and the analogy between his eternal procession from the Father and Son, and his temporal mission into the souls of men, Greek theology paid greater attention to the activity of the Spirit than did the Latin. The latter, at least until very recent times, has been somewhat neglectful of the personal indwelling and operations of the Holy Spirit. Nevertheless, in the final analysis, it has been in Latin theology that these topics have been investigated with the greater precision and detail.

This has come about in two overlapping phases. The first, which lasted until about the Reformation, was decidedly Christocentric; the second, which began to get under way in the high Middle Ages, has been progressively more and more "pneumatocentric."

St. Augustine (354-430), whose mind was destined to dominate western religious thinking down to the twentieth century, is often blamed for the lesser attention paid to the Spirit in the West. This is unjust unless carefully qualified. More than anyone else, Augustine is responsible for the formulation and promulgation (in opposition to the Pelagians) of the doctrine that man cannot be saved, cannot even take a single step towards salvation, except by the grace of God; and in the mind of Augustine, grace was always conceived as the action of the Holy Spirit. Augustine also made two special contributions to pneumatology. It was he who first proposed that, just as the eternal generation of the Son was conceived as analogous to the formation of a word or concept in the human mind, so the eternal emanation of the

247

Spirit could be conceived by analogy with the emanation of love in the human heart. Likewise, his exegesis of the seven "spirits of the Lord" which Isaiah 11:2 (LXX, Vg.) foresaw resting upon the messianic king, was the main root of the mediaeval doctrine of the "Gifts of the Holy Spirit."

On the other hand, however, it must be admitted that Augustine's approach to the theology of the Trinity did have the effect, in the long run, of weakening the popular consciousness of the proper role of the Paraclete. The earliest theologians of the Trinity had started with the Father, Son and Holy Spirit, and had labored (against vehement opposition) to demonstrate that the second and third are equal to and coeternal with the first. This approach kept the distinct characteristics of the three persons vividly in sight. Augustine's *De Trinitate* sets the one divine nature in the foreground and then within it distinguishes the three persons. This has great theoretical advantages, but tends to obscure the individuality and distinctness of the persons. When this occurs, the Holy Spirit inevitably loses out most of all because, as we have seen, he is in any case the most difficult of the three for human thought to capture.

The distinctiveness of the Holy Spirit was also obscured by the theory of appropriations, which has its roots in the doctrine of Augustine. Tradition had attributed the work of creation to the Father, redemption to the Son, and sanctification to the Spirit. But critical reflection led the Latin Church to recognize that in fact all three persons collaborated equally in all their works (with due reserves being made for the special instance of the human activity of Christ). Hence, when a certain work is regarded as proper to one of the persons, this is only because it bears a certain privileged resemblance to him. As this principle became established in the consciousness of the Church, it had unfortunately, and unnecessarily, the effect of causing people to pay less heed to the appropriations, which are biblically founded and render important service in enabling us to identify the divine persons. Once again, it is the Holy Spirit who has suffered most, because he, unlike the Father and Son, is known almost exclusively through the works attributed to him.

As regards these works of the Spirit, Western thought has focused on the effects occurring in man, rather than on the action of the divine person. This is not necessarily a fatal defect; the same thing can be said of the synoptic gospels, which are much more concerned with what man must do to enter into the kingdom, than with the gift of the Spirit, about which we get our information mainly from St. John and St. Paul. Nevertheless, it does have the effect of diminishing the distinct consciousness of the Spirit's action.

The practical, anthropocentric bias of Western theology certainly antedates Augustine; but it was powerfully confirmed by the Pelagian controversy. And while this controversy had the effect, through the genius of Augustine, of enriching our understanding of grace through the distinction of its various kinds and functions, it also tended to direct attention to the human rather than the divine coefficient of the mystery of grace. At a later epoch, the Reformation, Jansenist and Molinist controversies reinforced this concern with created, as opposed to uncreated, grace.

Medieval religious thought proceeded in the direction taken by Augustine. Not only the pastoral preaching of bishops, but even the monastic treatises on spirituality, such as Bernard's *Ladder of Humility* (ca. 1124), or Bonaventure's *Mind's Road to God* (1259), dealt chiefly with the practice of virtue by which man prepares for the supreme gift of (infused) contemplation, or the stages of growth by which the soul ascends to it. That the grace of contemplation, and even the virtues themselves, were gifts of the Holy Spirit was clearly recognized; but the anthropological rather than the theological aspect was directly in view. However, the two great hymns, *Veni Creator Spiritus,* and *Veni Sancte Spiritus,* which were composed approximately in the ninth and

249

thirteenth centuries respectively, warn us not to exaggerate the forgetfulness of the Spirit attributed to this period. The first ample treatise on the seven gifts of the Spirit was the work of a twelfth-century theologian, Rupert of Deutz. And while St. Bernard did not make much reference to the Spirit when explaining the stages of spiritual growth, elsewhere, for example in his moving description of the Spirit as a divine kiss (Sermon VIII on *The Canticle*), he makes it evident that he knew by personal experience whereof he spoke. There are many similar signs in the saints of this period that the relatively little attention given to the Spirit in their writings was not an index to the neglect of the Spirit in their life. It was merely that their system of ideas was not yet adequately adapted to the mysterious realities of which they spoke.

During the twelfth and thirteenth centuries there arose that devotion to the humanity of Jesus which has made the Christmas crib and the Way of the Cross staples of Catholic religious life ever since. This development merely carried onto the plane of piety the Christocentric character which had taken hold of theology since the third century. Naturally, it strengthened still further the tendency to leave the Holy Spirit in the background, so far as conscious ideas are concerned. But the warm piety which led this epoch to "discover" and hold dear the sacred humanity could hardly have come from any other source but the Spirit of Jesus. Francis of Assisi (1181-1226), the first person known to history on whose hands, feet and side the stigmata of Christ's passion were imprinted, is the exemplar of this piety. But the body of the saint would hardly have received this miraculous emblem of the passion of Christ, if his soul had not been filled with the Spirit of Christ.

Furthermore, the case of Francis reminds us that it was out of the Christocentric piety of the age that there welled up in the twelfth century the great wave of mysticism which spread across Europe in the thirteenth century, and reached its climax in England and the Rhineland in the fourteenth and fifteenth. Finally, as the flame cooled in the North, it burst out anew in Spain, with the Carmelites Teresa (1515-1582) and John (1542-1591), the greatest expositors of the mystical life.

If ever there have been Christians who "walked by the Spirit," and "lived in the Spirit," it was these privileged men and women, who were brought into an intimate and quasi-substantial contact with the divinity, which transformed and radically spiritualized them, and utterly transcended their efforts, sometimes lyrical, sometimes stammering, to describe it. And yet, for the most part, even the mystics make little express mention of the Holy Spirit. This is particularly striking in the case of John of the Cross, despite the fact that on occasion he represents the Holy Spirit as the *Living flame of love* that enflames the soul in perfect union with God. As a theologian, John is perfectly well informed about the workings of the Spirit, and as a mystic he has a rich personal experience of them; nevertheless, in conceptualizing the spiritual life, and even in representing the passivity required of man, he writes in terms of what man undergoes rather than of what the Spirit does. *The Imitation of Christ* (1418) may or may not be classified as mystical, but it is by far the most popular and influential expression of late medieval piety, and it has only two brief and uninspired chapters on the Holy Spirit.

The scholastic theologians of the Middle Ages also perpetuated in their own mode the Augustinian approach to grace. They amplified and systematized the various divisions of grace inherited from Augustine. They created a new and original theory of virtue which fused the biblical doctrine on faith, hope and charity, and the Augustinian doctrine that whatever is good is of grace, with the philosophical traditions on virtue inherited from Greece and Rome. They were far from being Pelagians; in fact, the tendency prevailed among them to hold that every genuine virtue is infused by God (Lombard's *Sentences* I, 27). For a moment they were even tempted to identify charity with the person of the Holy

Spirit (*ibid.* I, 17), until saner reflection led them to distinguish between the divine person who is cause and the created qualities and actions which are his effects in the human soul.

The structural needs of the great theological systems of the thirteenth century required that the uncreated person be treated separately from his created works. For a reader alert to the connection of cause and effect, this did not imply regarding them as separate in reality; but many of the later popularizers were not so alert. As a result, the theology of grace in the late medieval and modern periods tended to grow more oblivious to the Spirit's personal presence and sanctifying action than earlier medieval throught had been; in a way that was more harmful because it was more systematic.

The scolastics had even stressed the bond between the Spirit of God and the sanctification of man in their treatises on the invisible mission of the divine persons and the "Gifts of the Holy Spirit." The latter concept is a creation of medieval reflection on the spiritual life (evoked by Augustine's comments on Isaiah 11:2) and was brought to perfection by Thomas Aquinas (1224-1272). He was the first to hold that the characteristic of the gifts is to make the soul docile to the inspirations of the Holy Spirit, in contrast with virtues which are exercised according to the judgment of man's own reason. Furthermore, he maintained that the inspirations are not an extraordinary supplement to the normal Christian life, but are indispensable for salvation. In taking this position, Thomas goes well beyond his predecessors and brings out into the light of clear, firm declaration a truth that had been latent in the early medieval preoccupation with the seven gifts. In so doing, he took what was perhaps the decisive step toward the rediscovery of the Spirit by the modern Church.

His initiative, however, was not carried forward by the scholastics of the fourteenth and fifteenth centuries, who lost touch both with the Word of God and with the life of the Spirit. It was rather the mystical and spiritual life of the faithful that led the theologians of later ages to come back to the one ultimate root of

252

Christian spirituality. But this development was to be retarded several times by the vagaries of false mysticism and the reactions it provoked.

Already in the twelfth century, Joachim of Fiore (ca. 1132-1202) had prejudiced this development by proclaiming that the Age of the Son, which had succeeded that of the Father, was in turn soon to be supplanted by an Age of the Spirit.

While the Hospitalers of the Holy Spirit (1198) were devoted to genuine works of Christian charity toward the sick, the amorphous groups known as the "Brethren of the Free Spirit" regarded themselves as freed from the authority of the visible hierarchy of the invisible Spirit who led them.

Martin Luther (1483-1596), in his ambition to supplant scholastic theology with a purely biblical style of thought, did perhaps as much as anyone to bring the Holy Spirit before the religious consciousness of the modern mind. His beautiful lines on how the Spirit opens men's hearts to receive the Word of the gospel, and inspires those good works that are a sign of the "new creation," would have been welcome in any Catholic spirituality. But Luther exalted the Spirit by radically depreciating the role of the sacraments, the hierarchy and man himself in the work of salvation. As a result, all appeals to the interior work of the Spirit tended to become suspect in Catholic eyes, and the tendency which had set in during the late Middle Ages, to regard the Church as a juridical structure rather than a community of believers, was confirmed. The Spirit's role in guiding the hierarchy was stressed at the expense of his vivifying and illuminating activity in all the faithful. Protestantism itself, recoiling from the radical spiritualism of the Anabaptists, soon lost its own attention to the Spirit, which would later be recovered sporadically by the Quakers, the Pietists, the Camisards, the Moravian brethren and the Wesleys. Some of these movements may in turn have influenced the Catholic revival in the Romantic period.

Meanwhile, the Thomistic doctrine on the Gifts of the Spirit was being kept alive by a thin stream of scholastic theologians, mainly the great commentators, Cajetan (1469-1534), the Carmelites of Salamanca (1631-1701) and John of St. Thomas (1589-1664). The latter's treatise is a masterpiece. Denis the Carthusian (1402-1471) made this doctrine accessible to a wider public.

But it was the French spiritual writers of the seventeenth century who effectively began to bring about an authentic sensitivity to the Spirit in the Church. The simple, fresh, all-embracing spirituality of Francis de Sales (1567-1622) prepared the way, although still very implicitly. The Jesuit novice master, Louis Lallemant (1588-1635), aimed his spiritual direction very expressly at the goal of docility to the Holy Spirit as the interior master of souls.

De Berulle (1575-1629) and his disciples are chiefly known for their intense and methodical cult of the mysteries of Christ, thus prolonging the piety of the high Middle Ages. They advanced beyond the latter, however, in focusing attention on the interior states of Jesus' soul, rather than stopping at his exterior actions. The attitudes and dispositions of Jesus, in short his spirit, were to be relived by his disciples. It is a short and inevitable step from the "spirit of Jesus" in this sense to the person of the Holy Spirit, who inspired the human life of Jesus and alone can create the "mind of Christ" in his followers. The Berullians made this step consciously above all Olier (1608-1657), who insists upon the need of following the Holy Spirit in all things in order that Christ might live in us.

Although it made a permanent contribution to the heritage of Christian spirituality, the French school itself was short-lived. An anti-mystical reaction built up alongside of it, led by men such as Pierre Nicole (1625-1695) and Louis Tronson (1622-1700), who adhered to the safer, more human ways of discursive prayer, intense self-examination (Tronson's *Particular examens*) and resolute practice of virtue. (It should not be forgotten that even Francis de Sales had for a long while mistrusted the passive prayer into which Jeanne de Chantal was being led.)

Then, at the end of the seventeenth century appeared the pseudo-mystic quietism of Molinos in Spain, and of Fénelon and Madame Guyon in France. Their condemnations in 1687 and 1699 respectively achieved the disrepute of mysticism in general, and of the ideal of docility to the leading of the Holy Spirit in particular. Confirming the suspicions already provoked by Lutheranism, it produced that attitude of mistrust of religious experience which has so shackled Catholic spiritual writing of the past two centuries. This attitude tends to regard mystical experience as so exceptional that it hardly need be taken into account in ordinary spiritual direction, reacts instinctively to "consolations" by warning against the danger of illusion and excess, and leads one to expect that he must walk in the darkness of pure faith all his life long, with never a ray of light or taste of divine love until the beatific vision bursts upon him in full splendor.

Such a mentality leaves nothing for the spirit to do except to bestow an invisible grace that can only be taken on faith. But at the very epoch when this mentality was settling upon the Church, the means to dissipate it were also being disseminated, in the devotions to the Sacred Heart of Jesus and to his holy Mother. Critics often charge that these devotions came to take the place of the cult of the Holy Spirit that was wanting to Catholic piety. There is some truth in this view, for those devotions were a concrete embodiment of and exercise in that warm and simple spirituality which the Spirit of Jesus effects. Thus, in a hidden and indirect way, they prepared minds for a full and explicit appreciation of the doctrine of the Spirit when this would be possible.

The revelations of the Sacred Heart to Sister Margaret Mary (1647-1690) imparted to the Berullian cult of the interior states of Jesus the concreteness and fire necessary to touch the hearts of the masses. At the same time it disposed one immediately for, and as it were called down from heaven, the manifest and plenary action of the Holy Spirit, who alone can inflame hearts with that knowledge of the love of Christ that surpasses knowledge (Eph. 3:17, 19).

Similarly, the Marian piety which flowered with the French school and came back to life in the nineteenth century, after the Enlightenment had turned to dusk, was in its deepest sense a piety of simple docility to the Spirit, of which the Virgin of Nazareth is the supreme type. St. Louis de Montfort (1673-1716) made this connection expressly. He sees as the goal of Marian devotion being filled with the Spirit of Jesus. The first rule of true devotion is to do all things "through Mary," that is, to obey her in all things and conduct oneself by her spirit; for "the spirit of Mary is none other than the Spirit of Jesus."

Similarly, the "little way" of Thérèse of Lisieux (1873–1897) with its appeal to simplicity, humility and brotherly love, which is such a natural prolongation of the spirit of Francis de Sales, and anticipation of the spirit of Vatican II, is in effect an appeal to infuse the Spirit of Jesus into the most ordinary activities of life. Without being explicit, it is a kind of training for the Paraclete's plenary intervention.

The explicit appreciation of the Holy Spirit in modern theology has come about largely through three trailblazing thinkers of the nineteenth century. The first is Adam Moehler (1796-1838), whose patristic and ecumenical studies led him to react against the prevailing juridical and structure-conscious theology of the Church in favor of a theology which looks upon the Church primarily as the community of those animated and brought together by the Spirit of Jesus. In this he gave a powerful impetus toward the movement in twentieth-century theology to regard the Church as the Body of Christ, with the Spirit as its soul, and as the People of God, sanctified by his presence.

Cardinal Newman (1801-1890), in studying the development of doctrine, became aware of the active role that had been played by the faith of the laity, which he expressed in his famous discourse on the consultation of the faithful in matters of doctrine. The foundation of his stand is the fact that the Holy Spirit illumines not only the hierarchy in their teaching office but all the faithful in their belief.

Finally Matthias Scheeben (1835-1888) was led by the study of Petau (1583-1652) and the Greek Fathers to formulate the theory that the divine indwelling is not merely appropriated to the Holy Spirit, but pertains to him in a proper way, distinct from that of Father and Son. Later scholarship (Gardeil) has challenged the correctness of Scheeben's reading of the Fathers, but his position focused the attention of theologians on the doctrine of the divine indwelling and the work of the Holy Spirit.

Due to the impetus given by these men, as well as to other causes, many currents of contemporary theology and spirituality are conspiring today to highlight the action of the Holy Spirit. Thus, there is a powerful inclination to emphasize that grace entails not only a created quality but the presence of an uncreated Person. The sacraments are being viewed as personal encounters with God (and especially with the Holy Spirit), and not merely as sacred rites which produce that which they signify. Revelation is coming to be regarded as a personal divine communication more than an objective formulation of truth. New theories of inspiration and tradition also raise the question of the Spirit.

The liturgical movement has reminded us that Christ is present through the Spirit in a special way wherever two or three gather in his name; and this same consciousness has inspired the rapid growth of non-liturgical, informal prayer groups led by laymen. The modern biblical movement, at least when linked with piety, has drawn attention to the Spirit's role both in the prophet and in the hearer of the Word of God. The ecumenical movement gets its dynamism from the conviction that the Spirit is present and active in all those communities which believe in Jesus as Lord. Moreover, an almost militant determination to acknowledge the Spirit's action in every form of religion sincerely professed extrapolates this movement even beyond the confines of Christianity. In both theology and spirituality today, there is a powerful yearning to return to "the sources," among which must be numbered the Spirit as he was active among the early Christians. There is a clamor for the hierarchy to lay aside its material trappings in order to be more transparent to the Spirit. The appeal for the laity to recognize and exercise their special charisms is so powerful that this age in the Church is already being called the age of the laity. Never in the past has theology been so acutely conscious of the charismatic dimension of Christianity.

Even modern culture, with its exaltation of freedom, democracy and personal values, is furnishing a climate favorable to the recognition of the presence and work of the Spirit in each individual. Simultaneously, of course, secular humanism tends to turn away from any power in man other than man himself. The false spiritualisms that have proliferated amazingly in the present century are themselves a sign of the times, as counterfeit is of true coin.

The hierarchical magisterium has fostered, and to a large extent led the way in, this rediscovery of the Paraclete. Pope Leo XIII enunciated the traditional Catholic teaching on the Holy Spirit in the encyclical, *Divinum illud munus* (1897). Pius XII encouraged most of the above developments by his encyclicals on the Mystical Body, the liturgy and the study of scripture. Led by Pope John, the whole Church prayed that the Holy Spirit would renew his wonders in our time, as in a new Pentecost. The second Vatican Council was an extraordinary manifestation of the Spirit's action in the College of Bishops. In its documents, especially those on the Church, the missions, the laity and ecumenism, the Council spoke of the place of the Holy Spirit in the Christian economy with a fullness and vision unprecedented in Church teaching.

Thus, the tone of modern culture, the currents of modern theology, the aspirations of modern spirituality, and even the ravages of fraudulent spiritualism have conspired to focus attention on that "other Paraclete" through whom Christ guides his Church more divinely than the Israelites were led by the pillar of smoke and fire. As Cardinal Suenens declared to the Vatican Council, "The time of the Church is the time of the Spirit." Finally, the reappearance in the past few years of charismatic

258

activity on a scale comparable to that of the primitive Church compels us to ask whether Pope John's prayer for a new Pentecost is not being answered beyond all expectations by the arrival of an age of the Holy Spirit that will not supplant the age of the Son (as Joachim of Fiore imagined), but will consummate it, just as the latter had brought to fulfillment the age of the Father.

III.

The Spirit in Orthodox Theology and Life

THOMAS HOPKO

THE FEW THEMES touched upon in this paper are taken from the writings of modern thinkers of the Russian Orthodox tradition. Although being very different types of men, and some not theologians at all in the strict sense of the word, they have shown a remarkable unity in their interpretation of the thought and experience of the Eastern Church concerning the person and action of the Holy Spirit in the life of men.

In his letter, *On the Holy Spirit,* Father Pavel Florensky, the Russian priest, scientist, philosopher and theologian who is believed to have died in a Soviet prison in the fifties, sketches a history of the doctrine of the Holy Spirit which is essentially confirmed by his like-minded and much more famous friend, Father Sergius Bulgakov (d. 1944), as well as by the man who was perhaps the greatest contemporary Orthodox theologian of the strictly patristic tradition, Vladimir Lossky (d. 1958). In his letter, Florensky reveals the impossibility of elaborating any precise doctrine of the Holy Spirit comparable to the dogmas of the Holy Trinity and the Person of Christ which have been elucidiated in the history of the Church and which carry official commendation in conciliar decrees. What has been said of the Spirit dogmatically has almost exclusively been an extension of the doctrinal assertions about the Logos, with the formally required exchange of "procession" in place of "generation" in relation to the Father as the only significant adaptation. "Since such and such is said about the Son," writes Florensky, "so by the same token we are compelled to say such and such about the Spirit." This is the type of "false window" pneumatology which is found in doctrinal history, the contrived and somewhat artificial method of gaining a "symmetry" in trinitarian theology beyond which there is only silence about the Spirit himself.

The silence concerning the Holy Spirit, however, is considered to be not merely the result of an accidental lack of interest in this particular area because of the more urgent problems concerning the person of the Logos in his eternal and incarnate existence. Nor is it understood to be the result of the absence in the Church of dogmatic theologians capable of rising to the heights of doctrinal articulation concerning the third person of the Godhead such as that of the great church fathers of the trinitarian and christological controversies. On the contrary, the silence concerning the Spirit is understood to be demanded by the Paraclete himself who has remained, and by nature will always remain, hidden as a person in his divinity before the freedom of the human persons in whom he reveals himself in his indwelling; the Spirit who remains himself, as the Church sings on Pentecost, the feast of his coming, always and forever "sovereignly free."

The famous passage of St. Gregory the Theologian in his oration on the Holy Spirit, a passage of great popularity in contemporary Orthodox thinking, is quoted in full by Florensky. This is the place where the church father develops the doctrine of an order (taxis) in theology in which the Trinity is gradually revealed to men "as they can bear it"—the Father in the Old Testament, the Son in the Incarnation, and the Holy Spirit in the Church. Lossky recalls this same text in his *Mystical Theology,* and adds the commentary that as the Father finds the "express image of his person in the Son," and as the Son is manifested in the Spirit, the Spirit himself has no divine person in whom his image is expressed, and his manifestation to the world, the confirmation of his divine person and power is accomplished in human persons and always carried, therefore, the "character of a secret."

261

"The Spirit remains unrevealed, hidden, so to speak," writes Lossky, "by the gift (of his presence) so that the gift which he imparts may be fully ours, adapted to our persons . . . he mysteriously identifies himself with human persons while remaining incommunicable. He substitutes himself, so to speak, for ourselves; for it is he who cries in our hearts, *Abba*! Father! as St. Paul puts it. We should rather say that the Holy Spirit effaces himself as person before the created persons to whom he appropriates grace. . . . It is then that his divine person, now unknown, not having his image in another (divine) hypostasis, will manifest himself in deified persons: for the multitude of saints will be his image."

These words of Prof. Lossky form the foundation of the Orthodox theology of the Holy Spirit in the life of the Church: the multitude of holy men will be his icon.

In Orthodox theology the Church has one two-fold foundation, Jesus Christ the Lord and the Holy Spirit. The accent on the Spirit in the Church depends on and flows from the person of the incarnate Word who sends his Spirit to his people from God his Father so that they may become corporately his body, and individually members of it. The Spirit completes the mission of Christ and makes him present in the world in the unity of the one body, as well as in the multiplicy of the "brothers" who are anointed with him as "christs" to be also the sons of the heavenly Father: gods by the gracious unction of the Spirit.

Just as the work of Christ would be devoid of power without the "power from on high" in a Pasch without a Pentecost, so would the Way remain unwalkable, the Truth unknowable and the Life unlivable. The Spirit comes to make possible in men all that Christ is by nature by the gracious gift of his presence. This is what St. Maximus means when he says that men are called to be by grace all that Christ is by nature. And what St. Basil means when he announces so boldly that men are "creatures who have received a command to be god."

The two-fold polarity of the Church's dimensions—Word and

Spirit, incarnation and inspiration, passover and pentecost, nature and person, body and members, unity and multiplicity, ontological assumption of full humanity by God and personal participation in full divinity by men—all this is made alive in the sacramental mysteries of the Church in the Eastern tradition, especially in the two-fold character of its rite of sacramental initiation into the churchly life.

The originating events of the Church, the New Passover of Christ and the New Pentecost of the Holy Spirit, are ever renewed in the messianic age as the Church is continually fulfilling itself in baptism and chrismation (confirmation), and continually celebrating this new covenent of the new creation in the eucharistic mystery. In baptism the human person is born into the new humanity of Christ by dying and rising with him in the "tomb and womb" of the baptismal waters. In chrismation the human person is personally empowered to live the life of the new humanity with which he is clothed in baptism by the "seal of the gift of the Holy Spirit" who comes as a person to persons to enable each one in his own unique and individual way to "attain to the fulness of Christ." In the eucharist, the multitude of human persons become one body in Christ as the Holy Spirit comes "upon us and upon the gifts here offered" to manifest all things as communion with God through Christ in the Spirit. The sacramental foundation of the Church reveals the essential and existential unity and collaboration of Christ and the Spirit in God's redemption and glorification of the world of his original creation. God creates and redeems through Christ in the Spirit. And the created and redeemed return to God through the same Christ in the same Spirit. For here, rooted in the paschal, pentecostal, all-fulfilling events of the sacramental baptism, chrismation and eucharist, man gains "access to the Father" through Christ in the Spirit, and becomes his dwelling-place, filled with the "fulness of him who fills all in all . . . filled with the fulness of God."

With this fundamentally sacramental vision and experience of human life, the modern Orthodox theologians have continued to defend what was often criticized as an ecclesiological deficiency from the one side, and an anthropological utopianism from the other, in their own particular developments of the well-known sentence of St. Irenaeus of Lyons: "Where the Holy Spirit is, there is the Church; where the Church is, there is the Holy Spirit." This doctrine is understood to be the only logical and theological conclusion of the central Christian affirmation, to quote Irenaeus once more, that "God became what we are to make us what he is"—the introduction of Godmanhood into the world, the fulfillment of God's destiny for the one created in his image.

Father Bulgakov exemplifies this tendency very clearly when he defines the Church as "the blessed life in the Holy Spirit, or the life of the Holy Spirit in humanity" which "exists in us not as an institution or society, but first of all as a spiritual certainty, a special experience, a new life." For this reason, both Bulgakov and Lossky, albeit with quite different emphases and conclusions, are agreed to see in Mary, the *Theotokos* and Mother of God, the personal icon of the Church, the image of the perfection of life in the Holy Spirit, the bride of God glorified already now through the fullness of the Spirit's gracious indwelling; the personal, hypostatic pledge of what is given to all men in the Church who are "blessed" because "they hear the word of God and keep it."

In recent times the accent on the Holy Spirit in the Russian Church tradition, undoubtedly not unconnected from the rigid institutionalism of the church and society in the last century, and the Marxist experience in our own, was exceedingly widespread. The great father of the spiritual renaissance, directly or indirectly, and indeed the one whose life is the perfect living testimony to the life of the Holy Spirit in men, was St. Seraphim of Sarov (d. 1833). Called by G. Fedotov, the unique scholar of the Russian religious spirit in recent times, as the "latest and perhaps the greatest of Russian saints," St. Seraphim is most famous for resurrecting and popularizing the patristic formula of the goal of Christian life as the "acquisition of the Holy Spirit."

"The fire-infused grace of the Holy Spirit" is given to all people, even the simplest of men, in the sacramental mysteries of faith; and though sin darkens the Spirit's light and corrupts his power in the time of the "ordeal" ordained by divine providence, through sincere repentance, and good works done in the name of Christ, and especially through prayer invoking the name of Jesus, man can acquire the Holy Spirit in his life "who operates within us and establishes the kingdom of heaven in our hearts." Although the recorded words of even this greatest "icon of the Spirit" in modern times did not escape the "benevolent censorship" of the church hierarchy, the witness of this man stands as the first and most perfect sign of Spirit-centered Orthodoxy, in both theology and life, which began to blossom a century ago.

Within the framework of the traditional monastic spirituality, Seraphim was not alone, either in his penetration to the depths of the tradition, or in his emergence with prophetically inspired forms of its expression. There were also the "elders" such as those of the famous Optina monastery, with their often quite worldly, practically-oriented spiritual counsels. And there were also the writers and teachers of the life of the Spirit who exercised important influence on the lives of countless souls, especially with relation to prayer and the practice of the Jesus Prayer, such as the bishops Ignatius Brianchaninoff (d. 1867) and Theophanes the Recluse (d. 1894). At this time mention also should be made of the Spirit-centered literature of the novelists, poets and philosophers such as Dostoevsky and Tolstoy, A. Khomiakov (d. 1860) and V. Solovyev (d. 1900).

The turn of the century also marked the turn "from Marxism to idealism," and the creation of a number of religious-philosophical circles in Russia by a considerable number of the intelligentsia whose own personal lives and ideas and forms of expression are vastly different, but whose original inspiration by the same "great ideas" of Christ and the Spirit, freedom and creativity, human community and cosmic beauty, is undeniably one. Here we find not only Berdyaev and Bulgakov, but Floren-

265

sky, Frank, Fedotov, Struve and a truly significant number of others among whom we may even include the free and inspired souls of a number of contemporary poets, led by Boris Pasternak whose work is really a spiritual event.

The beginning of this century also witnessed the life of the acknowledged saint and "all-Russian pastor," Father John Sergieff of Cronstadt (d. 1908). This parish priest was in every way the antithesis of the free-thinking liberals, and yet even he demanded the friendship of czars to preserve him from the pressures of ecclesiastical officials so that his renewing inspiration and example could manifest itself as the clearest beginning of what Fedotov has called "A new 'spiritual' type of priest" in the Russian tradition. Among these "types" whose manifold gifts were so fruitfully expressed in rarely brilliant pastoral lives—a charisma so sadly missed in the church—are the fathers A. Elchaninoff, S. Chetverikoff and V. Zenkovsky. And in this respect Metropolitan Eulgious, the post-revolutionary bishop of Western Europe, must be named as a hierarch of incomparable inclusiveness and openness for everyone and everything, a pastor whose last will and testimony for his flock were the words: "Preserve the freedom in the Church."

"The Lord wants us to love one another . . . in this lies freedom. As God is love; so the Holy Spirit is love. By the Holy Spirit I came to know the Lord. . . . Ask, and the grace of the Holy Spirit will enter your souls and you will cry: This is true freedom. True freedom is in God and of God. He who is in the Holy Spirit can realize that paradise is the kingdom of the Holy Spirit within us."

These words, scribbled down on scraps of paper in the kitchen where he worked on Mount Athos, are just a token sampling of the thoughts of the unlettered peasant monk Silouan who died in 1938 after forty-three years in seclusion. Invoking the memory of St. Seraphim and John of Cronstadt in his "markings," almost every one of his sentences makes reference to the Spirit of God who abides in us granting knowledge and love, and a foretaste of the joy of paradise. No one in contemporary Orthodoxy has spoken of the Spirit with such simplicity and conviction as this divinely-anointed brother in his kitchen retreat. When considering the place of the Holy Spirit in contemporary Orthodox life, the living testimony of this man without a doubt holds the most extraordinary place.

And at almost exactly the same time that Silouan was alive on Athos, a Russian nun was walking the streets of Paris, through its slums, saloons and asylums. Aristocratic and sophisticated from her childhood, she plainly scandalized many with her un-nun-like association with philosophers and poets as well as drunkards and lunatics whom she took into her house. And when she finally went to her death in a Nazi gas-chamber on Good Friday, 1945, together with the Jews whom she protected, Mother Maria also had said her word to the world. "If Christianity is not fire," she said, the Fire which is the Spirit whom Christ has come to cast upon the earth, "then it does not exist."

The theologians and religious thinkers of the recent Russian experience had many things to say about the person and action of the Holy Spirit. And much of what they said was in fierce opposition to the Christian West and to what Father Georges Florovsky has called the "Western captivity" of the thought and spirit of their own church and nation. A large part of their criticisms are considered today to be grossly one-sided, uninformed and exaggerated. And many of the specific problems which they discussed have simply disappeared in history or have fallen into obscurity before the new theologies and new religious understanding of the contemporary world. But yet, despite all the changes in history and men, and the enormous multiplicity of new approaches to things, the newness itself is very often just a newness in forms and expressions of fundamentally unchanged positions, and the insights of these particular men continue to be meaningful for us, especially as they touch the person of the Holy Spirit of God.

When asked a few years ago before an audience of Catholic educators what was in his opinion the one great obstacle to

267

Christian renewal, especially as it effects the relations between East and West, the Russian theologian Father John Meyendorff made immediate reference to Dostoevsky's *Legend of the Grand Inquisitor*. Although Dostoevsky may have had a distorted image of the Church of Rome, and although his stabbing points about the institutional church may have been directed against his own Russian Church without impunity, the inference of Father Meyendorff remains, that behind all of the formal, specific thelogical issues which divide the Christian world—the Vatican dogma, the procession of the Spirit, the conception of Mary, the nature of grace, the understanding of the sacraments, the place of the bible—there lies a more original, more synthetic spiritual vision of reality, of God and man, the Church and the world, which keeps Christians apart, particularly the Orthodox East and the whole of the West, both Roman and Reformed.

The key to the problem which underlies all problems, and here we must leave Meyendorff specifically for a whole school of like-minded men, is the meaning of freedom and authority and their relation to truth. And this is basically a problem of the Holy Spirit in the life of man and the Church.

The forgetfulness of the Holy Spirit has caused men to search for what Khomiakov has called "an external criterion of truth," an "authority" which yields a doctrinal certainty and a spiritual security which is alien to the Christian idea of man as created in the freedom of God's image for life in the Spirit. The only authority for truth, if we might use the term "authority" in this way, is the Holy Spirit. He is the Spirit of Truth who proceeds from God, who brings to remembrance all that Christ has said, who teaches all things and guides into all the truth. The Spirit alone is the sole existing criterion for truth, its only guarantee. He is the unique Advocate who bears witness of the Truth. In the Spirit, Christ remains with us "even unto the end of the ages" and thus he needs no other guarantee for his presence; and indeed no one to represent him in his absence. Christ has given his own Spirit to make himself present in his body and its members which every man is called to be if only he has a hearing of the faith, and is ready and open to receive the Spirit, not being fearful or suspicious of his genuine coming.

Neither hierarch nor magisterium, council or decree, the Book or the multitude of books which may have the gift of serving to manifest Christ in the Spirit can ever pretend to jurisdiction over this divine Spirit who is "sovereignly free" and who, in the freedom of his holiness, imparts freedom to human persons to know the truth, and to "know that they know" by no other criterion than that of the certain conviction of the Spirit within them.

The only authority for truth which exists is the Truth itself, seen and embraced in the Spirit of Truth. And this is freedom: "For you will know the truth and the truth will make you free. I am the Truth. And I will send you the Holy Spirit, the Spirit of Truth. And where the Spirit is, there is freedom."

And where the Holy Spirit, there also is the Church. As "the blessed life in the Spirit" the Church must never yield to the temptation to offer something different or something less, not even to those "poor souls" whom, in a compassion ostensibly greater than that of Christ Himself, it judges as unworthy or unable to bear the glory of such gracious exaltation. The Church must not allow itself to become an "institutional authority," nor must it allow any of its external expressions within it, either living or printed, to take the place of the Holy Spirit, the only advocate and guarantee of freedom and truth.

But it is precisely here, on this point, that we discover the pathetic and tragic crisis in the Church—and even in society— today. It is not a "crisis of authority" as so many think it is, be it of the papacy or hierarchy or canons or scriptures or denominational disciplines in the churches, or social, political or family structures in society—which has resulted in the hard-line defenses of the authorities and the wild cries for revolutionary emancipation of the freedom-seekers. On the contrary, it is a crisis of a spirit which has been pushed to the point where it can only understand truth as necessarily bound to external authorities, and can only understand freedom in its negative relation to authority and not in its positive relation to authority and not in its positive relation to truth.

The very putting of the questions: How much freedom? How much authority? How much institution? How much individual conscience? The very existence of such questions put in this tightly-sealed framework betrays the futility of the situation as it stands, which can only burst open with a destructive power that can destroy the Church as well as any secular structure built on the same premises, and even man himself. For no matter which side ultimately emerges victorious, the human person himself is lost by the very categories themselves which deny him his destiny as the image of God, created to know the truth in perfect freedom by the indwelling inspiration of the divine Spirit who is indeed in every man who "comes to a knowledge of the truth" whatever his individual awareness may be.

The Church must remain as the herald and protector of such a human experience, the active witness of such an understanding of man. It must constantly insist, even to itself, that every law and authority, formulated within its own body or outside it, has ultimately the very restricted function of serving as a pedagogue, a tutor or custodian, to the life of perfect humanity in which men arrive to truth in freedom, and to freedom in truth.

After the Russian experience of our own day in which not only millions of bodies were destroyed, but hundreds of millions of souls, an experience prophesied with such penetrating analyses of the human spirit by a Dostoevsky and confirmed after the fact with such equally inspired insight by a Pasternak—after all this, one can only wonder how men, especially Christian men, can fail to see the seeds of destruction in the closed ways which they continue to pursue.

In much the same way, and because of the same forgetfulness of the Spirit, we are also given to believe today that we are confronted with a radically dualistic choice between our sacred and secular hopes. We can either choose "religion" in the sacral sense,

270

with its totally other-worldly substance which finds in the natural world, in human history, society and culture, nothing but dust and ashes; *profanity* which must be escaped as it will ultimately be eternally destroyed. Or we can choose "secularism" which either sees this world as God's area of activity with nature, history, society and culture as the place of his presence; or these same realities as autonomous from God in his "economic," or plainly ontological absence. This second choice, which is clearly more fashionable at the moment, contains the strange spectrum of a cryptic predestinationism on the one extreme, which can see God as the final determiner in the most capricious acts of nature and history; and cryptic and even openly revealed humanistic atheism on the other, which gives sovereign autonomy to man alone. But whatever the choice here—sacred or profane, religious or secular, churchly or worldly, divinely determined or humanistically autonomous—at least according to the witness of Orthodox thinking today, the choice is seen once more as a destructively false one. And here again the Holy Spirit moves in the center.

The work of Father Alexander Schmemann may be taken as an example of an Orthodox approach to this question. Summarizing his position, it may be said that there must first be an immediate disavowal of any sort of "sacral religion" which radically denies the world of God's creation and redemption in the name of some "other world." There must be an equally resolute "no" said to "secularity" in any of its forms; both to those which divinize this world and its natural and historical processes and to those which emancipate them in a radically independent autonomy from God. And there must still be the third absolutely categorical rejection that the relation between God and the world can even be put into such closed and mutually opposed positions.

There must be instead the sacramental vision of reality, the affirmation of the fact that this world in which Christ has been killed has forever lost its chance to become the kingdom of God through any natural process or development, even, of "God acting in history"; or through any autonomously human "reshaping of

271

the planet," to use the expression of Pasternak's Lara. But yet the foolish and scandalous paradox must remain that this very world which has condemned itself through the Cross of Christ has also, through the same Cross, been forgiven and saved, since by the humiliation of Christ, God has poured forth his Spirit upon men so that all of creation, already now in the mystery of the indwelling of the Spirit of God in human persons, may be experienced as now given back to men filled with the fullness of God.

Such theologians as Lossky and S. Verkhovskoy speak in very different terms from Father Schmemann, and yet they too are explicit witnesses of the theology which finds the overcoming of the closed option between the religious and the secular, the sacred and the profane, the other world and this world, indeed between God and man, in the concept and experience of the kingdom of God in the midst of the earth, present in those men who have received the Holy Spirit.

The Church in the Orthodox tradition is popularly called "the kingdom of God on earth." The kingdom is not of this world and cannot be identified or essentially tied to any of its "elements." And yet the kingdom is in the world, and it may even be dared to say that the kingdom is the world as it is, dead and resurrected, rejected and restored, condemned and then glorified in men who have passed through the death and resurrection of Christ and have received his Holy Spirit. The Church offers the experience of God's kingdom in sacramental mystery made possible by the presence and action of the Paraclete, the seal and pledge and guarantee of the age to come when "this world" will pass away and the new creation will be revealed filled with the presence of God. The Holy Spirit is the hidden presence among us of the kingdom of God. This doctrine has been developed in detail by Florensky where he refers to a gloss of the Lord's Prayer in the writing of St. Gregory of Nyssa where "thy kingdom come" is read as "the Spirit come upon us and cleanse us"; and goes on to quote the same St. Gregory when he says simply: "The Holy Spirit is the Kingdom."

272

The Holy Spirit, the kingdom of God, comes to persons. It does not come to the world in general, to nature, to history, to society or culture. It does not even come to the Church understood as a human society or an institutional authority which is identifiable with any "element" of this world. The kingdom comes to persons who form the body of Christ. It may reveal itself outside of the walls of the institutional society for, as we are told so frequently these days, "the Spirit blows where he wills." However, the Spirit over whom no man or institution holds jurisdiction is the same Spirit whom Christ has sent to those who consciously believe in him and who is given to men in the sacramental experience of life in the Church. If it were not for the experience of the Spirit in the Church, the Spirit "whom the world does not know," then there could be no possibility at all even to know that there is a Holy Spirit, like the men of Ephesus in the Book of Acts, not to speak of discerning the action of the Spirit in men in the world.

The kingdom of God, the Holy Spirit, comes not with observation, but with power. The power must be received, built up, acquired. It must be invoked and prayed for. It must be nurtured and not "quenched." It may never be taken for granted as it is exclusively personal and sovereignly free. It always, and even in the Church, has the "character of a secret."

The events of history and the achievements of society and culture have an eternal meaning, not in themselves, but as the events and achievements of human persons. There is no "holy history" after Easter and Pentecost, nor any secular restructuring or revolution which can bring about the kingdom of God. History has come to an end with the crucifixion of God in history and with the mystical breaking in of the "kingdom to come" by the outpouring of the Holy Spirit. The age to come has entered with the "eighth day" of Pentecost, and since that "final day," the building of God's kingdom is accomplished in human persons whose greatest achievements are lost in history and culture, but whose smallest achievements are not lost for eternity in the mystery of their persons, the persons of other men and the persons of God. Not only do the events in the time and space of this world find their eternal worth and salvation as they remain alive within the unending personal life of humanity, but even the groaning and travail of natural creation finds its transfiguration into rejoicing in the "revealing of the sons of God," the personal acquiring of the Holy Spirit by human persons. In this age, the Church must remain as the witness to these things until all things are fulfilled in the appearance of its head, the Lord of Glory.

The Church must remain—this is the message of Orthodox theology and life—to bear witness to the mystery of Godmanhood, the mystery of the Spirit in us, the mystery of the fulfillment of human destiny and the destiny of the world in the gracious deification of human persons in freedom and in truth. The "new religious understandings" which appear in every age and generation from Pentecost to our own and which, according to Florensky, have always tried to bring about the manifestation of the Spirit "prematurely or willfully," above and beyond the Church of Christ, have always condemned themselves to failure. This is not because the Church has dominion over the Spirit, nor because it is suspicious of or denies his free and genuine presence and action in men. It is because the Church must fulfill its function to preserve the mystery of the Holy Spirit whose presence remains always hidden, and whose very revelation is in his own self-effacement in freedom before the freedom of human persons, so that the grace of the fulness of the divine kingdom which he brings may be fully and completely our own. It belongs to the Church, in the face of so many more easy ways, to quote Florensky for the last time, to insist that "all the perplexities, difficulties and torments of our life are gathered around the Holy Spirit; and yet all of our hopes are also found in his revelation."

IV.

The Spirit and Protestantism

HERBERT RICHARDSON

How would you write the closing section of the Apostles' Creed?

Possibility 1: "I believe in the Holy Spirit, the holy catholic Church, the communion of saints, the forgiveness of sins, the resurrection of the body, and the life everlasting."

Possibility 2: "I believe in the Holy Spirit;

[And I believe in] the holy catholic Church;

[And in] the communion of saints;

[And in] the forgiveness of sins;

[And in] the resurrection of the body;

and the life everlasting."

Which of these ways seem right to you?

"I sort of like the second possibility," said my wife. "It looks more like a poem to me."

Now that's just the trouble with marrying a poetess instead of a theologian. You get gut reactions, not deep thinking. O.K., suppose you would write the last section of the Creed as a series of statements rather than just one, long complex statement. How then, would you write the middle section of the Creed?

Possibility 1: "And [I believe] in Jesus Christ, His only Son, Our Lord, Who was conceived by the Holy Spirit, born of the virgin Mary, suffered under Pontius Pilate . . . etc."

Possibility 2: "And [I believe] in Jesus Christ, His only Son, our Lord, Who

[I believe] was conceived by the Holy Spirit;

275

[And I believe] born of the Virgin Mary;

[And I believe] suffered under Pontius Pilate; . . . *et cetera.*"

To be consistent would you once again choose the second possibility?

To see what is at stake in these questions, ask yourself whether you believe in "the virgin birth" or in "Jesus Christ Who was born of the Virgin." If you believe in "the virgin birth" and such other things as "being conceived by the Spirit" and "descending into hell," it may be that you are separating—in your mind, at least—the possibility of such events from the person of Jesus Christ. It would then follow that you understand the Christian faith to involve a belief in (1) Jesus Christ, the Son of God and (2) the possibility and occurrence of several rather unusual events such as virgin births, spiritual conceptions, and resurrections from the dead. And you might find yourself reading reports on cases of supposed partheogenesis or communications with the dead, thinking that such reports suggest the possibility of a certain kind of occurrence which is also said to have happened to Jesus. And you might find yourself admitting that unless such things could be conceived to happen to other human beings (thereby becoming available for scientific investigation) that they couldn't be said to have happened to Jesus.

But is this really the way Christians understand these ideas? Isn't it rather the case that we hold our belief in the person of Jesus Christ and the account of the events in his life together as a single complex belief? If so, then when we say "And [I believe] in Jesus Christ, His only Son, Our Lord, Who was conceived by the Holy Spirit . . . etc. etc. . . . thence He will come to judge the living and the dead," we are not affirming either the natural possibility or the scientific inspectability of virgin births, descents into hell, resurrections, and spiritual conceptions. Rather, we are affirming these things as actions possible only for a divine person, the Son of God. And if this is the case, then we would say that any person who talks about virgin births

276

or spiritual conceptions apart from the Son of God—supposing that such things could happen to other men—would not be understanding what the Christian means when he says the Apostles' Creed.

In the same way, the first part of the Creed is not an affirmation that the world—considered as a thing in itself—began to exist in time (and hence possessed some potentiality to exist even before it existed). Rather, the first part of the Creed is one complex statement affirming "God the Father Almighty, Maker of Heaven and Earth." So both the first and the middle parts of the Apostles' Creed contain but two propositions.

The problem with supposing that the last part of the Creed contains *six* more propositions (in accord with the second way of writing it, above) is that to believe in the general possibility and occasional or eventual occurrence of such things as "the resurrection of the body" or "the communion of saints" seems very much like believing in the general possibility of virgin births and descents into hell. For the second rendering separates these events from their divine Agent, the Holy Spirit, and thereby forces us to think of them as if they were marvelous, exceedingly rare, but still quite natural events—a bit like giving birth to octuplets.

In order to clarify still further the problem involved, consider the following illustration: in Lewis Carroll's well-known story, Alice is said to have stepped through the looking glass into a strange new world. Now suppose you were to give a multiple choice questions to a student, which would be the correct answer? "In Lewis Carroll's story, the girl Alice

    a.——stepped through the window.

    b.——stepped through the looking glass.

    c.——neither.

    d.——both."

Could you now ask a student who gave answer "b" whether he believes (1) that stepping through looking glasses is possible, (2) that the girl in Carroll's story is called "Alice," and (c) that the girl Alice did this thing that is possible in general, that

is, also possible for you and me? You could ask him this—
though, of course, he will think you are being silly. For both you
and he know full well that stepping through looking glasses is
here meant as a possibility for a special story-book girl—and
not for human beings like you and me.

Now the spiritual conception of Jesus is affirmed by the Christian as a possibility for the Son of God—not for human beings
like you and me. Since this is the case, we have absolutely no right
to assume that this conception in any way resembles such fanciful
occurrences as parthenogenesis. In the same way, the resurrection
of the body, the life everlasting, and the communion of saints are
possibilities that can be worked by the Holy Spirit; they are His
acts. Hence, we should not try to explain them as general possibilities that might occur through some other agent. And we would
say to any person who tried to prove or interpret any of these
from psychological, historical, or physical evidence or in terms
of analogies with any natural events that he was not understanding them correctly because he had separated them from the more-
than-natural being who alone possessed the power to cause such
things to happen. Apart from the Holy Spirit, neither the resurrection of the body nor the forgiveness of sins could occur—since
the sole possibility of their occurring is in His power to do them.

Suppose, now, that we turn to the Church. Do we believe that
the author of the Church is the Spirit, that He is the immediate
agent of its existence? Or do we believe in (1) The Holy Spirit
and (2) the Church—which has its charter and character not
from the Spirit, but from another. Actually it was traditional in
medieval theology to separate the Spirit and the Church, sometimes even regarding the Church as the agent of the communion
of saints, the forgiveness of sins, the resurrection of the body, and
the life everlasting. On this view, the characteristic marks of the
Church in her unity, catholicity, and holiness often seem to resemble other natural forms of unity, holiness, and catholicity. It is
against such a distorted understanding that arises when the
Church is separated from the Spirit that the Eastern Catholic

278

Archbishop Elias Zoghby warns when he argues that to conceive the unity of the Church as an agreement between the heads of churches and make them the chief and only agents of this unity is to reduce the Church of Christ to the level of ordinary human societies.

Rather, he argues, it is "the Holy Spirit who is the source of all sanctity and all union." And the unity of the sanctity authored by the Spirit is an expression of the unique unity and holiness proper to the Spirit alone and hence not to be found in any other natural thing. But is it really true that we think of the unity of the Church in this way? Don't we usually think of the unity of the Church in a purely natural way—as a kind of organizational unity that is also found in many other institutions—and then claim that this natural unity is supernatural? No wonder we confuse people when this occurs. But focusing on Christ's "legal commission" to Peter as the founding of the Church, rather than the Pentecostal descent of the Spirit from heaven to create among men a new understanding that transcended linguistic differences, leads to such difficulties. For it suggests that Christ rather than the Spirit authors the Church.

The purpose of this essay is not, however, to debate with theologians who separate the Church from the Spirit, but to focus on the misunderstanding of the forgiveness of sins that occurred when the Protestant Reformation theologians separated this action from the Holy Spirit. For the Protestants thought of the forgiveness of sins as the work of someone other than the Spirit. They displaced the forgiveness of sins from the last to the middle section of the Creed. Here is a typical example—from the Thirty-Nine Articles:

The son is one Christ, very God and very Man; who truly suffered, was crucified, dead, and buried, to reconcile the Father to us, and to be a sacrifice, not only for original guilt, but also for the actual sins of men. /As Christ died for us, and was buried, so also is it to be believed that he went down into hell.

279

This displacement of the forgiveness of sins to the Christological section of the Creed was the fulcrum exploited by the Protestant theologians to "naturalize" the meaning of forgiveness itself. For if the Holy Spirit authors the forgiveness of sins in a man, he does so by overcoming sin in a man and making him truly holy (sanctified) by virtue of his indwelling presence. By making the agent of forgiveness Jesus Christ (one who is "outside" man), the Protestant theologians were also able to claim that a man's righteousness and forgiveness are also "outside" him. For Christ's death can be construed as changing God's attitude toward sinful man rather than changing sinful man himself. The forgiven man, on this view, thereby remains a natural man in a fully worldly condition; he is said to be *justified* (God accepts him), but not *sanctified* (he is really still a sinner).

The Protestant notion of forgiveness is very peculiar—to say the least. For it assumes that what keeps God from accepting man is God's wrath rather than man's sinful condition. It asserts that it is God who needs the therapy, not sinful man. This misunderstanding of forgiveness provides a rationale for worldliness and undercuts the claim of the Catholic Church that a religious vow and withdrawal from the world is the way to holiness. Such a rationale was needed by the emerging middle class—and it was needed because the Church had failed to affirm the full value of creation. But if the Protestants regained a positive appreciation of the creation in this way, it must also be said that they did so by distorting the idea of Christian sanctity. For the separation of the forgiveness of sins from the Holy Spirit allowed the Protestants to claim that God accepts the world as it now exists rather than requiring and causing it to be made anew.

The political consequence of the separation of justification and sanctification is to allow men to believe that they can accept an essentially unjust world because God himself does. That is, it provides an excuse for the *status quo,* a legitimation of political conservatism. We should not think that such thoughts were not in the minds of those who developed and applied these doctrines.

They knew the troubles stirred up by those *spiritualists* who held that since the Spirit authored the Church and forgave man his sins, the Church should be truly holy, a man should live a saintly life and society should be totally reformed. This would be a very embarrassing thing for the new Church of England which—as a national church—had to include both saints and sinners; and it would be very hard on the new Protestant bourgeoisie, who certainly did not intend to conform to the spiritualist demands to create spiritual cities with community of goods (communism!) or to restructure society to alleviate the tragic conditions of the poor, just then beginning a Peasants' Revolt. The Church and the sanctity of the Christian had to be defined as "invisible," "forensic," or "alien" if the political and economic interests of the emerging bourgeoisie were to remain undisturbed. The Protestants were so aware of this problem that, in a document like the Westminster Confession, it is specifically said that neither the sanctity of individual Christians nor the spiritual communion the Bible says they have with one another could be understood to take away or infringe the title or propriety which each man has in his goods and possessions.

So we see that the Reformation displacement of the forgiveness of sins into the second article of the Creed allows a Christian to have Christ's righteousness and not have any of his own that might "take away or limit the propriety" he has in any private property. Nor does it require from him concern for the poor, any change of social structures or titles. Then how, we might ask, do the two Reformation confessions quoted above treat the Spirit? And the answer reveals their distaste for this subject. The Westminster Confession does not even include an article on the Holy Spirit—an embarrassment that American Presbyterians finally corrected about 1900 when they put an appendum on the Spirit in the Westminster Confession by a special vote of their General Assembly. And the Thirty-Nine Articles, while including a statement on the Spirit, carefully gives Him no functions. It says simply that "The Holy Spirit, proceeding from the Father and the Son, is of one substance, majesty, and glory with the Father and the Son, very and eternal God."

The magisterial Reformers and their immediate successors did not exclude or depreciate the Spirit as a vital part of the communal life of the Church unwittingly. By their very omission of this emphasis—an emphasis that was central to the Anabaptist, Quaker, Leveler, and Antinomian groups that were also emerging at this time—they arranged to keep the Church, the forgiveness of sins, and everlasting life out of the hands of the Spirit (represented by the revolutionaries) and in the hands of Christ who, being absent, had to be represented by His vicar on earth —whether pope, preacher, prince, or presbyterian (the representatives of established privilege and property). "The time of the Spirit is not yet," they said. "And the place for the Spirit is not here. The Spirit belongs to eschatology; the Spirit belongs to another age." And when the Spirit started speaking to the enthusiasts, mystics, and Schwärmer, then the Protestant Reformers thanked God for the *filioque!*

The *filioque*—marvelous invention! What it says is that the Spirit doesn't come from the Father alone (in contrast to the Son). No, the Spirit comes from both the Father "and the Son" (*filioque*). This is what tames the Spirit and makes it ecclesiastically safe. For since "No one has seen the Father, but the Son." we have to believe the Son's word about the Father. But since the Spirit comes from *both* the Father and the Son, we do not have to believe what the Spirit says unless it can be shown by us to be in accord with our understanding of Christ. "Shown *by us?*" I mean by those who are properly accredited members of the magisterium of the Church. Not surprisingly, it turns out that the Spirit never speaks a truth that disturbs or embarrasses the Church—for any disturbance or embarrassment would itself be an evidence that it was not the Holy Spirit speaking, but some other spirit. The effect of the *filioque,* then, is to insure that God shall never be able to fulfill his promise, "Behold, I make all things new."

The Protestant Reformation of the sixteenth century was a reformation that never really took place. Fortunately, before things got out of hand, Luther saw the light and exhorted the princes to put down the murdering, thieving hordes of peasants. Anabaptists were drowned by the tens of thousands. Revolutionary Utopians were destroyed by the sword. And the Protestant-Catholic axis finally worked out a solution that evidences the real interests at stake. *Cuius regio, eius religio:* "Let the religion of each land be the religion of its king." This insures that God supports the existing politico-economic order, an order that has been expanded now just enough to allow the rising bourgeoisie a share of the wealth and a share of the say.

The question whether the Spirit is the immediate author of the Church and the forgiveness of sins is in large part a decision bearing on God's attitude to the *status quo* and the amount of sin that the Christian can regard as acceptable. For surely if God accepts a sinful world, the enthusiasts who refuse to do so and who promote utopian visions can be disregarded as dangerous eccentrics. The question whether the Spirit is the author of Christian holiness, so that the Christian must be really and visibly different in his behavior, presses us to ask whether the Christian gospel is not to proclaim a future kingdom of God, but to establish a present kingdom of righteousness—where there will be no war, no poverty, no sickness or death, no ignorance, no fear. Because the Reformation Protestants shied away from the reformation of the world, the Protestant reformation never took place.

"But, Mr. Wesley, it is in such bad taste to be running around the countryside in the company of all these poor, ignorant, and stinking people. How can they understand the subtleties of Christian metaphor, much less appreciate the fine things of culture? And yet you are said to go out into the open fields and preach to gathered masses of these vulgar persons, telling them that God not only seeks to make men perfect simply by sending the Spirit

283

into their hearts, but that God is going to make them perfect right here and right now. Why if God makes them holy simply by the Spirit, then what will happen to their obedience to the Church? And if they are to become perfect by faith, then how can an Oxford education increase a man's perfection? You are preaching a dangerous doctrine, Mr. Wesley, when you go out into the fields and into the city homes. Let the vulgar, if they wish perfection, be obedient and attend to the sacraments of the Church; and let them listen to instruction from their betters.

"What more dangerous than to separate the Spirit from the sacraments—as if a man could become holy simply by some fancy that the Spirit enters his heart and causes him to be 'born again.' 'Born again,' Mr. Wesley? What a strange and arrogant presumption. Bloated with pride, they rant and rave that they are new men and that even the king, the theologians, the professors, and even I must be born again. I do not choose to be born again; I am perfectly satisfied with the station I was born into the first time. And I wonder why they cannot be likewise satisfied. Humility, Mr. Wesley. Tell them about the virtues of humility, obedience, suffering, and patience. But do not rant on about the holiness, peace, and joy of the Spirit. Peace shall come, Mr. Wesley, to every man when he is raised beyond the grave. For the time being, we must be satisfied with an imperfect world, with a vale of sorrows. So preach to them the humility, obedience, and suffering of Christ, Mr. Wesley. Tell them of God's compassion, not this utopian perfection. Speak no further about the Spirit's making men to be born again. God loves the poor just as they are, Mr. Wesley. He loves us in spite of our imperfections. And we cannot overcome these, Mr. Wesley."

"Madam, we shall overcome."

"Overcome sin, Mr. Wesley?"

"Madame, we shall overcome."

"Overcome all fear, all rage, all injustice, Mr. Wesley?"

"Madam, we shall overcome."

"Overcome poverty, Mr. Wesley?"

284

"Yes, we shall overcome poverty and slavery and war—and men shall be free at last, free at last. Thank God Almighty; we're free at last."

"Don't be so unrealistic and impatient, Mr. Wesley. You want things to change too fast. Call home your outside agitators who travel throughout our land preaching a revolutionary doctrine that undermines its law and order. I fear for the life of men like you who think it is their business to reform the world."

"They shall murder me in Memphis, madam. But we shall overcome."

The true Protestant reformation—a reformation of the Church which also requires the reformation and sanctification of the world—took place in the eighteenth century. Wesley and Edwards—rather than Luther and Calvin—were its prophets. The sixteenth-century "reformation" never found a new positive principle of holiness. It exposed that depreciation of the world and all the goods of creation implied by the medieval notion of a state of grace that was "higher" than the state of nature. It guarded its new insight by mastering the methods of historical exegesis earlier than its adversaries and by the artificial device of setting scripture in opposition to tradition. It legitimated the admission of a new commercial bourgeoisie to a share in political-economic power. But it never discovered a new *religious* principle, a new understanding of holiness, a "machinery" for transforming and sanctifying man and the world. And it brutally exterminated the anabaptists and spiritualists who had won a prophetic insight into the true meaning of the Holy Spirit and who struggled for a holy world.

Traditional histories of the Christian Church dependent, as they are, upon European scholarship and the sixteenth-century perspective overemphasize the significance of the evangelical-catholic controversy and depreciate, or completely overlook, the eighteenth-century "Later Reformation." In this "Later Reformation," a new religious principle is given definite expression: the idea of a holy worldliness, a sanctified creation. This new move-

285

ment presupposed what the sixteenth-century magisterial reformers had won, namely, that the creation and the goods of creation provide the context within which man's religious destiny must be worked out. It presupposed there is no "higher order of grace" that stands against nature. It assumes these theological gains and then goes on to introduce its new positive principle: that the creation must be transformed by the Holy Spirit into a holy and perfect community. A comprehensive inventory and ordering of the new themes and tendencies of this spiritualistic reformation is presented in my *Toward an American Theology*. Within the confines of this essay, I can only indicate a sampling from this rich new lode.

First, I have indicated that the true fathers of the Protestant reformation—that is, that reformation of the Church which also implied the reformation of the world—were John Wesley and Jonathan Edwards, men who crystallized the insights of the radical and spiritualist sectarians into a powerful new missionary and ecclesiastical Awakening. Wesley's personal experience and scriptural studies led him to the conviction that the period of God's administrating the world through law had been brought to an end by Christ, and that God now was working to recreate a new humanity by the power of the Spirit. The key to this transformation in the life of an individual man is his being "born again," a total psychological reconstruction that roots out the effects of original sin—namely, death and the fear of death—and makes possible, in principle, the living of a perfect life.

To view all men as possessing this potentiality for moral perfection (since we now live in the age of the Spirit) opens the way for a new attitude toward law and a new task for the Church. Whereas classical Christian anthropology presupposed the inevitability of sin and, hence, the religious necessity of law and police power as dikes against sin, the new vision of the Spirit's working shifted the task of the Church to the actualization of those potentialities in man that would allow him to be perfect and live without the law. The classical view, by its intrinsic logic,

286

forced the Church to legitimate the existing political order—since this order wielded the law needed to restrain sin. The new spiritual anthropology now put the Church on the side of the potentialities of man's living perfectly without law—thereby opening the way for revolution against unjust rulers for the sake of a reconstructed, truly just state.

The spiritualist move toward Church-State separation, be it noted, is not simply a political accommodation to a pluralistic religious situation (as certain historians, even today, seem to conceive the matter). It is rather a logical consequence of the spiritualistic anthropology, the new vision of Christian perfection. In Europe, where the true Protestant reformation never took root, the Churches found themselves inextricably bound to the vested interests of the governing and propertied classes and the later proletarian revolutions were carried out in the name of atheistic and secular ideologies. In England and in North America, however, the true Protestant reformation itself was the revolutionary vanguard. It was Wesley who mobilized the poor in England—though it was Marx who mobilized the poor on the continent. It was Wilberforce and Parker and the revivalists of the second Great Awakening who mobilized the conscience of men against slavery. It was the *Baptist*, Walter Rauschenbusch, who formulated the definitive theology of the social gospel and the *Baptist* Martin Luther King who led the struggle against the use of war and violence as methods for settling human conflicts. Such movements presuppose the spiritualist vision of man.

The new vision of man and society is rooted in an exegesis of scripture that is guided by the experience of the Holy Spirit. The magisterium for this new movement is the experience of the sanctified man who, because he has experienced the new birth and intimations of a holy community, reads scripture as a testimony to its possibility. *Lived spiritual experience* rather than obedient belief in things taught by an authority (for the sake of attaining eternal life in a world to come) is the new characteristic form of religious life. Not obedience, humility, suffering, and

287

belief; but joy, peace, creativity, and holiness are the marks of the spiritual man. These are, of course, the eschatological virtues. And, in fact, the new theological centrality given to the Holy Spirit is an expression of the spiritualists' faith that the eschatological age has now begun.

Jonathan Edwards, the American counterpart to Wesley, is credited with creating the form of the "revival," the central institution of the Great Awakening. Historians who interpret this movement too often do so from the classical perspective that regards spiritual feelings or testimonies to being "born again" as signs of human presumption and madness. They fail to see them as Edwards saw them—as psychological evidences that we are in the midst of a great historical transition to an age when a perfect human community can be established on earth. The Great Awakenings were not interpreted by their proponents primarily as methods for increasing church membership. They were interpreted rather as signs that the eschatological Spirit was at work in the world, as evidences that the foundations for a just society were being laid, as proofs that a new possibility was evolving within creation itself.

In the nineteenth century at the time of the second Great Awakening, another eschatological institution was created: the benevolence society. Benevolence societies were voluntary associations of men converted in the revivals, now working together to improve this or that social problem situation. Benevolence societies struggled against slavery, child labor, and rum; they fought for female emancipation, public education, and later for labor and its right to organize. By the end of the nineteenth century, the Protestant gospel had become a social gospel and the Protestant Church itself had become a complex conglomerate benevolence society—a *communis sanctorum* filled with the desire for holiness and struggling for the creation of a holy world. The Holy Spirit was conceived to be the Spirit of unifying and moving this community, the vanguard of the new humanity living for the sanctification of man. In this way, the techniques of the revival were harnessed to the social gospel.

In our day we have seen a still more effective fusion of these two institutions—the revival and the social gospel Church—in the dramatic confrontations and demonstrations against injustice and traditional privilege by Martin Luther King. King's gospel is that of the true Protestant reformation: that spiritual reformation of the Church requires also the sanctification of the world. The religious character of his political struggles, his commitment to the cause of a holy and righteous world, are evident in the rhetoric and ritual of the cause. Participation in this struggle is itself the new sacrament of holy life. Just ask your friends who have tried it! Just test the magisterial experience of someone who has tasted this new kind of holiness. This spiritualistic tendency has also become a central emphasis in such modern movements as Pentecostalism, movements that bear a marked affinity with eschatological Protestantism.

The recovery of the Holy Spirit in modern theology related to the discovery that the time and place of eschatological life is *here* and *now*. The true reformation—the reformation of the world—begins with this insight. A full theology of the Spirit still awaits being written; but the form of such a theology now seems to be emerging in the course of that consistent historical tradition discussed above. Moreover, the import of the question with which this essay began should now be clear. Do we believe that the Church, human forgiveness, and the life everlasting are the works of the Spirit—so that the Church must be a spiritual Church, forgiveness be true moral perfection, and eternal life be a sharing in the life and work of Him who is and who seeks holiness? And do we believe that the Spirit, whose works these are, is now working in our midst? If we do, then we share the vision of holy worldliness. And to share this vision is to share in the Spirit's work for a holy world.

Is such a holy world possible? It is for the Spirit!

V.

The Spirit and Pentecostalism

KILIAN MCDONNELL

PENTECOSTALISM as a movement dates from the turn of the twentieth century. It arose out of the social disorganization and spiritual rootlessness that accompanied the great waves of immigration to America. Indeed, immigration reached a record high, 8,800,000, precisely in the decade, 1901–1910, when Pentecostalism began to form as a movement. One would expect major social dislocations from the greatest movement of nations in history. But even earlier, in the latter part of the nineteenth century, social disorganization was fostered by the industrial revolution, which brought to an end America's primarily agrarian society despite the westward movement that temporarily prolonged the dominance of rural life. During this time of industrialization, the growth of the cities and rapid social change, people sought refuge from the grim realities of life in revivalism, which offered assurance of salvation when there were no other certitudes. The revival was eminently democratic: there was little esteem for clericalism, it was non-liturgical and it exalted personal experience and personal action. The touchstone of orthodoxy was in individual religious experience, continually renewed in worship.

The immediate forerunner of the Pentecostal movement was the Holiness movement, a primitive reaction against theological rationalism, secularism and institutionalism, stressing continual growth in holiness. The Holiness groups tolerated expressions such as speaking in tongues, falling, jerking, moaning. They conceived perfection in two stages: first, justification by faith alone

290

(or a conversion experience), then a full sanctification experience. Pentecostalism took over this pattern but made speaking in tongues (glossolalia) a proof that the second stage, sanctification, had been reached. This is about as close to a definition of Pentecostalism as is possible.

There is no doctrinal unity to the Pentecostal movement, and its manifestations are so varied that generalizations are more than usually hazardous. Walter Hollenweger, who has published a nine-volume *Handbuch* on the movement, contends that the ultimate common denominator is "an overpowering sense of the presence of God and personal involvement, whether in baptism by the Spirit or in worship around the Lord's table." The Pentecostal is concerned above all about fullness of life in the Holy Spirit. One moment in this fullness is the baptism in the Holy Spirit (which is distinct from water baptism). It is an experience in which the Christian knows that the Holy Spirit not only dwells in him, but that he dwells in the Spirit. Most Pentecostals believe that speaking in tongues is proof that this mutual indwelling has actually taken place. They do not believe that the Christian had been without the Holy Spirit before the baptism but that the baptism represents a new fullness, a new modality of being in the Holy Spirit. Although tongues plays a large role as proof, it is less important in the life of the Pentecostals than an outsider might think. For the Pentecostal what is important is fullness of life in the Spirit, being in the Spirit, and tongues is only one manifestation of the present and active Spirit. The baptism in the Holy Spirit can be a highly emotional event, but often it is simply an experience, calm and disciplined, of the presence of God.

Pentecostal prayer services are ideally unstructured; there is a kind of practiced spontaneity about them with hymn-singing, preaching, testimonies, reading of the word, extemporary prayer. The number of times either speaking in tongues or prophecy occurs in a public service is very small. The more the local congregation has taken over the features of the historic churches (often the worst features), the fewer are these charismatic manifestations. Worship services in a Pentecostal church on a Sunday morning usually last as long as those in the mainline Protestant churches (and tend to be more subdued than other Pentecostal services), but a week-day prayer service, or a revival meeting led by a traveling evangelist, can easily last three or four hours. But the change of tempo, the hand-clapping, the congregation's involvement (each member is a contributor, each has a message, each a testimony), the joy in the presence of the Lord makes three or four hours go very quickly. Pentecostals seem to enjoy their worship services, perhaps because they are more than a means of fulfilling a "Sunday obligation." They are oriented to re-actualizing the sanctification experience which is the baptism in the Holy Spirit, and thereby attaining the goal of continual revival.

The worship services are also means of evangelization and recruitment, necessary in any ecclesial group based on voluntary association. David du Plessis, who might be called "Mr. Pentecost," has noted the falsity of the common supposition that a Pentecostal group will always remain so. "Every generation must have its own Pentecostal experience, if the revival is to continue." Apart from the voluntary association which each generation creates, there is no supporting apparatus to carry on the spiritual momentum. Thus, Pentecostal statistics do not include the children of members, because the Pentecostal experience cannot be inherited or handed down. As du Plessis puts it: "God has no grandsons."

The Pentecostals are people of the bible and they are fundamentalist in their interpretation of it. Although usually innocent of a unifying biblical theology, they do have a profound knowledge of the sacred text. The Pentecostals' spiritual vitality, devotional ardor and their amazing growth is related to the clarity and immediacy of the sacred Word in their lives. They divide the world, with a very unbiblical incisiveness, into nature and supernature. God may break through into the world of nature but essentially it is at war with the things of God. Their rich, even

292

exaggerated view of the supernatural contrasts markedly with an impoverished, in fact rationalistic, view of nature. Expecting God to intervene in their lives, they can name place and date where they are convinced that God did break through and alter the course of their personal histories. The word "miracle" is often on their lips in public and private testimonies.

Many find the Pentecostal eagerness for miracles naïve, often a matter of wish fulfillment. On the other hand, one cannot accept the New Testament witness and then postulate a deistic God, who observes from afar but never manifests himself in history. In the book of Acts, the point of departure for Pentecostal thought, it is the Holy Spirit who inspires the decisions necessary to maintain the unity of the church (15:28) and who guides the apostles and preachers of the gospel in their missionary journeys (4:8; 6:10; 8:29; 10:19; 13:2-4; 20:23). It would be difficult to confine the manifestations of the Spirit to the apostolic age; there is no reason why persons in any age who open themselves to the Spirit should not experience the actuality of God's presence in their lives. Unless one is willing to admit the act of God not only in Christ but in the lives of Christians then one has to abdicate all pretensions to a biblical spirituality. It is appropriate to be somewhat skeptical about the miracles, prophecies and numerous divine interventions claimed in Pentecostal circles, but it would impoverish the gospel to rule out, *a priori,* the numinous and the wondrous from the lives of ordinary Christians.

Pentecostalism is popularly identified with speaking in tongues. It would be a mistake, however, to isolate this phenomenon, to study it exegetically, historically and psychologically and think that one has thereby studied Pentecostalism in depth. If Pentecostalism is to be identified with any one thing it must be with the fullness of life in the Spirit, including all the gifts and charisms of the Spirit, of which tongues is one. Even though most American Pentecostals speak of tongues as evidence that the baptism in the Holy Spirit has taken place, even the more intransigent leaders insist that the central issue is not tongues. On

293

the other hand, it was the linking of tongues to the baptism in the Holy Spirit which gave viability to the Pentecostal movement. Tongues is clearly not innate to the Pentecostal ethos.

Outsiders are much mystified by the phenomenon of tongues and their fascination with it makes them attribute an importance to it that it does not have in the life of the Pentecostal community. Pentecostals do not gather for the precise purpose of speaking in tongues. It may or may not occur at any given meeting. just as there may or may not be prophesying. The practice varies.

In the biblical sense, tongues is distinguished from similar cultural manifestations by its functions within the kingdom of Christ: to glorify Christ and to build up the community. These functions are not fulfilled by some kind of spiritual extravaganza, a grand display of strange utterances, but only by glossolalia as a prayer gift. It is precisely this point that outsiders fail to understand. The gift of tongues is a gift of prayer, and more particularly, a gift of praise (Acts 10:46). Researchers who have done field work and talked at length with those who "have come into the experience" know that the depth of their prayer life, their great love of prayer, their joy in praying and desire to praise and glorify God plus the transformation in their lives because of this new prayer dimension, are not lightly to be dismissed.

From a theological point of view, the question of whether or not tongues is a real language is irrelevant, although the Pentecostals insist that it is. Pentecostal literature is full of instances, admittedly rare in proportion to the frequency of tongues, in which the language was recognized. (In the original Pentecostal experience, as related in Acts, Chapter 2, the language was understood by the bystanders, while in the Epistles of St. Paul the phenomenon apparently was not understood by the listeners.) The difficulties of a scientific investigation in a controlled situation are almost insurmountable when one is speaking not about linguistic analysis (which has its own problems) but about recognition of a given tongue. (There are about 3,000 languages in the world, according to an admittedly low estimate by Carl F. Voegelin, director of the Archives of the Languages of the World.)

Scornful critics of the Pentecostal movement have dismissed the baptism in the Holy Spirit and tongues as "instant holiness." Some Pentecostal converts who thought themselves so transformed by the experience, have declared that they were no longer capable of sinning; most were proved wrong. For those entertaining such an illusion, the sense of God's presence is so immediate, and the realization that God's love is not a parable is so forceful, that the possibility of deliberately offending God seems impossible. To be sure, the concept of sin prevalent in some Pentecostal circles is superficial, but there is no ambiguity about the Pentecostal insistence that tongues is neither to be identified with holiness, nor is it to be considered a sign of spiritual maturity. Pentecostals would rather say that glossolalia is the lowest of the gifts—merely the first step in the full life of the Spirit—and, being the lowest of the gifts, it is a good place to start. Spiritual maturity is a process of growth, they would say; the profound and sometimes overpowering sense of God's presence which often accompanies the baptism in the Holy Spirit is not to be confused with spiritual maturity. Pentecostal history, like that of every religious movement, has ample evidence of leaders endowed with spiritual gifts of Christian morality. Pentecostals would even be willing to grant the possibility that the incestuous man spoken of by St. Paul in 1 Corinthians 5 was a spirit-filled Christian.

Some experts have called tongues "ecstatic speech," but that can be misleading. Those who speak in tongues are generally not in a trance; they start when they want and they stop when they want. They can pray in tongues without any emotional elevation. One can, of course, mention cases of persons who, in speaking in tongues, moaned, cried, rolled on the ground, etc., but these excessive manifestations are extraneous to the experience of the baptism and to glossolalia, and would be vehemently rejected by many Pentecostal leaders.

Dealing with tongues in this way, in terms of the criticisms posed by non-Pentecostals, has necessitated isolating the issue in a manner that only does violence to its essential meaning. The task of theologians and, I might add, church officials, is to take the admonition of St. Paul seriously: "Do not forbid speaking in tongues," (1 Cor. 14: 39), and, having adopted at least a policy of toleration, to situate all the charismatic gifts (not just tongues) in a broad ecclesiological framework. All the gifts have a proper role which should be worked out theologically as a part of an extensive ecclesiological reflection. If the early Pentecostals had been competent to undertake this theological work they might have avoided many a sad chapter in their history, as knowledgeable Pentecostals will themselves admit, and contemporary classical and neo-Pentecostals would not be repeating the earlier mistakes. Walter J. Hollenweger, the greatest living authority on Pentecostalism, has for years urged competent Pentecostals to pursue this task.

To millions of television-viewers Pentecostalism *is* Oral Roberts, and Oral Roberts is healing. Although he has recently renewed his affiliation with the Methodist church, he remains a Pentecostal in outlook. In 1962 both *Harper's* and *Life* published articles about Roberts. Both were essentially negative and pointed up the difficulties in evaluating a man who belongs to a subculture without a real awareness of its structures, modalities and patterns. Without a truly socio-cultural approach, entailing a study of the man within his own subculture, no valid judgment can be made. There is a Pentecostal logic and a Pentecostal vocabulary stemming from this experiential knowledge of God's presence and from the manifestation of the Spirit through his gifts. Although the root experience may be valid and even biblical, the logic and vocabulary need not be a pure expression of it, undiluted by cultural determinants. Oral Roberts uses a logic and speaks a vocabulary which is rooted in a biblical experience. However, they are also reflections of a given socio-economic level and historical setting. To understand him one must know how to distinguish between the biblical and the socio-cultural; further, one must understand the dynamics of the cultural components within their proper secular context. Here only a few random remarks can be made.

When Roman Catholics approach the subject of miraculous healing they use the filter of their own subculture; that is, they filter out certain events as undesirable and admit others as desirable. Thus, for a Roman Catholic to believe himself healed by the Blessed Virgin at Lourdes is a mark of childlike piety; to believe in a healing by the Holy Spirit through a charism is a mark of rank hysteria. Using the Catholic filter, the faithful son of Rome has no alternative but to label Oral Roberts a fanatic and a huckster; whatever he is, however, Roberts is neither of these. If one accepts the biblical witness that there are "gifts of healings" (1 Cor. 12:28) one need not accept the style of healing ministry which Oral Roberts represents. Proceeding exegetically from the biblical component of his subculture, one would have to have very serious reservations about his claims. On the other hand, it is difficult to dismiss all of the healings as psychic, although even the Pentecostals will admit that many of them can be attributed to psychological "adjustments." Oral Roberts himself says of his failures: "No one has prayed for more people who have *not* been healed than I." Like most faith healers, he publishes a magazine, *Abundant Life,* the most restrained and dignified of the healing magazines, in which, he prints only the testimonies of those who have been under a doctor's surveillance for an extended period of time.

Apart from Oral Roberts, there is a difference of opinion within Pentecostalism on the role of healing ministry, and in particular about the big healing campaigns. Donald Gee, undoubtedly the most articulate leader Pentecostalism has so far produced, has written extensively on this subject. Although he truly believes in the manifestation of the Spirit in healings, he is severely critical of healing demonstrations. "Solid missionary work is not fulfilled by attracting huge crowds to witness a ministry of healing in a revival campaign. That is easy. It needs solid

297

preaching and teaching to produce fruit that remains." Gee counsels the honest admission of failures. There is a "place for wise and courageous facing of 'failures' to receive miraculous answers to prayer, including honest exposition of passages in the Bible where miracles did *not* happen. The weakness of faith-building propaganda that does not face all the facts is that in the end it can leave people more hopeless and distressed than ever."

The campaigns are often accompanied, says Gee, by commercialization and exaggerated reports. While granting that true healings have occurred, he suggests that "there has been a misguided attempt to make a habit of that which should be unusual and therefore impressive and sanctifying. It is cheapening the holy to attempt to play upon people's love for the wonderful by systematizing it." Finally, he claims that the healings claimed are often ephemeral and that after a spectacular healing campaign one is left "with the stark fact . . . that most often very little remains of permanent value." Carl Brumback, also a Pentecostal, accuses some local healing preachers with immorality, vanity, arrogance, too high an esteem of bodily healing and the false doctrine that health is the decisive sign of piety. This accusation prompted the *Pentecostal Evangel* to stop printing reports of the successes of the healing preachers. Many Pentecostals recognize that healing is not the most important aspect of the gospel and, as far as I have been able to determine, Oral Roberts has never suggested that it is.

In all of this the Pentecostals have a reputation of being very gullible. It would surprise many therefore that some Pentecostal pastors with little or no education, but with years of experience in the movement, manifest a remarkable sophistication and are not easily taken in. More officially, the General Presbytery of the Assemblies of God, one of the largest of the Pentecostal denominations, issued a report in 1952 calling attention to the abuses in the healing ministry. This report, issued by a highly responsible group of men, is as sober and circumspect as any of the staidest of the historic churches. It laments the attempt on the part of healers to diagnose diseases, condemns the financial gimmicks sometimes employed ("Is selling prayers any more religious than selling indulgences?") the unfounded claims of success and the emotional excesses.

It should not be thought that Oral Roberts is the object of all these allegations. Whatever negative judgment one feels bound to make on certain elements in his style of ministry, he is a dedicated, talented and sincere servant of the gospel. Finally, any man who has been able to realize his ambitions to found a multi-million dollar university is a man to be reckoned with. Oral Roberts University in Tulsa, Okla., has not yet earned its academic spurs, but it is a step in the right direction.

Questions about the psychological stability of Pentecostals are based on two factors: the emotional content of their prayer services, and their practice of what in Western society is socially unacceptable behavior, speaking in tongues. Depending on the socio-cultural situation, the emotional level can either be excessively high (by Roman Catholic standards) or restrained and contemplative.

It was recognized very early in Pentecostal history that the movement did attract some neurotic types. Frank Bartleman, who has described Pentecostalism's early history—one which he helped to form—wrote: "We had plenty of wrongheaded and wayward people with us. . . . Persons who would not listen to reason and violent characters have tried to cast their lot with us." Experienced Pentecostals will readily admit that in given cases tongues can be a merely hysterical manifestation. Where it is evident that a person needs help Pentecostals are not above urging their members to seek psychiatric counseling.

Some scholars take a dim view of the psychological make-up of glossolalics. The standard treatise on tongue-speaking is by George Cutten who contended (in 1927) that glossolalia is related to schizophrenia and hysteria. Lapsley and Simpson (in 1964), while denying that glossolalics can be considered mentally ill in any clinical sense, still consider them "uncommonly disturbed." In their judgment, tongues fill the psychic function of reducing conflict brought on by a "developmental 'fixation' at an early age in their relationship with parental figures" and is a "dissociative expression of truncated personality development." William W. Wood (in 1965) came to the conclusion that "Pentecostalism attracts uncertain, threatened, inadequately organized persons with strong motivation to reach a state of satisfactory interpersonal relatedness and personal integrity." In an unpublished paper, Andrew D. Lester noted that glossolalic groups he studied manifested childish megalomania, had weak egos, confused identities, high levels of anxiety, and were generally unstable personalities. In a survey of the pertinent literature (in 1968) George J. Jennings came to the conclusion that "most scholars and observers maintain that glossolalists are usually characterized with some personality deficiency."

Many researchers would not only reject these negative judgments, but also would reject the assertion that any such consensus as Jennings postulates exists. Taking up the conclusions of Cutten that glossolalia tends to be related to schizophrenia and hysteria, Alexander Alland (in 1961) countered that the sociocultural data no longer supports such a view. The members of the Negro Pentecostal church that Alland studied were well adjusted to their social environment and, by the norms of socially acceptable behavior, normal in every respect except for speaking in tongues. In 1939 Anton Boisen wrote that: "the rapid growth of eccentric religious cults in recent years may be regarded as a direct result of the shared strain due to the economic depression," but he found no mental illness among the people he studied. Indeed he found several disturbed individuals who found the Pentecostal experience psychologically beneficial. E. Mandell Pattison (in 1964) rejected the position that economic deprivation is a necessary factor in explaining growth. Pattison also found that glossolalics are neither contentious nor emotionally maladjusted. In an early study Lincoln Vivier (in 1960) showed

300

that Pentecostals scale lower on suggestibility than non-Pentecostals; in a later study (1968) he asserted that "glossolalia, as practiced in its religious context, is manifested in normal, non-neurotic persons." Vivier found that glossolalia brings a change in the ego complex which "tends toward the more mature and tends, furthermore, to add quality and enrichment of feeling and depth of meaningfulness." Speaking of Pentecostals within the historic churches, A. W. Sadler (in 1964) contended that the psychic force of glossolalics may not be neurotic but rather the unconscious expressing itself postively in a creative way.

Anxiety and tension, Vivier says, are obliquely associated with glossolalia, that is, not with the practice but with the frequency of tongues. One of the most interesting studies is that of the Jewish sociologist, Nathan Gerrard (1966, 1968), who observed a snake-handling Pentecostal church, using a conventional denomination as a control group. He concluded that there is very little difference between the two groups with regard to mental health, "but whatever differences there are seem to indicate the serpent-handlers are a little more 'normal' than members of the conventional denomination." The list of studies finding good the psychological health among Pentecostals could be extended. These studies and yet unpublished material show that to argue the dubious character of the Pentecostal experience or persons on the basis of psychological data is to argue from very shaky premises.

Before considering the rise of neo-Pentecostalism, a word should be said in criticism of classical Pentecostalism. Classical Pentecostals tend not to distinguish sufficiently between what comes from the human psyche and what comes from the Holy Spirit. As Father Lepargnier has pointed out, the criterion for identifying charisma is not phenomenological, as the Pentecostals generally contend, but functional. Most Pentecostals are given to a fundamentalistic interpretation of the bible that pushes *sola scriptura* principle to its ultimate. Walter Hollenweger insists that even within the Protestant tradition the *sola scriptura* principle holds only within the framework of the church, and the Pentecostals are extremely weak on ecclesiology. Pentecostals tend to absolutize Lukan theology—as Catholics tend to absolutize the Pastoral epistles and the Lutherans a Pauline anthropology and conception of the Spirit. The radical nature-supernature dichotomy of the Pentecostals is hardly biblical, but is familiar to the decadent scholasticism in the Roman tradition and to the tradition in Protestant orthodoxy going back to the 16th and the 18th centuries. The Pentecostals' total approach is too subjective and too individualistic, which has been one of the causes of the fragmentation so characteristic of Pentecostal history. In their devotional literature, not in the life of the church, they give the impression that tongues is the dominant New Testament reality. In defense of the Pentecostals, it should be said that there is hardly a criticism mentioned in this article which Pentecostals have not already made of themselves.

About 1955, Pentecostalism moved into the historic churches, advancing from the lower socio-economic groups to the higher and thus, with one fell blow, shattering all the neat categories researchers had carefully worked out, especially their economic-deprivation theory. From this point on there were to be found large numbers of persons of wealth, education and social position among Pentecostals: doctors, lawyers, university professors, business executives. This movement, which is called neo-Pentecostalism, has had the most profound effect on churches which historically, doctrinally and liturgically, were the farthest removed from Pentecostalism: Episcopalians, Presbyterians, Lutherans. The groups that had the most in common with Pentecostals, that is the Holiness churches like the Church of the Nazarene and the Christian Missionary Alliance, were the least affected. In the spring of 1967, Pentecostalism appeared as a movement within Roman Catholicism. As far as I have been able to ascertain the Catholic bishops are mystified, cautious and basically unhappy (mostly because they lack information), but they have made no overt measures to stem the movement. It is still too soon to assess the reasons for this relative calm within Catholicism in contrast to the vigorous opposition often experienced by Protestant neo-Pentecostals, even to the point of excommunication.

In order to understand the negative reactions within the historic churches, Protestant and Catholic, some attention should be given to the difficulty of an objective evaluation of Pentecostalism. Obviously the first obstacle is the dearth of critical studies by those who have studied in some depth the movement within the classical Pentecostalism and in the historic churches. Church commissions set up to study the problem frequently are inadequate to the task simply because they cannot do the primary research themselves and do not have sufficient scholarly research on which to draw. The result is that judgments are made with only superficial knowledge.

The most formidable obstacle, however, is the public image of Pentecostalism. It is so bad that Pentecostals, classical or neo, never really receive a fair hearing. To the public, Pentecostalism conjures up images of emotional fanaticism, religious mania, illiteracy, messianism, credulity and panting after miracles. It cannot be denied that there is both historical, and to some extent, contemporary justification for this image. But for large segments of the Pentecostal community the image does not reflect the Pentecostal reality. It no more reflects the true nature of Pentecostalism than the Inquisition, the massacre of St. Bartholomew's Day or Alexander VI reflect the essential quality of Catholicism, although all belong to Catholic history.

Fear of religious experience also constitutes an obstacle to an objective evaluation of Pentecostalism. If I approach a lay person, priest, bishop or religious superior with an abstract theological statement he will consider its orthodoxy dispassionately. But if I face him with a religious experience he panics. We have taken the position that religious experience does not belong to the normal Christian life. This is not formulated theologically, but is rather a psycho-theological stance. Catholics inherited this sus-

303

picion from the era of John of the Cross and Teresa of Avila who wrote at a time of some grave scandals; contemporaries claiming to have had religious experiences were later proved to have been either dupes or impostors. A heritage of suspicion was created that is with us still. Within Protestantism the fear of religious experience stems from a too-radical rejection of pietism.

The norms of socially acceptable behavior constitute another obstacle to evaluating Pentecostalism objectively: If one proceeds on the assumption that what is not socially acceptable, whatever its objective merits or demerits, is not worthy of a mature person, then social acceptability becomes the ultimate norm. Obviously, for the vast majority of Americans, and others too, speaking in tongues, prophesying and interpreting the bible are not socially acceptable ways of behaving, however authentic the manifestations may be.

A further difficulty is the very nature of the charismatic gifts. One can subject them to a rational inquiry, examine them psychologically and sociologically and study their economic implications (which do exist). In this way one can learn much about the gifts, but the ultimate spiritual reality eludes such methods. Spiritual gifts can only be discerned spiritually in the function of the kingdom of Christ. St. Paul said quite clearly that the gifts of the Spirit would not be understood, and therefore they would not be received. "An unspiritual person [that is, man left to his own natural resources] is one who does not accept anything of the Spirit of God: he sees it all as nonsense; it is beyond his understanding because it can only be understood by means of the Spirit" (1 Cor. 2:14).

There are some who will admit the existence of the gifts but object to what they consider their abuse. There are abuses and objections to them are well taken. But for large numbers of people what they object to in reality is not the abuse, but to the fact of the gifts. For many, any use of the gifts is an abuse, but as Larry Christenson notes "the cure for abuse is not disuse, but proper use."

304

Another obstacle to an objective evaluation is the history of divisiveness and fragmentation associated with Pentecostalism. Their causes are various. Some have interpreted baptism in the Holy Spirit and the gift of tongues as a direct authority to impose a personal theological view of the spiritual life, the nature of the church and the mechanics of parochial life. This supposed authority has been accompanied by a new legalism, messianic postures and disdain for the uninitiated. Others, on receiving the baptism in the Holy Spirit have, in the first joy of their discovery, been importunate in persuading friends and acquaintances to seek the baptism. This has resulted in alarm, resistance and open opposition. But even when all is in order, when there are no expressions of superiority, messianism or hard-sell, even with the greatest circumspection, opposition has developed; not infrequently it has been an irrational opposition whose vehemence is difficult to account for logically.

A final obstacle to an objective evaluation is the fear on the part of ecclesiastical authorities when they are forced to deal with a dimension which knows no jurisdictional boundaries, which cannot be regulated by decree, which cannot be pre-programmed, pre-planned or pre-structured. In such a situation ecclesiastical authoritarian figures often over-react. This could force a showdown in which persons are faced with the temptation to choose between the structural and the charismatic church, a fatal choice. Structure without the pneumatic, prophetic element is a corpse. But the pneumatic prophetic element without the structure is only charismatic chaos. One might ask whether a purely charismatic ecclesiology is viable. The church order without definitive offices (sacramental orders) as seen in the Corinthian epistles seems to have been rejected even in Paul's lifetime.

Despite all these fears and obstacles, Pentecostalism is growing, in some countries from 9 to 15 times as fast as the historic churches. How is this growth to be explained? Why are Roman Catholics joining the Pentecostal movement?

In the first place, Pentecostals offer not a doctrine, but an experience of God. For persons brought up within the tradition of an arid intellect-and-will, catechism-Catholicism and within the ambience of a raging objectivism (in liturgy, piety, prayer, law), an experience of God in the Pentecostal sense can be the discovery of a new dimension in life. Beyond that, Pentecostals promise that the experience of God will be power-generating, so that one's whole life will be transformed. This power is not hidden in the recesses of the soul, access to which is only through some abstract faith-act; rather it is power experienced within the room in which man experiences his concrete, historical self. Protestant and Catholic neo-Pentecostals share the whole spectrum of problems, personal and social, common to their contemporaries, but one of the problems so acute for others is greatly diminished for them: relevancy. The immediacy of the presence of God, the reality of his love, the power of his mercy, the clarity of his voice in his Word are all so real that they see God active in their personal history. A social psychologist might see in Catholic Pentecostalism the attempt to interiorize the authority which the now-suspect structural church exercised in the past, an attempt to find a new anchor for an institutionally nervous Christianity. Pentecostalism in any of its forms is an attempt to reach behind the formalities and structures which sacramentalize the original Christian experience, and to recapture the original experience itself without the visible sacrament. To this extent Pentecostalism is reductionist.

Even in their impatience with the structures of the Church, Catholic Pentecostals are usually profoundly loyal and have a great compassion for the episcopacy, in marked contrast to their attitude before their Pentecostal experience (which prompted one bishop to remark, "May their tribe increase"). A number of priests and nuns who were uncertain in their vocations have been reconfirmed in them. Neo-Pentecostals are also strongly drawn to prayer, so much so that one might be led to think of Pentecostalism simply as a prayer movement. The prayer meetings of Protestant neo-Pentecostals tend to be much more restrained than those of classical Pentecostals; Catholic Pentecostal meetings are even more so, being indeed the height of propriety.

The neo-Pentecostals are only one manifestation of the contemporary quest for transcendence and a new synthesis, a quest which has religious and secular branches. In the secular branch self-transcendence is sought through the use of LSD, pot, through T-groups, sensitivity sessions and yoga exercises. Two representatives of the religious branch would be neo-Pentecostalism and the underground church. The sociological similarity of Catholic neo-Pentecostalism and the Catholic underground church, to limit the scope, is striking. Father Caporale's characterization of the underground as "covenanting ecclesial units, neither territorially nor hierarchically located, which maintain functional identity boundaries and generate more or less enduring autonomous systems of symbols, control and rewards," is a fairly accurate sociological description of Catholic Pentecostal groups. The whole quest for transcendence tends in both its religious and its secular branches to be a white middle-class activity.

Those in the historic churches who have found a measure of success in their quest for transcendence through the Pentecostal experience are faced with temptations to prophetic enthusiasm. Donald Gee, a classical Pentecostal, gives this advice to the neos: "Do not allow the first rush of novelty where prophetic gifts are concerned to sweep you off your feet. It is all so wonderful, and is such a liberation of spirit, that it is easy to become unbalanced, with speedy disaster. . . . Beware of making too much of 'messages' whether through tongues and interpretation, or any other way. The Spirit of God is not so prodigal with these things as we, in our folly, would have Him to be." Gee has also noted the frequency with which men of academic background seemed to forget all their scholarship and learning; this seems to be especially true of people with theological training. The essential reality which classical Pentecostalism has brought to the attention of the historic churches, the fullness of life in the Spirit and the exercise of the gifts, is of unassailable validity. But Pentecostalism is very weak in exegesis and in doctrine. Classical Pentecostalism cannot make a contribution here, and it is sad to see men of theological attainments taking over the whole Pentecostal vocabulary, exegesis and doctrine, simply because the experience has validity. All too often the result is simple, that neo-Pentecostals repeat the same mistakes that classical Pentecostals made and now regret. Also tragic is the unthinking way in which neo-Pentecostals adopt all the cultural baggage of classical Pentecostalism. Frequently no distinction is made between the experience and socio-cultural components which are not transferrable. Baggage here is not necessarily a pejorative term. It simply means the accoutrements with which one passes through time, which are historically and culturally determined, belonging to a style of life that is not universally valid. The pattern of classical Pentecostalism may have validity for a classical Pentecostal but not necessarily for others. A Lutheran or Presbyterian or Catholic who tries to squeeze himself into this pattern can only be the loser.

VI.

The Spirit as Philosophical Problem

DAVID TRACY

PERHAPS IT WOULD BE most helpful to state immediately one's basic reservations concerning the recent phenomenon of "Spirit-talk" in contemporary American Catholic practice and theology. At the price of sounding world-weary at best and irreligious at worst, the phenomenon seems to this observer significant but certainly not unprecedented in the history of theology (cf. Yves Congar's *History of Theology,* Garden City, 1968, esp. pp. 144–154; 166–168). Positively, the present phenomenon allows a genuinely religious spirit some breathing room within what have often become stifling institutional forms. It also provides for some intellectual flexibility within the often too rigid categories of the Catholic theological tradition. Negatively, however, the phenomenon bears very little long-range theoretical importance for theology. Of course, many in the "underground" church or in the Pentecostal movement find such lack of theoretical significance itself insignificant to their religious concerns. But any of them who have attempted or will attempt to construct a theology from their religious experience of the Spirit must be willing to face up to the strictly theoretical difficulties of their position. Nor does one have to adopt the purely rationalist stance of Brand Blanshard (vis-à-vis Kierkegaard) or the purely naturalist stance of Sidney Hook (vis-à-vis Paul Tillich) or the "linguistic stance" of Anthony Flew (vis-à-vis any "religious" thinker) to share what would undoubtedly be their lack of enthusiasm for the new Spirit-Theology. In the short space available

here, we will try to elaborate and exemplify how such a probably unpopular judgment is possible without forcing one into
an anti-religious or anti-Spirit stance.

At first sight, a specific treatment of the nature of judgment
may seem rather extrinsic to present purposes. Indeed, to consider
it here may risk taxing the prospective reader's patience more
than is judicious. But a number of considerations seem to demand
precisely that risk. For do we not really have to ask ourselves
anew, just what anyone means when he states that he is attempting a philosophical-theological judgment-discernment upon any
phenomenon—especially upon a religious phenomenon that explicitly claims to be able to *discern* the Spirit? Is not such a question particularly exigent at a time when the Kantian critique
of judgment and its influence on Protestant theology have come
under serious questioning from a number of perspectives? Is it
not equally urgent when the Thomist notion of judgment has
become widely recognized as too explicitly objectivist to allow
any immediate aid for the discussion of the presumably psycho-
logical-ontological factors involved in all "Spirit-Talk"? Or can
we really content ourselves with the consoling but probably illu-
sory thought that we somehow possess Pascal's *esprit de finesse*
or Newman's illative sense on the question of "Spirit-talk" and
may, therefore, sidestep a defense of what we mean by judgment at all and move immediately into often exhilarating but
rather short-runned joys of judging in the style of "it seems to
me that," etc. . . .

Indeed, within a context in which the very word "judgment-
discernment" is open to so many meanings it becomes imperative
for any prospective "discerner" of the discerners of the Spirit to
state as clearly as possible just what he thinks he is doing when
he attempts some judgment on their expressions and meanings.
For in this as in any other critical attempt one must be willing
to ask a few relatively uninteresting questions before the more interesting ones can even be formulated. In the present context,
before one may attempt to formulate a language for the Spirit-

phenomenon (section two) or, *a fortiori*, articulate the necessary conditions of possibility for a positive theology of the Spirit and attempt to judge the present American Catholic Spirit phenomenon (section three), one may do worse than say what he thinks judgment itself is. In this article, then, the last two sections are attempts at judgment; while this first is more simply an attempt to say what such an attempt presumes. But it is time to turn from an apologia for the discussion to the discussion itself.

I. The Nature of Inquiry and Judgment

"Judgment," of course, is a very elusive word: the histories of philosophy and of theology are strewn with theories of judgment (Aristotelian, Kantian, Whiteheadian, etc.) each one of which must ultimately defend its position psychologically, epistemologically, and ontologically. This is obviously not the proper place to enter into a discussion of these philosophical dialectics. For present purposes, I prefer to content myself with a brief exposition of the best theory in the nature of theoretic inquiry in general and of the act of judging in particular with which I am familiar, Bernard Lonergan's in *Insight*. While assuming the possibility of different analyses from other philosophical viewpoints, therefore, we will later be employing Lonergan's theory in order to locate some of the more important conditions that impel a relatively negative judgment on the recent theologies of the Spirit.

However, three precautionary notes should first be added. Caution one: the theory is not arbitrarily chosen. For as any careful reader of *Insight* realizes, the core of that work is Lonergan's careful and gradual movement up to, explicitation of, and development from, his peculiar explanation of judgment as a "virtually unconditioned." Caution Two: Lonergan's theory does not occur in a vacuum innocent of the more general philosophical dialectic. Indeed, it bears important and intrinsic connections with a long and respected intellectual heritage (principally,

311

its obvious connections with contemporary theories of the nature of scientific judgments and its historical connections with Aristotle, Augustine, Aquinas, and Newman). Caution Three: Lonergan's theory is employed here not to impose a rigid set of *a priori* categories upon the Spirit phenomenon. Rather, it is chosen precisely because it avoids such rigidity by elaborating an explanatory but flexible theory on the nature of inquiry and judgment which may help to elaborate the necessary "conditions of the possibility" for judging the Spirit phenomenon. In fact, in the present writer's judgment, the Lonerganian language merely (but importantly) provides the most helpful heuristic approach for expediting the discussion.

To recall a central and often overlooked factor in Lonergan's argument, his analysis of the dynamism of human questioning reveals four differentiated, functionally interdependent, and indeed self-structuring levels of inquiry (experience, understanding, judgment, and decision). The original data (the "religious" experience) provokes a whole series of questions: psychological, sociological, anthropological, philosophical, and theological. But before moving into any of those specifications, one should recall that the question impels one to a second level of the cognitional process: All the questions for intelligence (what? why? how often?) provoke insights and concepts on the level of understanding. But the questions for reflections (is it so? is it verified? is it true?) provoke the further and quite distinct kind of critical insights and judgments. For it is on this third level alone that there emerge the notions of truth and falsity, of certitude and probability, of yes or no. On this level, there arises the personal commitment that makes one responsible for one's judgments: for on this level there come the utterances that express one's affirmations or denials, one's assents or dissents, one's agreements or disagreements. In a word, one expresses oneself. With La Rochefoucauld (if less cynically), one really understands why "Everyone complains about his memory, but no one of his judgment." It is time, however, to allow La Rochefoucauld's insight to take a more technical turn.

Accordingly, in the short section, "The General Form of Reflective Insight," lies much of the strength of the entire argument of *Insight*. In Lonergan's terms, the grasp of the sufficiency of evidence for a prospective judgment is a grasp of that judgment as a virtually unconditioned. The meaning of each part of the phrase is critical. "Virtually," first of all, refers to the fact that there are conditions for the judgment but that such conditions are fulfilled. In short, the inquirer is not dealing with a "formally" unconditioned, (that is, a judgment which has no conditions at all) but with a "virtually unconditioned," involving three principal elements:

(1) a conditioned,

(2) a link between the conditions and the conditioned, and,

(3) the fulfillment of the conditions.

Hence, any prospective judgment (for example, Am I understanding this argument, Do I grant the possibility of 'spiritual' religious experience?) will be a virtually unconditioned (and thereby a grasp of the evidence as sufficient) if:

(1) it is conditioned: but the very fact of the actuality of *question for reflection* (Am I understanding?) shows that it is. For the posing of the question itself indicates a conscious recognition of the need for evidence that will insure a *reasonable* pronouncement.

(2) the conditions are known and (3) they are fulfilled (for example, Am I alert at present? Have I understood the context and meaning of the question? Am I detached and disinterested in my inquiry? Am I asking the question in an already differentiated intellectual pattern of experience? And not in any spiritually undifferentiated state? Do I realize the meaning of the word "virtually?" Am I seeking a matter of fact judgment or an absolutely necessary one? etc., etc.) In short do I realize that the very meaning of reflective insight is the power of my own ration-

ality to make precisely that move? Indeed, Lonergan's explicitation of this universal reflective process as the movement of a prospective judgment from a conditioned to a virtually unconditioned by means of a grasp of the (usually) myriad conditions (see sections 2 and 3 for some of these conditions on Spirit-talk) of the conditions and their fulfillment is meant to be not some "deus ex machina" (illumination, "intuition," "vision") to save the epistemological day, but rather a relatively simple explanation (that is, explicitation) of the matter-of-fact (*not absolutely* necessary) behavior of all rational activity. In other words, if the critical inquirer in any theoretical question (for example, what is the relevant question to provide the needed conditions of possibility for Spirit-talk?) grasps that the correct question for reflection, in each case, actually constitutes the conditions, then he may further grasp that behind, within, and grounding the "link," the fulfillment of the known myriad conditions of every case for reflection, is *the condition* of all rational behavior: that rational and structured exigence immanent and operative in all cognitional process—an exigence which always demands a sufficiency of evidence and is satisfied to cease its inquiry only when its own high ideals are fulfilled. It is, then, the immanent cognitional structure itself, set into operation by the reflective question (for example, Is religious experience verifiable and is this experience verifiable as religious?) and finding fulfillment only in a reflective act of understanding, which allows, indeed impels the critical inquirer to make the judgment *it is* (or *it probably is*) or it is not (or probably is not).

II. The Horizons of Religious Inquiry

If the nature of inquiry and judgment can be described in that general way, then the next heuristic necessity becomes to articulate the complexity of the "religious" phenomenon (that is, the data or experience in question here) and the consequent complexity emerging on all levels of inquiry into that phenomenon. For in the present case, the data alone (as "human meaning" or "behavior") are manifold and extremely difficult to determine. For example, even the relatively minor phenomenon of "speaking in tongues" associated with the pentecostal experience has yet to develop measurable criteria. Secondly, the questions of the intelligent inquirer (in, for example, psychology, sociology, or anthropology) upon this manifold and not easily measurable set of behavioral data are also as varied as the various theories in the various human or behavioral sciences. Thirdly, the questions for judgment (for example, What are the conditions of the possibility of religious speech? Are they fulfilled here?) are likewise as varied as the criteria and categories employed by a particular philosophy of religion or a particular theological method and language. Once again it is impossible to enter fully into these many dialectics. Instead, we will again introduce a category— "horizon"—which may expedite the possibilities of the present discussion while forestalling a peremptory approach to the question.

Before defining "horizon" technically, however, it would be well to attempt to set the descriptive mood whence such concerns and categories may emerge. "Mood" here, moreover, refers not to some fleeting and unimportant phenomenon but to the Heideggerian reality described by Macquarrie as a moment of heightened awareness by means of which the right questions may begin. During the few years, for example, every American is, if anything, all too familiar with phrases such as "generation gap," "credibility-gap," etc. By now, moreover, every serious contemporary theological student presumes that he is also familiar (precisely as "post-existentialist") with the much discussed "existential gap." But are we really? As Americans and Catholics, I suspect that just the reverse is true: that we are just beginning to *experience* that gap, however well we may be able to define the category. In fact, as we continue to lose our formerly treasured American and Catholic innocence, is it not far more likely that we will continue to be rapidly and sometimes desperately tossed into the crisis-situation exposed in the late nineteenth and early twentieth centuries by the philosophical and Protestant "existentialists"? For behind the use of the category "existential gap" lies the reality of a fundamental alienation of the horizon-threatened subject from his former world of meaning and, at the limit, from himself and reality. And the self at stake here is not merely the "self" revealed by the sciences of biochemistry or depth psychology or sociology but the yet more basic self as the opening to and/or creator of one's meaning, one's intelligence, one's freedom, one's ability to love, one's very ability to get some positive hold on the complexity of human and cosmic reality. In short, it is the self who has known dread. Even if one cannot express that experience, he knows that somehow and irretrievably his entire former interest, orientation, concern, horizon have become threatened on some basic level. At least two features of such dread are clear and commonplace: a non-specifiable anxiety in the face of such a threat combined with a spontaneous, ingenious, and often subconscious resistance to the demands for radical change now put upon one. From such an experience the only possible liberation is, psychologically, a new self-identity and, ontologically, what can only be called a conversion, that is, an entire shift from my present orientation direction, and concern; a radical transformation of myself, my operations, my worlds of meaning.

Within such an "existential context," the category "horizon" may first be defined metaphorically: as such it is the limit or boundary beyond which one simply cannot see. What lies beyond my present horizon, then, lies not principally in unresolved answers but in unrecognized questions which the phenomenon of dread has finally forced upon me. More technically, a horizon may be defined as a maximum field of vision from a determinate standpoint. It possesses both an objective and a subjective pole, each one of which is conditioned by and conditions the other. The subjective pole refers to the intentionality-meaning possibilities of the present stage of development of the subject. The objective pole refers to the "worlds" of meaning achieved by or open to the subject at his present stage of development. His world, in other words, may be defined as that totality of objects by means of which the subject in his present intentional development can operate.

For example, the subjective pole of an expert in a particular field would be comprised of that set of scientific operations with which he is familiar, while the objective pole is the field or fields (worlds) that such operations may reach. More philosophically the objective pole of a philosopher in the Christian Wolff tradition is all possible being. His subjective pole would be the logical operations of necessity and possibility establishing the relationships between possible and necessary "beings." Or, more to the point, the subjective pole of a philosopher employing transcendental method (Coreth, Rahner, Lonergan) is that method itself; the objective pole is the being intended by and critically grounded in such method. Finally, in such a framework, one may recognize that any man at any stage of his life is open to at least refinement of his horizon, usually development and sometimes even what we have called above conversion (that is, radical transformation).

In his most recent work, Lonergan has not remained content with his earlier analysis of man's horizon constituted by six differentiated worlds (common sense and theory; sacred and profane; interior and exterior) along with various possibilities of integration (for example, elimination, transposition, oscillation, mediation, etc.). Rather he has attempted to formulate a basic theological method whose full complexity (for example, the key concept of functional specialization) cannot be investigated here, but one of whose features merits attention for all theologians, that is, the attempt to allow a genuinely collaborative effort by differentiating the notion of horizon into what he calls with increasing frequency relative and basic horizon. The distinction, I believe, is fundamentally the fruit of Lonergan's (and most

317

Catholic theologians') deeper reading in the problematic of the human sciences (especially psychology, sociology, and cultural anthropology) and in the contemporary philosophical movements of phenomenology and existentialism. But whatever its origin, the distinction itself is clear enough: Relative horizon is one's present horizon relative to one's psychological (education), sociological (society), and cultural (epoch) development. It depends for its articulation on the present stage of development of those varied human sciences. Basic horizon, on the other hand, is the horizon of any man in relation to the presence or absence of what Lonergan begins to call the four basic, that is, transcendental conversions (intellectual, moral, religious, Christian). The key, once again, is conversion. As an operative definition of this central category, one may say that conversion is the actual transformation of the subject, his orientation and operations and therefore his worlds. While it is normally a prolonged process, it is often remembered as concentrated in a few key judgments and decisions. And when we refer here to the four *basic* or transcendental conversions, we are referring to the horizon-factors that must be operative in any genuinely theological inquiry: intellectual (or, more properly, philosophic) conversion; moral conversion, that is, the transformation involved in moving from the level of judgment to that of decision and action: in short, the questions of value, of ethics, of self-constitution; religious conversion, that is, the transformation of the subject when he is aware of himself as possessing an openness not merely as fact and achievement (self-appropriation) but as gift: it is the level, for example, of Jasper's *Eksistenz,* of self as gift of the self by God to the self; Christian conversion, that is, that transformation-in-faith of the subject into the "contagious," if you will, life of the Spirit, into the death-resurrection of Christ Jesus. This later transformation, moreover, must be made in the face at once of one's highest possibilities (cf. Bonhoeffer) and of one's own recognized inability either to indefinitely sustain one's development or to avoid the reality of the surd, the irrational, the genuinely evil factor in one's own life and that of one's society and culture, one's own or other epochs (cf. the "existentialist").

III. The Horizons of the Theologies of the Spirit

A few summary observations, then, are in order here. Judgment (precisely as a grasp of a virtally unconditioned) becomes increasingly difficult as the myriad conditions for critical inquiry expand. For example, on our present question, what we have called "relative-horizon" factors have formerly been either ignored (for example, Luther on the Anabaptists) or treated in purely literary terms (for example, Ronald Knox's treatment of the Anabaptists in *Enthusiasm*). Today, on the contrary, such factors are imperative for the philosophical theologian to absorb especially as the human sciences in question grow ever more complex and technical. In psychology, for example, the conquistador attitude of Freud towards religion is now in fairly widespread disrepute among psychologists as the post-Freudian attempts to deal with the religious phenomenon continue to emerge (most recently, for example, the far more positive approaches of Abraham Maslow or Paul Pruyser or especially the far more rigorous approach of Paul Ricoeur). In sociology and anthropology, Marx's and Durkheim's critiques have yielded to the far more complex languages and more sophisticated data of such very different figures as a Claude Lévi-Strauss or a Peter Berger.

And in a directly parallel fashion, a philosophical theologian's judgment on the basic-horizon factors intrinsic to any religious phenomenon becomes ever more difficult as the philosophical and theological dialectics grow ever more complex. In contemporary theology, for example, it is by no means the "Death-of-God" theologians alone who are fully involved in the philosophical-theological discussion of the God-Talk (or *a fortiori* of "Spirit-Talk"). In fact, the present dialectic has become so complex that merely to list some of the more obvious options demanding

319

serious and prolonged study by anyone in the field is itself a reasonably lengthy task: the contrasted availabilities of the "early" or the "later" Heideger; the use of Whitehead and Hartshorne; the possibilities of the "later" Merleau-Ponty; the subtle employment of American naturalism and pragmatism; the transcendental method of Rahner, Coreth, and Lotz and its historic-political critique by John Baptist Metz; the approach to the question of God by the Lonergan of *Insight* as compared to his more recent work and the work of some of his former students (Novak, Burrell, Dunne, *et al.*); the use of empirical "models" or linguistic analysis (especially, the possibilities of the "later" Wittgenstein), etc. etc.

If the reader acknowledges the accelerating complexity of all serious theoretical study of the religious phenomenon; if he further acknowledges the legitimacy of some kind of distinction between relative and basic horizon factors and finally, if he acknowledges the need on the level of basic horizon first to consider intellectual and moral conversion-factors before differentiating the possibilities of specifically religious "conversions," then he will be in a critical position to recognize the principal conditions that must be considered before making any definitive philosophical-theological judgment of the "underground" and pentecostal phenomena and their resultant Spirit-theologies.

Moreover, if the critic is attempting to judge what claims to be an explicitly *Christian* conversion (the "Holy Spirit") then, besides the conditions listed above, the following must also be studied: the widely acknowledged underdevelopment of a theology of the Spirit in the Western theological tradition; the gradual emergence (in the wake of the scriptural revival) of the needed biblical understandings of the Spirit; the scholarly recovery of the great theologies of the Spirit of the Eastern tradition (especially Origen and Gregory of Nyssa); the studies, in the Western tradition, of such central factors as the distinction between Thomist prudential *discretio* and Ignatian personal 'discernment'; the recovery of the Western mystical tradition and the

320

development of new and largely phenomenonological categories to explicitate and communicate that tradition (for example, Morel on John of the Cross, Fessard on Ignatius of Loyola); the contemporary emergence of a whole series of problematics each of which serves to highlight the inability of traditional categories for the Holy Spirit to handle certain theological tasks (for example, the "Kingdom-Church" relationship; the intrinsic role of the resurrection in redemption; the nature and function of the "magisterium"; the nature of the sacraments and their relationship to faith).

Perhaps it may seem that I have set so many conditions for the prospective judgment that any such judgment is really an impossibility. To state the matter as bluntly as possible, I hope I have. For actually, the more one tries to judge any religious phenomenon, the more the hopes for some classical synthesis or neo-Romantic *tour-de-force* dissolve. Indeed, unless philosophical theologians become willing to recognize, on a purely practical level, the crying need for a collaborative enterprise and, on a more theoretical level, the centrality of the methodological question, the present impasse will continue. And, if one may be permitted to indulge in apocalyptic imagination for a moment, a few more years of this impasse and a few more desperate mythic attempts to save the theological day may well allow the few remaining practitioners of theology to become the alchemists of the behavioral sciences.

But this discussion still leaves me with the need to defend my relatively negative judgment of recent theologies of the Spirit. The basic defense of that position can now be defined: as far as I can see, all of the "Spirit" practitioners and theologians are quite innocent of the nature of theoretical inquiry, of the need to differentiate the myriad conditions before judging, and of the contemporary inadequacy of a return to undifferentiated expressions of religion. But that judgment may best be defended by a specific example: aside from the "underground" and "Pentecostal" movements themselves, probably the most influential "Spirit-theology"

321

among American Catholics at the present time is Dr. Rosemary Ruether's in *The Church Against Itself*. Readers of that often brilliant work and the discussions it provoked (especially the Callahan-Ruether exchange) will recall that besides its more obvious limitations (for example, its too heavy dependence on one school of biblical exegesis or its often dogmatic statements on involved historical questions) there remains a central flaw in the whole enterprise: How in the world is Dr. Ruether able to speak so knowledgeably (that is, so theologically) of the Holy Spirit? Does she realize the sociological, psychological, anthropological philosophical, and theological presuppositional difficulties of her work? Her reply to Mr. Callahan (who wrote a largely sociological critique inspired by Peter Berger along with his own philosophical critique disguised as an incarnational theology) leads me to suspect that she does not.

A second reason for a negative judgment is fundamentally a relative horizon factor, but an extremely important one. It involves what many commentators consider the most important cultural determinant in contemporary Catholicism, namely, the much-discussed shift from classical to historical consciousness. That shift is by now familiar fare to most readers of contemporary theology and we will not belabor it here. Briefly then, in the theoretical realm the shift is one from classical Aristotelian science's concern for the universal, the necessary, the essential, to contemporary science's search for the complete explanation of all the data in terms of their intelligible relationships and its attendant concern for the changing, the probable, and the pluralism of perspectives involved in "the best scientific opinion" on a particular question in a particular period. On a more "existential" level, the collapse of classical theological systems and the slow transformation of classical institutional structures have forced most contemporary Catholics (*pace* Brent Bozell *et al.*) into a development of a genuine historical consciousness. Indeed somewhat hesitantly at first on the level of *aggiorniamento* and now in a full-fledged way on a widespread post-Vatican II and even post-ecumenical front, most Catholic thinkers no longer feel embarrassed to declare both their Catholicism and their contemporaneity.

Besides the generally acknowledged fact of this cultural shift, two factors involved in it seem especially pertinent to a discussion of the "Spirit-phenomenon" and the varied reactions it provokes. In the first place, historical consciousness occurred not first in the Catholic context but outside and often against it (the seventeenth century scientific revolution, the Enlightenment, the nineteenth century German Protestant domination of philosophical and theological thought). It is hardly surprising, then, if those trained within the structural and ideological security of the classical Catholic world should immediately distrust and/or reject any such "Spirit-talk." Their present dilemma is most graphically expressed by the desperate rapidity with which they find themselves quoting Luther's cries against the Anabaptists before returning to their anti-Luther polemics.

In the second place, the previous entries of historical consciousness (notably into the empirical and human sciences, into philosophy and into Protestant theology) have all been attended by a Romantic period. Indeed, such a period almost seems to be a necessity: to allow the newly-liberated culture to experience its varieties of spare, strange, original uniqueness again; and to allow time for the theoretic exigence to emerge anew and to formulate the methods and categories needed for its new tasks (for example, the experience of the young Hegel or the Protestant development of a hermeneutic from the Romantic hermeneutic of Schleiermacher and Dilthey through the more complex technical developments of Husserl, Heidegger, and Gadamer). Once again it is hardly surprising if the Catholic (especially the American Catholic) community should feel compelled to indulge in its own Romantic revival. Now, this is not to argue with supremely Toynbeean serenity that history must repeat itself. Indeed all the previous historical situations are only analogous to ours and certainly not definitive. For example, the American

323

Catholic theological situation has for so long been strained by the pure rigidity of the manualist approach and the inflexibility of many of its institutions that the short space of time available to it either to recover its own theological sources (the biblical, patristic, mediaeval, liturgical, philosophical revivals) or to enter and understand the modern and contemporary periods may well prolong and intensify the Classicists' antagonism towards the Romantics and the Romantic distrust of theory. In fact, the original difficulties attendant upon the classical Greek and medieval movements into the differentiated consciousness of *theoria* and the still further difficulties of the collapse of that movement into the sterile rigidity of the manuals along with the later and still-evolving transformation of that movement into the yet more complex and demanding exigencies of historically conscious *theoria* have tempted many Catholics to abandon the demands of theory and content themselves with the enriching but ultimately disappointing delights of an undifferentiated, that is, romantic consciousness.

It is true, of course, that these shifts in Roman Catholic theology and practice have not yet occurred upon a universal front. But that they have occurred is indisputable—and not merely on the 1950's level of Toynbee's "creative minority," but also on the widespread and far more influential front represented most clearly by the majority of the documents of Vatican II and most graphically by the creative and inevitably controversial "Dutch" catechism. Indeed the earlier struggles of the biblical, partistic, liturgical, and ecumenical "return to the sources" have already found eloquent and irreversible expression in the decrees and reforms initiated by that council. In that return, a clear, indeed, a radical openness to judgment by the "Word of God" is especially prominent—and, I suggest, the key reason for the two-edged success of the "aggiorniamento." For the classical consciousness of the Catholic Scholastic tradition (including most of "neo-Thomism") *has* yielded to a gradually evolving historical consciousness represented first by positive empirical studies of the bible, fathers,

councils, liturgical decrees, etc., and secondly by the exigencies of
continental personalism and phenomenological existentialism.
One need only recall the careful historical work of a Congar, a
De Lubac, and a Küng, the aesthetic and kerygmatic impact of a
von Balthasar, or the interpersonal categories of Schillebeeckx's
sacramental theology to taste anew the freshness of recovery in
the best thought of that period. Still it may be well to recall that
the European Catholic theological context has, by and large, not
abandoned a theoretic critique of its religious tradition but has
attempted to restore and restructure that critique in the light of
the richer context made available by its return to the sources and
re-emergence of a rigorously philosophical pluralism. The work
of Karl Rahner from his earliest articulation of a transcendental
method through his development of the notion of the "supernatural existential" and its many applications, to his present theoretical struggle with the historico-political factors exposed by his
former student, John Baptist Metz, reveals but one outstanding
example of a more widespread European Catholic phenomenon.

In American Catholic thought, with which this article is principally concerned, the situation is far more difficult to understand.
In the first place, our own historical sense of our relatively brief
American Catholic past has not received any definitive treatment—perhaps because many of us vaguely suspect that there is
not too much to recover. Yet such vague suspicions cannot veil
the need for such recovery—and on a level coincident with the
highest demands of contemporary historical scholarship and the
most rigorous critique of the cultural and theoretic expressions of
the American Catholic religious experience. But instead of such
a recovery the present situation seems, to this observer at least,
rather disheartening. The liturgical movement, once so promising, seems not to have returned to a more rigorous theoretic
critique of its foundations but seems to have retreated into a
basic lack of trust of its own foundations combined with somewhat vague and critically innocent calls for joyful "revolutions."
The American Catholic biblical revival still seems reluctant to

325

enter fully into the theoretic demands of the Bultmannian and post-Bultmannian hermeneutic problem. And, on a more practical level, attempts at structural reforms in the American Catholic Church too often collapse into an impasse in which neither side seems quite able to risk even trusting the other—much less entering into fully critical, that is, theoretical and factual, discussion of the relevant issues. It is true that the American Catholic philosophical situation seems at present not only promising but possibly salvific for theology: the genuine revival of different traditions of Thomism; the accelerating interest in transcendental method or phenomenological ontologies; the full-fledged entry into the Anglo-American philosophical traditions. But for reasons which only some future historian may properly unravel, the full impact of those revivals have yet to transform American Catholic theology. For example, a philosophically very American—and religiously (perhaps to his surprise) very Catholic—thinker like Daniel Callahan seems lately to prefer psychological and sociological critiques of theological phenomena rather than the philosophical critique and constructions which he might well achieve. But we must not paint too bleak a picture. For there still remain many (Burrell, Dunne, Dupré, Lonergan, Dewart, Richardson Fontinell, *et al.*) who, in their very different ways, do attempt to recover and reconstruct a philosophical-theological critique of religious experience in a context both contemporary and, in the best sense of the word, Catholic.

In the meantime, however, central attention must probably be accorded to the not anti-theoretical but simply a-theoretical attempts of the at first expanding and now exploding American Catholic Romantic religious phenomenon. And since I doubt that either of the earlier two sections would convince most of the present members of the "underground" and "pentecostal" movements on the need for theory, perhaps a consideration of some more pragmatic factors may prove more effective, namely, the inherent religious dangers of a long-range anti-critical stance.

Indeed, in a day when the popular American "religious"

Weltanschauung can collapse any genuinely religious basic horizon into the complacency of the "everyday" speech of fundamentalism (from Heidegger's *Gerede* to Simon and Garfunkel's "dangling conversations") the pentecostals and spirit-theologians might well reconsider their own mistrust of theory. For unless theological inquiry of religious practice and speech begin once again to take the theoretic enterprise in earnest (not necessarily, of course, with the articulations given above) then the general distrust accorded all "conversion" experiences and "religious" speech by that highly elusive and, at his best, highly differentiated consciousness called "contemporary man" must be judged well-merited. For notice what can all too easily happen to once genuine speech if it becomes content with itself too readily and criticizes itself too lightly. It almost inevitably arrives at the dead-end of "everyday" (theologically, read fundamentalistic) and eventually corrupt religious speech. Nor is that phenomenon confined to religious conversion. For example, "intellectual" conversion can become reserved in the popular mind for now mythic figures like Einstein or Teilhard (what splendid poster-materials their extraordinary faces provide!). Or "moral" conversion can become identified with the "Up With People" moral rearmament group. "Religious" conversion can become the reserve of eventually desperate proselytizers for the quickest "now" trip to the "Divine" like Tom Wolfe's Ken Kesey or Timothy Leary's Timothy Leary. Or "Christian" conversion can become identified, at once extreme, with mere church attendance or, at the other, with Oral Robert's faith-healing by placing one's hands on the television set. The problem is not that the originating moment in almost any of the above examples could not really open one's horizon to the transforming possibilities of conversion. But they do not. Why? At least a major part of the reason may well be that (short, of course, of Western *hubris*) it is impossible any longer for a sophisticated contemporary mind to allow such "conversions" to develop or even endure without engaging in the most rigorous inquiry upon even its richest moments and its

327

possible foundations. We have seen too often how "religion" can become no more than an intellectual failure of nerve. How "God" can become an emotional uplift for the "gaps" in our lives. How "Spirit" can become an unexamined blanket-word to cover a whole range of rich but too-fleeting experiences which may or may not be real (that is, true). For the perhaps unpleasant fact remains that no alert contemporary Westerner can really turn his back on science, on criticism, on *theoria* (in a word, on differentiated consciousness) even in his articulation of his "moral," "religious," and "Christian" life. More accurately, he can do so only at the price (too often and too willingly paid, I fear) of having that life, at first ecstatic, dissolve into the adventitiousness of a "religious" atmosphere or a "leisure" moment or harden into the brittleness of an ideology.

In my judgment, then, what the Spirit-theologies fundamentally represent is the cultural emergence in the American Catholic world of a basically healthy and widespread Romantic revival. But when the revivalists turn to theology they seem either to return to a classical biblicism or to create undifferentiated categories which are left theoretically undefended because usually indefensible. One may even agree that the contemporary under-thirty generation demands a McLuhanite world where they may live "mythically and in depth." One may also applaud those theologians who have attempted to capture that world, as William Hamilton does in his brilliant essay "From Prufrock to Ringo." One may further wish to encourage without patronizing a theologian like Rosemary Ruether in her plea for religious breathing space *via* some kind of recovery of the originating Christian eschatological spirit. And one may join this writer in refusing to label the present Spirit-movement as simply another kind of *Zeitgeist* theology. But still one's former theoretical reservations hold. And for one who does not claim to be a discerner of spirits but only a philosophical theologian such reservations are critically binding. Indeed, in a day when even the establishment journals like *Time* can list those who do or don't have soul or the

New York Times can list those who are and are not charismatic (and can even inform its quiet Sunday readers on the availability of Rock as Salvation) one need not search for what the great American Mainstream likes to call fringe groups in order to document the American Romantic revolt.

It had been said of Giambattista Vico, the great eighteenth century precursors of the later Romantics, that his insistence upon the "priority of poetry" against *philosophic* rigidity was a doctrine thought out at the end of the seventeenth century, written in the eighteenth, read in the nineteenth, and understood in the twentieth. I trust that our present theological Romantics will not have to wait that long for recognition. But I also hope that they may learn again not to distrust others or themselves when they find that they usually cannot reject the demands of critical investigation upon even their richest and most ineffable experiences—and that such investigation must be done in the light of the authentic traditions of our past and the almost incomprehensible demands of our uneasy present and our uncertain future. In the meanwhile, I hope that they have experienced God's forgiving Spirit deeply enough to pardon one who, at the last, must join Yeats to say: "So get you gone, von Hügel, though with blessings on your head."

VII.

The Spirit and Church Authority

DANIEL MAGUIRE

AT ROOT, we are all idol-makers who would capture God and truth in static form. We instinctively shy from the Spirit of God who is life and process and surprise. We are strangers to the mobile God of ancient Israel who in "great times" was active and poured out his living spirit on the dead bones of Israel and his people lived. At other times he slept and seemed uninvolved and his people protested this in their liturgies.

Rabbinic teaching was saying at the time of Christ that God's spirit had disappeared with the last of the great prophets. Yet hope perdured in the God who loved "with an everlasting love," who had promised new outpourings of his spirit "on all mankind." The faith of many found this outpouring in Jesus, the man who was "conceived of the Holy Spirit." "The Spirit of the Lord is upon me," he said, and for those who believed him, Yahweh was wide awake again.

Suddenly the Spirit was everywhere, building community, firing believers with love, filling all with understanding. Through the Spirit all know the things of faith; all "are taught by God"; all have gifts of understanding and "need be taught by no one." The Spirit gives each person the capacity to judge, to love, to be free and to be glad. The gift of the Spirit was lavish and without rules. Of unbaptized believers Peter could say: "they have received the Holy Spirit just as much as we have" (Acts 10:47). The earliest New Testament theology of the Spirit was an exuberant and optimistic religious anthropology. It was also a bit

330

naïve. Enthusiasm generated absurdities and joyously attributed them to the Spirit of God. (Some early gnostics interpreted Christian freedom as a repeal of the commandments . . . especially those regulating sexual conduct.)

Organization and the development of ministries was healthy and inevitable. It did, in fact, obtain, bringing with it, of course, the inherent danger of institutional religion, the danger of "localizing" by arbitrary *fiat* the God whose Spirit it seeks. The religious quest for the Absolute leads to the formation of the *QAHAL* and then, it would seem from history, the *QAHAL* is inclined to evade the quest for the Absolute by absolutizing and sacralizing itself, its history and its instruments. In Exodus they took their golden earrings, melted them into an image and said "Here is your God." The Church, like Israel, is tempted to idolize, to leave its God and to worship its own ornaments. Some historical perspective might help us to assess the extent of our modern idolatries.

The very early Church was not without ministries. It was versatile and liberal in creating, shaping and even discarding them. Aside from the apostles, prime witnesses of the Christ event, we find prophets, evangelists, teachers, pastors, overseers, presbyters, leaders, presidents, stewards or administrators. These ministries were not a primary reality around which the Church was structured, but rather involved functions within the Christian life of service. The lists of ministries (1 Cor. 12:28–31; Rom. 12:6–8; Eph. 4:11) vary without apology. One individual might claim several ministries. There is no indication of a fixed set of "offices" destined for all time.

More is known of the Corinthian Church than any other New Testament Church. Paul was convinced that this Church was enriched in every way and lacking in no spiritual gift (1 Cor. 1:5,7; 2 Cor. 8:7). In this Church, and apparently in all the Pauline Churches, there was little of the structuring later to be considered essential and divinely designated. There was no monarchical episcopate; there appears to have been no presbyters

331

and no ordination to office by the laying on of hands. In this Church, as Küng writes: "Anyone who is qualified for a particular ministry—as prophet, teacher, helper, superior, bishop or deacon, etc.—and who performs it properly, has received the call of God and the charism of the Spirit." Indeed in the indisputably Pauline letters, the term *episcopos* is found only once, and then in the plural, suggesting a collegial arrangement (Phil. 1:1). (Luke's contention in Acts 14:23 that Paul "appointed elders . . . in every Church" tends to be seen today as influenced by later tradition.)

The early Church did not see Jesus as having brought them the fullness of truth. The Spirit was expected to lead them "to the complete truth" (John 16:13). There was, however, great reliance on the power of the truth that was revealed in Christ. The term "charism of truth" was used by Irenaeus, not to describe the teaching power of Church officers, as it is in Vatican II, but to express the power of the truth itself. The title "vicar of Christ" was first applied to the Spirit. It was not in men of special rank that basic doctrinal security reposed, but in the power of the Spirit of truth. While the apostles lived and could provide living witness of the genetic Christian experience, the Church was adequately served by the rather fluidly and sporadically developed ministries of apostolic witnesses, and there was room for prophecy and charism. The death of the last apostles and the persistent influx of variant, interpretative theologies changed all this.

In the post-apostolic Church, the systematizing that had already begun became more intense and precise. In a true sense, there could be no "successors of the apostles" since the apostles were first-hand witnesses of the revelation which had been given, in Jude's words, "once and for all." Apostolicity, a property of the whole Church, came to be seen as the essential criterion of being "in the Spirit," of being in contact with the initial formative revelation. The notion of apostolic succession when it appears in Hegesippus, Irenaeus, Tertullian and Origen is understood in terms of the maintenance of apostolic doctrine. As Congar says, the "links of this succession are principally those of an authentic teaching."

The line of "succession" went like this: God spoke in Jesus; the apostles experienced the revelation of God in Jesus. After the death of the apostles, those who had heard them had prime credentials. Thus Irenaeus could claim instruction by Polycarp who had listened to John; Mark was thought to have been instructed by Peter and Luke by Paul. (The glut of pseudo-apostolic writings indicate this same system of dependence.) Cities such as Rome, Smyrna, etc., founded by apostles, were considered as specially reliable witnesses to truth. The custom of arguing from "Fathers," unimpeachable authorities from the past, began in the second century and by the time of the Nestorian heresy was an established technique.

The rise of the "bishops" was extraordinary. Though he did not use the later term "hierarchy," Ignatius of Antioch had a markedly hierarchical view of authority and church. He tells the Magnesians and Trallians that in being subject to their bishop they are subject to God. The bishop comes to be seen as a kind of personification of the Church in Cyprian, with his "bishop in the Church and the Church in the bishop." Old Testament notions of king and high priest, as well as the notion of prince, are applied to bishops by Origen and Hippolytus. Texts which originally were applied to all Christians were now limited in application to the bishops: "A spiritual man . . . is able to judge the value of everything and his own value is not to be judged by other men" (1 Cor. 2:14). From the time of the pastoral epistles, there are signs of a developing monarchical episcopate. This development could scarcely have been seen as divinely established since it did not become general practice until the middle of the second century.

Omens and signs were much heeded by the pagans in appointing men to high office. Something similar developed in the Church as historical backtracking became difficult and office-holders became the main guarantors of truth. Councils often

333

claimed the support of visions. Visions and supernatural communications are attributed to St. Cyprian. St. Bernard weights the "signs" in deciding between Innocent II and Anacletus II. Inspiration and revelation are loosely attributed to episcopal and conciliar statements.

The allusions to kings and high priests understandably diminished the stress on service in the development of the episcopal role. Still, Cyprian could say that he had made no decisions "without the approbation of the people." Bishops were elected by the people and were concerned to give reasons for their decisions. They were to be men excelling in love. To receive someone *episcopaliter* was to receive him with generous hospitality. An effort was made to choose genuinely holy men for the episcopal function. Authority continued to be seen as separable from ecclesiastical appointment. Holy men had an authority directly from God. (Later, in the monothelite and iconoclast crises, authority passed from hierarchical figures to the monks, whether priests or not, because of their undisputed sanctity.)

The rise of the episcopacy, however, was paralleled by the decline of the charismatic and prophetic in the Church. It is true that as late as the Didache (ca. 100) the prophets are in the highest regard in the community. Prophets still celebrate the Eucharist and are permitted to digress from the customary ritual. When there are not enough prophets and teachers, bishops and deacons are to be chosen. The Didache admonishes the people not to belittle bishops and deacons "for they are worthy of honor along with prophets and teachers" (15:2).

Although 1 Thessalonians urged the faithful not to "suppress the Spirit" or to treat "the gift of prophecy with contempt," prophets who ranked second only to apostles in early lists of ministries, were soon eclipsed by appointed officers. During the second century they are still to be found, but by the third century they disappear.

For the first Chrisitans, scripture meant what we call the Old Testament. Gradually, however, the Christian scriptures were formed. Again, apostolicity was the critical factor. By what Cullman calls "the principle of a canon," the Church "drew a line under the apostolic tradition." Without stating the invalidity of subsequent religious experience, the Church "subordinated the subsequent tradition . . . to the superior criterion of the apostolic tradition codified in sacred Scripture." (Oscar Cullman, *The Early Church,* Westminster, 1966, p. 90) Four gospel accounts were canonized in the Christian scriptures. Celsus wrote that the Christians treated the gospel "like drunkards" by "recoining it three and four and many times." Many Christians agreed. Strong efforts to reduce the "gospels" to one were made. Interestingly, the most notable efforts were made by men eventually recognized by the Church as heretics—Basilides, Marcion, Tatian, the Valentinians. The prevailing mind of the Church was not scandalized by the multiplicity. It made sense that the divine revelation should be refracted through a plurality of forms. Heresy, as ever, was guilty of reductionism and a narrow selectivity.

The establishment of a scripture did not mean the adoption of a *sola scriptura* stance by the Church. The Spirit was not to be limited to the pen. Tertullian, Clement of Alexandria, Basil, Epiphanius and others did not feel that all apostolic richness was contained in the sacred pages.

From the second century on, unanimity of the Churches was an authoritative criterion of truth. According to the classical and sanguine formulation of Vincent of Lerins, that was to be believed which had been believed "everywhere, always, and by all." Unanimity will be seen into modern times as a sure sign of revelation. (It was used by Pius IX and Pius XII to justify the dogmas of the Immaculate Conception and the Assumption.)

The Constantinian event had an influence on the developing Church that was nothing less than colossal. It created changes that linger on in present day Christian consciousness. Clerical separatism and juridicism become conspicuous presences in this epochal time. Bishops had become increasingly strong in the third century. In the Constantinian Church they became *illustri,* equal in prestige to senators. They were vested with honors, subsidies and civic authority. They and their clergy were draped in privileges and immunities. (The Theodosian Code has strong penalties for those who would fraudulently pretend to clerical status to reap its advantages.) Eusebius did not sing alone when he greeted these events in eschatological tones.

The wine of imperial favor was a heady one. Jesus had warned his followers of how the pagan kings ruled. "This must not happen to you." But the new status was beguiling, and heavily juridical notions of authority, society and office seeped into the Christian ecclesial mind. The osmosis of Roman legality was thorough and so the expression: *ecclesia viget lege Romana.* By the time of Gregory I (590–604), it was decreed that Roman law should be used whenever no relevant ecclesiastical law could be found.

The Constantinian experience also hastened the formation of a separate clerical caste. In the early Church the ministries were seen as functions. Now they constitute the minister a different kind of being. Gradually the notion of *character,* developed by Augustine in another context, was found admirably suited to give ontological basis for the new differentiation of clergy and laity. Pope Celestine I wrote the bishops of Narbonne that they should be distinguished by their knowledge and conversation, not by their dress or "manner of life." His enjoinder was overriden by the processes of clericalization. Special dress, which had not been required even for the liturgy, became common in the fifth century, as did the tonsure. Clerical celibacy made its uneasy but highly significant debut. The stage was set for Gratian's: "There are two kinds of Christians," and for Urban II's "two kinds of life . . . one to help the insufficiency of the weak, another to perfect the goodness of the strong." The creation of specialists is a classical retreat from the rule of the Spirit.

A revolution in the notion of authority occurred in the middle ages. It is sharply visible in the reforms of Gregory VII. In a desire to free the Church from its identification with political society, Gregory sought to establish the Church as a sovereign society in its own right with power over kings and their kingdoms. He commissioned scholars to comb Roman and ecclesiastical sources for supportive juridical texts. A narrowly juridical conception of Church authority emerged from the burgeoning canonical studies. In earlier thinking, authority was God's and was visibly and sacramentally represented in Church ministers and "vicars." God's authority and power could be vertically, iconologically *presenced* in his ministers. After the Gregorian reform, as Congar writes, *"vicarius* came to indicate, to a steadily increasing degree, a delegated assistant himself possessing an authority handed over by a founder in the past."

The apparently subtle change was massive in its consequences. Church officers, especially the pope (whose office in this period was much affected by what Weiler calls "totalitarian thinking"), rather than imperfectly reflecting God's authority came to be seen as *possessing* it through delegation. Indeed, authority came to be seen as embodied in the officeholder. A confusion of ecclesiastical with divine authority ensured in succeeding centuries. The change was marked by a switch from a sacramental and mystical to a juridical ecclesiology. Juridical categories converted the Church into what Stickler has called the *Corpus Christi juridicum.*

Though authority at the episcopal level was radically influenced by this thinking, the error was most telling in the subsequent history of the papacy. Papal claims in the ninth century, strategically buoyed by the False Decretals, already had an absolutist tinge. The twelfth-century renaissance of Roman law lent itself to a structuring of these claims. In Roman law the subject of law is the individual and in public law the subject is not the people but the state conceived of as a person. The roots of absolutism are contained in this abstractionism since the power of the prince can come to be seen as the personification and embodiment of the people with their rights and powers. Add to this the perennial temptation of any leader to say *"L'état c'est moi,"*

337

and it will explain how some deviant and stubborn forms of papalism rivaled the sovereignty theories of Bodin and Machiavelli in philosophical absolutism.

Aegidius of Rome said that the supreme Pontiff could be "called the Church." Sylvester Prierias believed the universal Church to be "virtually" in the Pontiff. The Church was described as "the body of the Pope." The confusion of divine and human authority can be seen in Tancred's: ". . . he represents God because he takes the place of Jesus Christ . . . he can grant dispensations beyond the law or against the law." Witness, too. Bernardus Palmensis: "In everything he wants, his own will is the only norm of action." Some went so far as to speak of the presence of Christ under the pontifical species. St. Catherine saw the pope as "gentle Christ on earth." Ockham reports some as saying that if the pope contradicted the gospel, they would believe him rather than the gospel. Others opined that by a special revelation the pope could change Church's nature and set St. Paul aside in favor of Roman law.

This pontifical fever was running high in some quarters at the time of Vatican I. Aubert records a remark of the bishop of Geneva to the effect that there had been three incarnations of the Son of God: in the womb of the Virgin, in the Eucharist, and in the old man of the Vatican. *La Civiltá Cattolica* explained that "when the pope meditates, it is God who thinks in him." Pius IX was not unaffected by all this. When Cardinal Guidi quoted tradition to ground his modest reservations about the definition of infallibility, Pius replied: "There is only one tradition; that's me." Recently, the American bishops' pastoral on *The Church in Our Day* says that "no one would maintain . . ." that even "all the laity together should be heard by the Christian community in the same way that the Pope in his office of Chief Shepherd" is to be heard.

Fortunately, these currents have not run unopposed. The expression attributed to Jerome had much resonance: *orbis major urbe.* Tradition also enshrined the axiom: What affects all should be treated by all. Gratian took the forgery: "The pope is to be judged by no one" and added "unless he should deviate from the faith." Cardinal Anibaldeschi in the thirteenth century said that any Church authority could be resisted on grounds of better information, even when there was threatened excommunication. Suárez countenanced disobeying a pope who blocked a necessary council. And Bellarmine, for all his stress on papal authority, conceded that the Church would be in a sorry state if it had to accept a pope who was doing it serious harm. Furthermore, the papal power was never ontologized and given indelible status, as is attested by the multiple depositions of popes in Church history. Important, too, were the moderate conciliar theories that developed widely in the Church of the twelfth and thirteenth centuries and which found blessing at the Council of Constance. These theories emphasized the inability of the pope to gainsay the faith of the living Church.

It was not just the papacy that was victimized by being molded into an image of divinity. The holy scriptures have been similarly treated. Tertullian felt that "a doctrine is false by the very fact that scripture does not speak of it." Irenaeus branded the scriptures "divine" and "perfect." For the early apologists, the Old Testament was the source of all truth. The Alexandrians emphasized the absolute authority of scripture. To establish the omniscience of scripture, the early Fathers took pains to show that the wisdom of the pagans was pilfered from our holy writ. After referring to the sciences of physics, ethics and logic, Jerome said that whatever man's tongue could speak, whatever his mind could encompass is contained in scripture.

For the men of the middle ages, the book of nature and the book of the soul could only be deciphered by reference to the bible. Roger Bacon wrote that all the wisdom useful to men can be found in the bible, although, he conceded, all of it is not therein explained. The Protestant reformers, reacting against the sacralization of tradition and office, cannot be excused of a sacralization of scripture.

The great councils, a perennially favored technique for probing ecclesial wisdom, fared somewhat better. The manifest humanity of their proceedings generally discouraged their excessive aggrandisement. Indeed, Gregory of Nazianzen was of the opinion that no council had ever turned out well. Augustine's remarks on councils are more helpful and realistic. He says that even in the case of universal councils, "the earlier are often corrected by those which follow them, when, by some actual experiment, things are brought to light which were before concealed, and that is known which previously lay hid." (He used the verb *emendare* to describe the correction of past councils)

In the period of the counter-reformation (a strange but not entirely undescriptive term), a further consolidation of the authority of officeholders took place. The experience of ebullient diversity banished hope that the power of Christian truth was such as to ensure decisive unanimity. The important magisterial role of the universities in the thirteenth, fourteenth and fifteenth centuries waned in the new climate. In subsequent centuries, the boundaries between the juridical and the epistemological blurred as Irenaeus' "charism of truth" no longer referred to the inherent power of revelation but to the power of officeholders to discern orthodoxy. At the hands of theologians "the rule of faith" which used to signify the normative content of the faith came to refer to the official proclamation of the faith by the "divinely assisted" hierarchical magisterium. The juridical metaphor was dominant in the understanding of hierarchical teaching. A doctrinal pronouncement was seen in a manner similar to the enactment of law. An "official" statement is binding if certain conditions are fulfilled and if the officials will to invoke their full authority. The will to bind would, apparently, be a sign of the activated assistance of the Holy Spirit. The modern Rahner-Vorgrimler dictionary puts it baldly when it says that the magisterium is a teaching competence "juridically embodied." The seductive comfort of such an approach is that it views the "official" as divinely blessed. The problems here merit further comment.

340

Vatican II confronts the illusion that we live in a post-magical world. It appeals for "a more critical ability to distinguish religion from a magical view of the world and from the superstitions which still circulate." Although magicians inhabit every forum, magic is a natural hazard for religion. The "magico-religious" category of anthropology shows that magic is stimulated when the achievement of results seems beyond our native resources. In the world of science, magic delayed technological growth. In religion it is the bane of creative response. The scantiest look at history shows that the Church, intent on finding God's will and mind, and aware of the insufficiences of its own criteriologies, has, at times, substituted magic for genuine religious dependence on the Spirit of God.

Sacralization has been our favorite magical indulgence. Sacralization occurs when persons, formulae or things are seen not only as manifesting the sacred or functioning in the realm of the sacred, but as somehow substantively embodying the sacred. Juridical trappings and categories have regularly attended this process, endowing it with respectability and order. It is important to see how the sacralizing process has affected the teaching and ruling function in the Church, the scriptures and dogmatic traditions, in order to determine the proper response of the Christian to these realities.

In the view of the magisterium that has prevailed especially since Trent, the magisterium has been thought of as hierarchical. The pope or the bishops with the pope can achieve infallibility in their utterances on faith or morals. In point of fact, there is no instance of hierarchical teaching on particular moral questions that is seen as "infallible." In other matters infallibility is rarely claimed, especially of late, as the complexity and history of doctrine and language is appreciated. (Vatican II was avowedly fallible.) More practical in this view of the magisterium is the assertion that the pope and the bishops are *ex officio* the "authentic" teachers of the faith. Such "authentic" teaching claims the "religious assent" of the faithful. According to Paul VI, the magisterium could "preserve and teach the faith . . . without the help of theology." It would not be easy, the pontiff concedes, since it would be done without revelation and inspiration and "only with the assistance of the Holy Spirit." Still, it is for the magisterium to "make an authoritative judgment in the light of revelation on new doctrines and on the solutions proposed by theology." Pius IX had put it as clearly saying that it was the duty of the hierarchy to direct theology.

Such a position has difficulties. It treats the magisterium as a preter-theological preserve. As soon as you begin to explain the Christian faith, however, you enter theology and the problems thereof. Scripture itself contains varying theologies. Furthermore, if the magisterium must direct theology and rule on its findings, it has set for itself a supremely theological task. This task, in fact, demands skill not only in historical theology but in exegesis, linguistics, philosophy, etc. The achievement of this theological task without an essential dependence on theological skills sounds dangerously magical. It is also redolent of docetism, which would escape the human condition in the pursuit of the sacred.

If the hierarchical magisterium purports to move amid theological findings and, as though with a diving rod, to discern truth from error, it must and does claim to do so through the assistance of the Holy Spirit. There is another difficulty here. The assistance of the Spirit is not pressed on unwilling subjects. The teaching grace can be blocked by sin. The American bishops' pastoral admitted that "those in apostolic office who violate the limits of their authority . . . diminish their effectiveness in echoing Christ authentically." The promise of Christ's ultimate victory does not allow us to prescind from the darkening influence of sin. If the magisterial reliability of officeholders, singly or corporately, is not dependent on their "disposition and cooperation" (Trent), then we have at once the heresy of forced grace and the "something for nothing" of magic. If it is so dependent, it cannot elude theological evaluation and the possibility of dissent.

342

Assent to the "authentic" teachers cannot be absolutized. (Thomas More is lauded for opposing his hierarchy in a serious matter.) Rather, if error in hierarchical teaching is recognized in a reliable fashion, it is *dissent* and not *assent* that is religious. The wide dissent of theologians and other Christians to the *Humanae Vitae* of Paul VI is, I believe, a good example of religious dissent. The distressing spectacle of the old teaching on contraception being brought forth again long after its philosophical and theological underpinnings had been cut away, is, among other things, a betrayal of the traditional notion of the oneness of truth. Relying on "the light of the Holy Spirit, which is given in a particular way to the pastors of the Church," the encyclical abstracted from the development of thought that has taken place in the entire human community on this subject. Whatever "light of the Holy Spirit" animated this development of human consciousness is treated as negligible. In the presuppositions of this encyclical, the Spirit, to be heard and to be deemed authentic, must "go through channels." The inevitably limited witness of deceased popes is heard with fixational intensity while the presence of the Spirit in the living Church is bypassed. Dissent to this limiting theology of discerning the Spirit is a religious necessity.

What then of the papal and episcopal roles? First of all, it is inexact to say that there is a revolt against authority today. There is a revolt against authority figures who appear like obstructive icebergs in shipping lanes, frozen fragments from another world. There is also a healthy revolt against sacralized pretenders in Church and state. But human hearts still long for leadership. Edward L. Long has said that the Christian Churches lack a science of leadership and when a great leader happens along we dub it a charismatic event. This lack should be met. Rulers and teachers in new forms are needed for a new age. Ruling leadership should be such as to create growth and peace. Where growth and peace are absent, it is a fair sign of deficient leadership. A breakdown of creative order will be diagnosed by leaders as disobedience or a lost sense of law and order. This is an understandable, defensive simplism. The challenge of leadership, however, is to motivate, not to importune compliance. Jesus, interestingly enough, seemed more interested in the use of authority than in disobedience. The message might be that when authority functions well, the community tends to do likewise.

The rule of the Spirit must be found in human processes and not treated as a *deus ex machina* substitute for the human realities. The authority to rule cannot be conceived as divinely imparted and existing independently of the will of the community. Rather, as Robert Johann writes, the power of authority is based on the "actual intention of unity, institutionally embodied and acknowledged by the plurality of persons as having a claim on them." Hence, authority depends essentially on community will and includes in its notion the possibility of deposition or recall. Unimpeachable authority is an idol.

On the other hand, the community which founds authority should not confound it by complying only when it agrees. Authority requires the community-building ability to yield one's preference at regular times. Without this ability to yield and to trust, community ceases and atomistic individualism prevails. This does not mean that there is a given "presumption in favor of authority"—civil or ecclesiastical. Better, it is the task of authority to create a presumption in its own favor. Authority figures must realize that what they command can be commanded because it is good; it is not good because commanded. Law is a "dictate of reason" by essence. When it is not reasonable, it ceases to be law. The will of the legislator cannot "bind under pain of sin"; sin results from the malicious rejection of a good which the legislator and his law may have exhorted us to embrace.

As to the teaching role of Church officers, it may once have been possible for the bishop to be the principal teacher of doctrine. Because, however, teaching competence must be earned and maintained and is not an *ex officio* endowment, no bishop today could easily achieve it. The "charisma" of the papal and episcopal offices does not impart a special "feel" for the truth that can be divorced from the development of expertise. The Christian duty to teach can best be fulfilled by Church officers if they use their influence to activate the teaching resources of the community, anointed by the Spirit as that community is in Christian faith. When they speak out and teach, they should do so in reliance on the best insights in the community. They should not indulge in a magical view of office that would see their teaching as uniquely authentic regardless of the quality of their learning and faith. They should imitate the Lord who "became as men are" (Phil. 2:7). An acknowledgement of their fallibility will not deprive them of a hearing in an honest world. Since the role of authority is to stimulate, Church leaders should promote a free and vigorous study of theology. A good relationship between authority figures and intellectuals (not that the twain never unite) is the mark of a healthy society.

Finally, in a time of rapidation and "gapping," it would seem that democratically-elected popes and bishops would most effectively serve fixed terms of office. After this time, these men (or women) could return to the Christian community in a priestly or lay role. Such a *kenosis* is not demeaning or dogmatically infeasible.

In asserting the authority of the Church councils, the juridical paradigm has been paramount. All ecumenical councils are thought of as having equal value, and papal approbation has been seen as determinative of ecumenicity. Ballermine said a council not ratified by the pope is "void." His position seems to be: "Wherever two or three are gathered together in my name, with proper approbation, there am I in the midst of them." A recent study wonders if Martin V might have been too distracted to ratify Constance validly and render it ecumenical. It is as though the pope had a power to will the council into ecumenical being, if he had his wits about him. Likewise, the unanimity of the council fathers is seen as a sign of divine approbation.

More realistically, a council is as valuable as it is representative of the work of the Spirit. Councils attempt, with varying

345

success, to reflect the purest streams of the Church's current doctrinal consciousness. Such serious attempts, as Calvin readily conceded, deerve a most serious hearing. But when a council has done its best, its words do not become the words of God. The American bishops' Pastoral, commenting on the witness of the faithful, says that it is not numbers that count but "who is speaking and what manner of faith is his. Numbers count only if those who comprise the total really know." This incontrovertible insight applies also to the teaching of bishops, whether conciliar or extra-conciliar. The value of their teaching depends on what they know and on the quality of their faith.

The definitions of past councils, then, merit deep reverence. They represent important efforts to give voice to the faith of the Church. If they should be later corrected, as has happened, it is because they are imperfect. Like maps made centuries ago with imperfect tools, they must be open to correction by subsequent discovery. A radical dispensability attaches to any verbalization of religious truth.

The authority of dogmatic traditions has been stormily discussed over the years. Some Christians saw only the scriptures as speaking for God and proclaimed revelation closed with the apostolic era. Others merited the rebuke of Jesus: "You put aside the commandment of God to cling to human traditions" (Mk. 7–8).

It is close to saying that God is dead if we say he is mute and no longer revealing. Without demeaning the fundamentally "normative" character of the revelation communicated through scripture in the Church, we must say that revelation is not closed. To dogmatize that post-biblical words deserve no hearing is dogmagenic deafness. The spirit of all religious experience must be tested to see if it is of God.

The ecumenical age need not shrink from the Marian dogmas or from purgatory, hell or infallibility. The question is not whether these dogmas are found in scripture or defined in council, but whether we can find in them meaningful expressions of

346

Christian experience. The tenure of dogmas does not establish them but it does recommend that they be taken seriously. Healthy traditionalism is concerned for the leakage that besets the collective human consciousness. The dogmas are deeply felt words from man's religious past, words which may represent peak experiences.

In approaching these polemic-scarred words, we must beware a literal fundamentalism. Fundamentalism is easily mistaken for orthodoxy since its rigid reductionism seems safe and preservative. Rather, in the freedom of faith could we not listen anew for accents of the Spirit? Is the Assumption another empty tomb to trouble the apologetes and brace the mariologists? Or, seeing Mary typologically, could the appearance of this dogma have been a strong mythic endorsement of corporality in an atmosphere tainted by Encratite, Manichean and Stoic poisons? The Immaculate Conception, rather than a juridical non-imputation, might express Christian joy and hopefulness at the appearance of life in a world that has heard God's voice. Rather than seeing purgatory in spatio-temporal simplicity as a punitive prelude to bliss, could this myth not be touching the great scriptural truths of God's holiness and man's radical sinfulness, and expressing the need for purification (purgare) before union. The term "infallibility" is clumsy in an age that recognizes the fallibility of language, the partiality of concepts and the processuality of truth. Yet, the dogma of infallibility might well transcend epistemology. It may be an appreciation of the power of God's truth and the already-begun victory of his Spirit. The old theological metaphor, *ex opere operato,* however infelicitous an expression, need not be discarded with the shortcomings of past theologians. This theology was replete with an appreciation of the reality of God's life-giving presence and the meaningfulness of man's approach to God. In whatever bedraggled wrapping traditions may come to us, we should not be too quick to discard them; we should rather be open to the possibility of enriching content.

Desacralization costs us the comfort of false security. Yet, nothing could justify the continued sacralizing of office and book. The urgent task of theology is to develop a criteriology for testing the Spirit. Contact with the ineffable can never be wholly methodized, involved as it is with mystery, with affectivity and intuition. Yet the task remains. Admitting where we have been and what we have done is a necessary first step.

Notes on Contributors

RAYMOND E. BROWN, S.S., is professor of scripture at St. Mary's Seminary in Baltimore. He was, most recently, translator and editor of *The Gospel of St. John* for the Doubleday-Anchor Bible Series.

DAVID B. BURRELL, C.S.C., is a professor of philosophy at Notre Dame. His articles have appeared in numerous theological and philosophical journals.

DANIEL CALLAHAN, former Executive Editor of *Commonweal,* is the author of *The Mind of the Catholic Layman* and *Honesty in the Church.* He is presently doing work on a grant from the Population Council and the Ford Foundation.

J. M. CAMERON, English correspondent for *Commonweal,* is a professor of philosophy and master of Rutherford College in the University of Kent at Canterbury. His most recent book is *Images of Authority.*

THOMAS E. CLARKE, S.J., is professor of systematic theology at Woodstock College. He is co-author (with James E. Carmody, S.J.) of *Christ and His Mission* and *Word and Redeemer.*

JAMES COLLINS is professor of philosophy at St. Louis University. He is the author of numerous books, including *The Mind of Kierkegaard* and *God in Modern Philosophy.*

BERNARD J. COOKE, S.J., is professor of theology at Marquette University in Milwaukee. The author of numerous theological articles, his most recent book is *Christian Sacraments and Christian Personality.*

FREDERICK E. CROWE, S.J., is a professor at Regis College in Willowdale, Ontario. A specialist in the thought of Bernard Lonergan, he recently edited two books on the subject.

CHARLES E. CURRAN is associate professor of moral theology at the Catholic University of America. He is the author of *Christian Morality Today* and the editor of *Contraception: Authority and Dissent.*

LESLIE DEWART is professor of philosophy at St. Michael's College, University of Toronto. He is the author of the much acclaimed book *The Future of Belief,* and most recently of *The Foundations of Belief.*

JAMES W. DOUGLASS is a member of the Department of Religion at the University of Hawaii, and is the author of *The Non-Violent Cross: A Theology of Revolution and Peace.*

AVERY DULLES, S.J., is professor of systematic theology at Woodstock College. A frequent contributor to *Theological Studies* and other scholarly journals, he has written *The Dimensions of the Church* and, most recently, *Revelation Theology.*

JOHN S. DUNNE, C.S.C., is a professor of theology at Notre Dame, and is the author of *The City of the Gods.*

LOUIS DUPRÉ is professor of philosophy at Georgetown University. He is the author of *Contraception and Catholics,* and the editor of *Faith and Reflection,* a collection of writings of Henry Duméry.

DR. J. MASSINGBERD FORD, an associate professor in sacred scripture at Notre Dame University, is the author of *Wellsprings of Scripture, and A Trilogy on Wisdom and Celibacy.*

WILLIAM HAMILTON is a member of the faculty of New College in Sarasota, Florida. The author of *The New Essence of Christianity,* he was also co-author with Thomas J. J. Altizer of *Radical Theology and the Death of God.*

THOMAS HOPKO is pastor of St. Gregory's Church in Wappinger Falls, New York, and lecturer in theology at St. Vladimir's Seminary in Crestwood, New York.

DANIEL MAGUIRE, an assistant professor in the Department of Religious Studies at Catholic University, contributed an essay on moral absolutes and the magisterium to *Absolutes in Moral Theology?*

KILIAN MCDONNELL, O.S.B., the director of the Institute for Ecumenical and Cultural Research at Collegeville, Minnesota, also teaches theology at St. John's University there.

GABRIEL MORAN, F.S.C., is chairman of the Theology Department at Manhattan College and the author of *Catechesis and Revelation, Vision and Tactics,* and, most recently, co-author with Sister Maria Harris of *Experiences in Community.*

EDWARD D. O'CONNOR, an associate professor of theology at Notre Dame University, is the author of *Faith and the Synoptic Gospels.*

HERBERT RICHARDSON is the author of *Toward an American Theology,* and a member of the faculty of St. Michael's College at the University of Toronto.

DAVID TRACY, a member of the faculty at Catholic University, has contributed to *Continuum, Theology Today* and other journals. He is the author of *The Achievement of Bernard Lonergan.*

BRUCE VAWTER, C.M., is a scripture professor at Kenrick Seminary in St. Louis. Associate Editor of *The Catholic Biblical Quarterly,* he is also author of *A Path Through Genesis.*